E294

TALES FROM THE TENNIS COURT

also by Richard Evans

Whineray's All Blacks
Match Point with Marty Riessen
Nastase
If I'm the Better Player, Why Can't I Win?
(with Allen Fox)
McEnroe: A Rage for Perfection

TALES FROM THE TENNIS COURT

AN ANTHOLOGY OF
TENNIS WRITINGS EDITED BY

RICHARD EVANS

SIDGWICK & JACKSON
LONDON

First published in Great Britain in 1983
by Sidgwick & Jackson Limited

This edition and selection © 1983 by
Richard Evans

Copyright in the extracts, articles and illustrations
published in this volume belongs to those
mentioned in the acknowledgements and on
the contents page

ISBN 0–283–99005–8

Photoset by Falcon Graphic Art Ltd
Wallington, Surrey
Printed in Great Britain by
Biddles Ltd, Guildford, Surrey
for Sidgwick & Jackson Limited
1 Tavistock Chambers, Bloomsbury Way
London WC1A 2SG

To my colleagues whose book this is
And to Reg Hayter who, with Ron Roberts
and Freddie Garside, gave me a chance and
set me on the road

CONTENTS

Contents

Contents

9

ACKNOWLEDGEMENTS

First and foremost I must acknowledge the debt I owe the Wimbledon Library where so many treasures can be found. My thanks, in particular, to Tony Cooper, Curator of the Wimbledon Museum, Alan Little, the Librarian, and, especially, to Valerie Warren, whose patient help was invaluable.

Also I am indebted to Lance Tingay, whose afternoons I disturbed with various queries. As usual Lance had the answers on the tip of his tongue.

The work of Charles Ambrose and 'Mac' provided artwork from another age while Mario Spezi, one of Italy's leading cartoonists whose work appears in *La Nazione*, Florence, used his skills to depict players of the more recent era.

Finally, my editors at Sidgwick & Jackson must take their customary bow, particularly Libby Joy whose meticulous eye for detail played a major part in the production of this book.

In addition to those publishers, magazines, newspapers and writers who appear on the Contents page – to whom the editor and publishers are grateful for permission to reproduce material used in this book – they would like to thank A.D. Peters & Co. Ltd for allowing them to reprint the extracts from *Big Bill Tilden* by Frank Deford and *Portrait in Motion* by Arthur Ashe and Frank Deford, and E.P. Dutton, New York, for reproduction of Herbert Warren Wind's material on Walter Wingfield which was also published in their book *Game, Set and Match*.

They would also like to thank the following for permission to use the illustrations reproduced here: The Wimbledon Lawn Tennis Museum for pages 22 (taken from *The Illustrated London News*, 24 July 1880); 33 (taken from *The Illustrated London News*); 36; 37; 43; 49; 58, 67 and 69 (all three taken from *The Bystander*, 26 June 1929); 71 (taken from *Piccadilly*, 29 June 1929); and Mario Spezi for pages 110, 162 and 216.

11

INTRODUCTION
RICHARD EVANS

The problem with compiling an anthology is always one of choice. Having muttered for years about the comparative poverty of tennis literature (I suppose I was dazzled as a schoolboy by the flowing works of Cardus, Swanton and Arlott) I discovered, after just a few hours in the Wimbledon Library, that if the game has not been blessed with quite as many well-turned phrases as have been bestowed on cricket, it does not lack for quality writing. Very quickly, I realized how much that was worthy of inclusion would have to be left out.

In the end I decided to forego the original idea of choosing a sample of my favourite pieces of tennis writing and to try, instead, to give the reader a broad picture of the game as it has developed ever since the earliest days of Wimbledon. So although it remains quite possible to hop about amongst the following pages, dipping in as we all like to do for a quick look at Tilden, Gonzales, or Ashe as the mood takes us, this is an anthology that can also be read from start to finish. Approached in that way, it should be possible to get a feel for the changing face and pace of the sport as selected extracts and articles throw a brief light on the exploits of the great players of each era.

Inevitably there are obvious ommissions for this is not an attempt at a complete history of the game. However, it has been a fascinating and exciting task to select little historical slices of a sport that is so rich in anecdote and tradition. In particular I am delighted to be able to focus some attention on one of the original dashing figures of international sport – Anthony Wilding, the New Zealand-born Wimbledon Champion from 1910 to 1913, who lost his title to Norman Brookes a year before he was killed in Flanders. Although no poet, Wilding epitomized the spirit of Rupert Brooke – a young and inspirational life abruptly ended when it still had so much to offer. But, as his own charmingly told story reveals, he made the most of that life; living it at a speed that would seem hectic even by today's standards as he hurtled from tournament to tournament all over Europe on a motor-cycle. Quite apart from

13

the state of the roads, where did you find a petrol station between Paris and Hamburg in 1910?

But, of course, it was Wingfield, not Wilding, who got the show on the road, and to trace the origins of the modern game I have used the meticulous research of Herbert Warren Wind, the soft-spoken tennis correspondent of the *New Yorker* magazine, to whom one can always turn for a carefully considered comment even when McEnroe or Connors are creating bedlam at Madison Square Garden. Herbert is very much a gentleman journalist.

My knowledge of H.S. Mahony is limited to the fact that he won Wimbledon in 1896, was sufficiently Irish, according to Wilding, to wear odd socks, and wrote with a deep and detailed knowledge of the game's first great champions. We will never be able to see how Barlow, Pim and the Renshaws hit the ball, but after reading Mahony we can get a pretty clear idea.

Norah Cleather, described by Ted Tinling in his book *Sixty Years in Tennis* as being surrounded in her office by bouquets of flowers and a huge display of crystallized fruit – an annual present from Jean Borotra – was secretary at the All England Club between the wars and her description of Wimbledon as it celebrated its fiftieth anniversary brings to life the attitudes and ambiance of a different era.

Few biographies of the game's earlier figures have been so widely praised as Frank Deford's book on 'Big Bill' Tilden, from which I have extracted the introductory chapter. Deford is a ubiquitous figure in these pages for he also helped Arthur Ashe put together his diary of a year on the pro tour, and he then wrote the definitive piece on the complex Mr Jimmy Connors. Frank, who emerges all too infrequently from his Connecticut home to report on tennis for *Sports Illustrated*, towers over us in the press box; a sort of Gary Cooper figure with a liking for Western boots and large hats. I always think of him as a kind of Connecticut Cowboy but, amongst cowboys, only Zane Grey would be fit to lick those boots.

If John Arlott's Hampshire drawl first wetted my appetite for cricket, it was Max Robertson who conjured up my first images of Wimbledon with his incredibly skilful descriptions of Sedgman and Drobny on BBC Radio. He produced a beautiful book on Wimbledon a few years ago and here expertly fills in the immediate post-war era of Kramer and Schroeder.

The game of doubles is too often overlooked so it was satisfying to be able to include a lovely piece which Fred Tupper wrote for *World Tennis* on one of the most memorable Wimbledon doubles finals, won by the veteran pair of Budge Patty and Gar Mulloy in 1957.

In those days Fred, an ace PR man, led something of a double existence himself, working for Pan American Airways in London and covering Wimbledon for the *New York Times*.

My total admiration of Gordon Forbes' writing is mingled with frustration, for *A Handful of Summers* is still the only book he has written – a wicked waste of a rare talent. The problem is that Gordon has been making a fortune selling lighting equipment for tennis courts all over South Africa, apparently oblivious to the fact that he has the ability to become one of those rare souls who could also make a fortune writing books. One day I shall spirit him away from his bright and beautiful wife and stick him in a garret, preferably on some misty Scottish moor, and feed him on a diet of haggis and Scotch. In desperation he might then be inspired to entertain us further with tales of the people he has met – all brought to life with such a wonderfully whimsical and luminous touch. In the meantime it is no chore at all to keep re-reading *A Handful of Summers*.

I wish I could read Gianni Clerici in Italian. I have a suspicion he is as delightful company in print as he is in person. Heaven knows what kind of inventiveness he brought to the tennis court in his days as a top-ranked player in Italy, but I suspect some of his eccentricities would have provided a marvellous antidote to the sterility of some base line styles he is required to write about today. Apart from his colourful contribution on Pancho Gonzales, I am indebted to Gianni for the opportunity to delve into his copious tennis library on the shores of Lake Como, where the extravagance of the hospitality and home-made wine make the task of research a highly enviable occupation.

Having an eye for the good things of life, Bud Collins is a frequent visitor to Casa Clerici and, were he not in love with Boston, would probably end up living there. Happily I have been able to share his good humour in such diverse places as Accra, Fiji and Prague over the years, and, in between, can marvel at the range of the imagination that is evident in his *World Tennis* columns. A television commentator of ribald style, Bud is also steeped in the game's history and here he remembers Forest Hills in a companion piece to my own contribution on the three leading centres of the European game.

The British colleagues who have shared deadlines with me for so many years at tournaments all over the world will be more familiar to readers in this country, and their contributions, written, as they mostly were, for a daily newspaper, throw vivid spotlights onto some of the great players and significant events that have shaped the professional game in the post-war years.

There will probably never be a more respected or widely read tennis writer than Lance Tingay, who has now handed his *Daily Telegraph* reporting over to John Parsons. There was a time, before computerized ranking lists, when Lance's world rankings were accepted as the official yardstick for determining who was the world's number one player. No more need be said of his stature in the game.

Rex Bellamy's turn of phrase has not only delighted readers of *The Times* ever since that august organ started using by-lines, but has also impressed the players to such a degree that he received the ATP's JAKS award for Writer of the Year on no less than five occasions.

If awards were given for knowing how to live life to the full, Laurie Pignon and Geoffrey Green would have been toasting each other's success in even greater style than has been their custom – if that were possible. Their writing has given almost as much pleasure as their company.

Frank Rostron is another *bon viveur* who used to be the terror of his rivals in his days as a hot-shot *Daily Express* man. But, having scooped you, Frank was always the first to offer the low-down on the best and most reasonably priced meal in town.

The Observer's high standard of writing is well represented by such diversified contributors as Yorkshire's Arthur Hopcraft, Australia's Clive James and America's John Crosby, while this section, which I have called 'Moments in Time', also includes an analysis of Ashe's superb Wimbledon triumph over Connors, written by one of the world's greatest exponents of the original game, Real Tennis.

But Gene Scott is better known as the publisher of his excellent newspaper *Tennis Week*, as well as for playing the modern game with above average skill on the Grand Masters tour.

Two other good friends, David Gray, formerly of *The Guardian* and now secretary of the ITF, and John Barrett, the former British Davis Cup captain and BBC commentator, recall the career of Wimbledon's first committee woman, Virginia Wade, and to round it all off another talented *Sports Illustrated* writer, Curry Kirkpatrick, takes us on a farewell tour with Bjorn Borg – his erudite tongue firmly in his cheek. H.S. Mahony, odd socks and all, would have been quite flabbergasted.

I hope, at least, you are entertained.

Richard Evans
London, May 1983

MAJOR WALTER WINGFIELD

HERBERTWARRENWIND

Major Walter Clopton Wingfield, the man who invented tennis, must surely rank among the most colorful and controversial figures in the history of sport. A cavalry officer in Victorian England, Wingfield was a scion of an ancient and prominent family whose ancestral seat, a castle in Suffolk near the Norfolk border, is said to have been erected in 1362, though there are those who contend that it antedated the coming of William the Conqueror. A good many of the Major's forebears had distinguished themselves as soldiers and diplomats. For example, Sir Richard Wingfield was Marshal of Calais in 1511, and later, as the Ambassador to the Court of France, was present at the Field of the Cloth of Gold. Beginning in 1521, Sir Robert Wingfield served as Ambassador to the Court of Charles V. In the middle of the sixteenth century, Sir Humphrey Wingfield put in a stint as Speaker of the House of Commons, and Anthony Wingfield, a kind of maverick, was a reader in Greek to Queen Elizabeth I. However, by the early eighteen-sixties when Major Wingfield returned home from China, where he had commanded a cavalry troop, the family had long since lost most of its eminence and wealth. Wingfield Castle, no longer inhabited, was fast becoming a ruin, the outline of its towers obliterated by a rank growth of vines, the drawbridge across its moat rusted and broken. Major Wingfield, who was assigned after his China command to the Montgomery Yeomanry, a Welsh outfit, had enough money to get by on, but a few extra pounds would not have hurt, and he began to ponder how he might go about acquiring them. A tall, athletic young-middle-aged man with a handsome face framed by a full beard, he got around a good deal socially, and one of the things he noticed about the Britain

17

he had returned to was how mad everyone was for sport. Organized cricket, soccer, Rugby, and rowing had become enormously more popular, but the rise of team sports wasn't the particular development that caught the Major's shrewd eye. What did was a new facet of the cult of games – the games that ladies and gentlemen played together on weekends on the wide, well-kept lawns of the fashionable country houses. Croquet, the oldest of these games, remained the leader, but it was obvious that many of its practitioners, including the females, were finding it too tepid. A good many of them had already switched to badminton, originally called Poona, that was imported from India in the early eighteen seventies by some British Army officers and re-named after the country seat of the Duke of Beaufort, where the first important demonstration of the game had taken place. The trouble with badminton was that it required an absolutely breezeless day; otherwise there was no controlling the shuttlecock. Wingfield was certain that the national passion for sport would keep on growing, and it struck him that a small fortune along with a substantial renown any man would be pleased to have awaited the person who could devise a really fascinating lawn game. He began to think along those lines himself.

Wingfield had the background for it. In his youth, he had played the various forms of handball and just about all the racquet games. (According to Edward C. Potter, Jr., in his book 'Kings of the Court, there had been a court-tennis court in Wingfield Castle. Moreover, as Potter brought out, among the people who had supposedly made use of it was Charles d'Orléans, a grandson of the King of France, who had been captured at Agincourt by the English and consigned to Wingfield Castle during part of his long captivity.) In any event, in 1873, after considerable deliberation, the Major came up with a game that contained certain features of these earlier games – the net came from badminton, the ball from Eton fives (a form of handball), the method of scoring from hand racquets, and so on. (Until special racquets were manufactured, the player was free to use the racquet from his favorite game.) Wingfield called his amalgam Sphairistiké, or Lawn Tennis – 'Sphairistiké' because he had heard that there was an ancient Greek game of that name, and 'Lawn Tennis' because it seemed a natural spinoff from 'court tennis', and thus suggested a game that was both old and aristocratic. (As Potter has pointed out, 'Wingfield had little idea how Sphairistiké was played but . . . he could be sure that even antiquarians had forgotten its rules.') Another advantage gained by calling his game Sphairistiké was that it emphasized its originality, and this, Wingfield felt, would greatly increase his chances of obtaining a patent for it. That was crucial – a patent. Once he had it, he would be able to manufacture and sell sets of his game and, he hoped, reap a small fortune. His concern about gaining a patent also prompted several of the new wrinkles he had introduced into his game, such as decreeing that the court not be rectangular but shaped somewhat like an hourglass – thirty feet wide across the baselines and only twenty-four feet wide at the net. In December 1873, Wingfield tried out the game with a group of young people who were members of a houseparty at Nantclwyd Hall, the country estate, in Denbighshire, Wales, of the family of a good friend of his, Thomas Naylor-Leyland.

On February 23, 1874, Major Wingfield was awarded a preliminary patent for his game, and the patent was confirmed five months later. The moment he received word in February that the patent office had registered his application for 'A New and Improved Portable Court for Playing the Ancient Game of Tennis' (in his presentation the Major had heavily emphasized that tennis in its earlier forms had always been an indoor amusement), he arranged for sets to be manufactured and for the Messrs. French & Company, of 46 Churton Street, Pimlico, to act as his exclusive sales agent. A set cost five guineas – a fairly substantial amount in those days. Encased in a wooden box thirty-six inches by twelve by six and bearing the label 'Sphairistiké, or Lawn Tennis' on the cover, a set contained poles, pegs, a main net a little over four and a half feet high, two small side nets (they adjoined the main net like wings), a mallet, a brush, a bag of balls, and four tennis racquets, made by Jefferies & Mallings, which were a sort of cross between the conventional hard-racquets racquet and the conventional court-tennis racquet. Wingfield left it up to his clients to supply their own colored cord, tape, or paint for lining the court, but he did throw in a slim pamphlet called 'The Book of the Game', in which he set down the dimensions of the court and provided instructions for installing one in five minutes. The pamphlet also included a brief, if fuzzy, account of the game's history, along with an explanation of its scoring system and the rules of play. On the page facing the title page ('The Major's Game of Lawn Tennis, dedicated to the party assembled at Nantclwyd in December, 1873, by W.C.W.') were two interesting paragraphs. The one at the top went as follows:

> This game has been tefted practically at feveral Country Houfes during the paft few months, and has been found fo full of interuft and fo great a succefs, that it has been decided to bring it before the Public, being protected by Her Majesty's Royal Letters Patent.

19

There then appeared a facsimile of the royal coat of arms and, beneath it, a paragraph headed 'Useful Hints':

Hit your ball gently, and look well before ftriking, fo as to place it in the corner moft remote from your adverfary. A great deal of fide can be imparted to the ball by the proper touch, together with a nice appreciation of ftrength, adds much to the delicacy and fcience of the game.

The rest of the pamphlet similarly used the romantic, archaic 'f' instead of the modern 's'. The Major, Madison Avenue incarnate, never could stop selling.

Lawn tennis caught on instantly. In a matter of months, with the Major pushing it vigorously and using his influential friends with characteristic chutzpah, it became *the* social game, driving croquet and badminton from the velvet lawns of the stately homes of England and the rest of Britain, and also establishing itself with the better military garrisons around the world. With the boxed sets selling so rapidly, the Major brought out a second edition of his game before the year was over, defining some of the rules, modifying some of the equipment (the side nets, for example, were dispensed with), and also raising the price of a set to six guineas. Before many more months had passed, a third edition became necessary. At this time, bowing to mounting pressure, he gave up the name Sphairistiké. Thenceforward, the game would be known simply as lawn tennis. To Wingfield's deep gratification, the game had quickly gained many enthusiastic converts among the nobility. During the first year it was on the market, sets were bought by the Prince of Wales, the Crown Princess of Prussia, and Prince Louis of Hesse; by eight dukes, including the Duke of Edinburgh and the Duke of Devonshire; by fourteen marquises, including the Marquis of Lansdowne and the Marquis of Exeter; by forty-nine earls, including the Earl of Cadogan, the Earl of Leicester, and the Marquis of Salisbury; and by eight viscounts, including Viscount Halifax and Viscount Bangor.

For all its dazzling success, however, Wingfield's invention did not bring him the fortune he dreamed of, or anything like it. With the third edition, sales of the sets began to fall off drastically. One reason was that many of the people whom Wingfield had viewed as potential customers thought it foolish to lay out six guineas for the Major's equipment when they could make – or had already assembled – their own. Indeed, as a large number of them pointed out in irate letters to *The Field*, the leading periodical dealing with outdoor life, hard-racquet or court-tennis devotees in various sections of Britain had thought up and had been playing games very similar to the Major's long before he entered the picture. The dimensions of these other courts were somewhat different, of course, and so were many of the rules of play, but, essentially, these games were the same game as lawn tennis. Besides castigating Wingfield for his presumption in presenting his brainchild as a wholly original creation, the letter writers made it clear that they considered their own versions of tennis far superior to his. Other troubles lay ahead for Wingfield. For persons who did not have a spreading lawn of their own, an obvious site for a tennis court was the grounds of the local cricket club. By late 1874, the Marylebone Cricket Club, the governing body of the national game, was becoming a trifle worried over the inroads the fashionable new game was making. The fact that tennis players had appropriated the white shirt and white flannels of the cricketer as their own outfit was of no great importance, but lawn tennis had the look about it of a game that could cut deeply into cricket's vast popularity, and that *was* serious. The prudent course, the M.C.C. decided, was to step in and take over lawn tennis before the game became too big. The top men at the M.C.C. also had a few suggestions that they thought would make lawn tennis a much better game, such as lowering the net and adopting the method of scoring used in court tennis. On several occasions in 1875, a committee from the M.C.C. met with Wingfield to talk things over, but in the stormy sessions that inevitably resulted Wingfield stubbornly held his ground. Shortly after this, heavy pressure was exerted on him by another sports organization – the All England Croquet Club, which had been founded in 1868 in Wimbledon, on the southwestern edge of London. Commercially, croquet had fallen far short of the club's hopes for it, so in the mid-seventies the A.E.C.C. had, as an experiment, laid out a tennis court in one corner of the club property. As it turned out, the court was filled with players from morning to night. Obviously, the way to make money was to plunge into lawn tennis in a big way. Very much in the manner of the M.C.C., the A.E.C.C. was soon challenging Wingfield's right, patent or no patent, to run lawn tennis singlehanded, particularly since the game had already developed an alarming number of variations and seemed to be developing more. At length, late in 1875, his obstinacy worn down by months of slow sales and fast talk, Wingfield suddenly agreed to accept all the changes proposed by an M.C.C. committee, insisting only that the game be played on a court shaped like an hourglass. This peace treaty, however, turned out to be next to meaningless, because in 1877 control of the game was captured by the All England Croquet and Lawn Tennis Club – note the change of name – which, under the leadership of three members who were both veteran adminis-

21

trators and ambitious ballgame intellectuals, announced not only that it would be holding a national lawn tennis championship in July but that the event would be played on a rectangular court, under a new set of rules worked out by the club's high-powered troika. The M.C.C., after a session with the A.E.C. & L.T.C., gave in on every point.

Twenty-two men entered the first Wimbledon – the first lawn tennis championship put on by the All England Club, in its bailiwick in that suburb. The winner was Spencer Gore, an old racquets player from Harrow. He was succeeded by P.F. Hadow, another old Harrovian, and then by the Reverend J.T. Hartley, who had been a court-tennis champion at Oxford. In 1881 the first great tennis player arrived on the scene – Willie Renshaw. He won the singles at Wimbledon seven times and with his twin brother Ernest carried off the doubles seven times.

The Reverend J.T. Hartley

As for Major Wingfield, he lived on until 1912, the last thirty-five years in almost total oblivion as far as tennis was concerned. (Wimbledon, after appropriating control of the game, had simply shunted the Major to one side.) When he finally died, at the age of seventy-eight, the obituary in the London *Times* dwelt on his military career, his ties with the famous old Suffolk family, some pamphlets he wrote late in life ('Bicycle Gymkhana' and 'Musical Rides'), and a term he served as justice of the peace in Montgomeryshire. There was not a word about his being the inventor of the thriving international game of lawn tennis.

This spring, when I was in England during the second week of Wimbledon, I took a couple of days off from the tournament in order to visit two locales that had played a vital part in the fascinating saga of Walter Clopton Wingfield: Wingfield Castle and Nantclwyd Hall. Through the assistance of Ann Allison, of the British Information Services in New York City, I had learned that Wingfield Castle was still in existence. Just what condition it was in, Miss Allison had not been able to tell me, and her information about the village of Wingfield was limited, too. All things considered, she felt that perhaps the best procedure for me, if I was serious about visiting the castle and the village in this the centennial year of lawn tennis, was to get in touch with the Reverend W. G. Muir, of Wingfield. I wrote to him immediately. Through Miss Allison's good services, I also got in touch with Nantclwyd Hall. At her suggestion, I wrote to the clerk of the Rural District Council in Ruthin, which is the village nearest to Nantclwyd. The clerk of the council passed my letter on to Major B.G. Rhodes, the representative of the trustees of the Nantclwyd Settlement, which administers the Nantclwyd estate, and Major Rhodes sent me a long, friendly letter in which he said that he had cleared the matter with the trustees of the Nantclwyd Settlement, and that it would be a pleasure to welcome a lawn tennis pilgrim to the grounds on which Major Wingfield introduced his game to the world in 1873. 'Although the original lawn-tennis court is not still in use, it is clearly identifiable,' Major Rhodes wrote. He also explained that 'Nantclwyd Hall . . . has been and remains the home of the Naylor-Leyland family since 1840,' and that Major Wingfield's friend Thomas Naylor-Leyland was 'the great-great-grandfather of the present baronet, Sir Vivyan Naylor-Leyland, who now lives in Nassau.'

I decided to undertake the expedition to Wingfield first, because it was the more chancy of the two: I had received no answer from the Reverend Mr. Muir, and I would be descending on the village cold. To get to Wingfield, I took a train from London to Colchester, in Essex, and there hired a taxi to take me the remaining forty-odd miles. As we began our drive northeast across the deep green dales of Essex and Suffolk on a typical English summer's day, the dark-gray clouds in the wide sky occasionally pierced by bolts of brilliant sunshine, I noticed in talking with my driver, a cheerful middle-aged man, that he spoke

23

with a slight European accent, and I asked him about it. He told me that his name was Tony, and that he was born in Italy and had been living in England since the war. 'I was captured by the British at Benghazi,' he added, breaking into a radiant smile. 'Happiest day of my life!' It took us about an hour to get to Wingfield, which lies in an out-of-the-way part of East Anglia, about thirty miles by road from Bury St. Edmunds, about twenty-five from Lowestoft, and about twenty-five also from the local metropolis, Norwich. The area around Wingfield grows good wheat, oats and barley, and also has a reputation for raising good pigs. The village now has a population of two hundred and twenty-nine, and just about all the farmhouses and other buildings are set along a narrow, winding paved road, which another narrow, winding paved road meets at a right angle. Wingfield's handsome old stone church lies two hundred yards down the second road. The side door to the church was open, and, entering, I asked the only person in sight, a well-dressed elderly lady, where I might find the Reverend Mr. Muir. I learned that he had left the village almost two years before and that his successor was currently on holiday. I then asked her about Wingfield Castle, fearful that I would learn that it had slipped into the moat and disappeared from sight. Here the news seemed definitely better. Not only was the castle standing but it had been meticulously restored by its present owner and resident, Baron Ash. That put a whole new complexion on things. The next step, obviously, was to speak with Baron Ash, if this was possible, and, at the lady's suggestion, I went into a small, bleak pub almost directly across the street from the church to see if I could reach him by telephone. I learned from the barmaid, who bore little resemblance in looks or manner to the enchanting breed that has been a staple of English films since the first camera handle was turned, that the pub had no phone but that I would find a phone box at the corner.

'You won't get to see the Baron, I can promise you that,' she added, with a rough little laugh. 'I don't care what your business is. The Baron's not seeing anyone these days.' And with this she broke into that unpleasant laugh again.

To my surprise and relief, there was a Norwich Area directory in the phone box. Not only that, but a number was listed for G. Baron Ash. Tony dialled the number for Wingfield Castle, and handed me the phone. A deep-pitched, edgy voice at the other end said, 'Yes?'

I asked to speak to Baron Ash.

'This is Baron Ash,' came the reply. 'Who are you and what do you want?' All this in a most peremptory tone.

I explained that 1973 marked the hundredth anniversary of the invention of lawn tennis by Major Wingfield, and asked if it might be possible to visit Wingfield Castle.

'No, you can't,' Baron Ash answered, his voice rising to a roar. 'That's absolutely out of the question. I have a right to my privacy. I'm eighty-three years old. Don't you think that at that age I have a right to my privacy?'

I said I certainly did.

'The last thing I want is publicity,' he went on, dropping his voice to a more conversational pitch and speaking with less petulance. 'Nevertheless, people are always bothering me. They drive right into the driveway, as if the castle were their home and not mine. It's a constant annoyance. It's twenty-five years since I bought the castle. I've loved rebuilding it. It's been my baby. But I'm not going to stand quietly by and let people I don't know invite themselves into my private grounds. This year, it's been far worse than ever before. People every day.'

I said I wouldn't have guessed that the centenary of the birth of lawn tennis would lead so many people to seek out Wingfield Castle.

'Good heavens, man, tennis has nothing to do with it!' the Baron roared. 'It's those blasted Wingfields. They're a very prolific family, spread all over, and they keep coming round to inspect the ancestral castle. Constant interruptions. This morning, there were five automobiles filled with people parked in front of my breakfast room while I was eating my breakfast.'

I was properly sympathetic. I went on to say that I had heard that the Baron had done a superb job of restoring the castle. Then I said, 'All I want to do is to take a very quick look around.'

'Don't you understand me?' Baron Ash boomed out. 'I don't want to be disturbed by you or anyone!' And with that he crashed the phone down into its cradle.

Wingfield Castle is fairly visible from the road, even though it is set back a couple of hundred yards and is partly hidden by a screen of tall trees planted along the front of the estate and along most of the rest of its perimeter. As Tony and I were driving over to get the catch-as-catch-can glimpse we would now have to settle for, we passed the village post office, and I decided to drop in for a moment. It took up less than half of a rather slapdash, faded white wooden structure, in which the postmaster, a man named Matthias, also ran a jumbled odds-and-ends shop. A tall, thin, middle-aged fellow, Matthias proved to be outgoing and highly articulate, and he seemed to enjoy filling me in on Baron Ash. To the best of Matthias' recollection, when the Baron came to Wingfield it was from Buckinghamshire or some place in that general

25

vicinity, where he had a palatial country home. The Baron, he had heard, was related to the Marlborough family. The trouble was that, being a real showplace, his home attracted tourists by the busload, and one day, his patience exhausted, he decided to get away from it all. He turned that estate over to the National Trust and bought Wingfield Castle, which had the advantage of being well off the usual tourist routes. The castle was then in terrible shape, but the Baron calmly went about fixing it up, from its drawbridge to its twin towers, pouring a small fortune into the project until, in the postmaster's phrase, 'the edifice was as neat as a pin.' Matthias went on, 'When he came here to Wingfield, the Baron had a staff of twenty-seven people looking after him – valets, maids, cooks, gardeners, and all the rest, you know. Now he's down to a staff of three. Most people of his class have had to do that in recent years. When he arrived here, he drove a Rolls-Royce. Now he's down to a Rover and an Austin. He pays the man from the local garage five pounds when he wants them washed. That's a generous sum, but the Baron is a very generous man. ·

The Baron Ash he was describing, I interposed, certainly didn't resemble the crusty character I had talked to on the telephone.

'Yes, he has changed,' Matthias agreed. 'When he first came to Wingfield, he was friendly with the people in the village. He attended the village functions, like the church fairs, quite regularly. When he went out for a stroll in the evening – he's an old bachelor – he had a cordial word for all of us. Then, I'm afraid, the local hooligans began to act up. Once, I remember, when he was away on a trip, they mucked up the cherry trees he had planted on his lawn. Baron Ash had been very proud of those trees. There were other incidents like that, and he gradually withdrew from the life of the village. I can picture him saying to himself, 'Well, if that's the way they want it!' or, you know, words to that effect. At heart, I think, he's a kind and friendly man. I think him being a bachelor and in his eighties is what makes him grumpy, you know. You would never guess his age by looking at him. He's a tall, slim, straight-backed chap who still rides a bicycle. He loves the castle.

In spite of his evident affection for Baron Ash, Matthias was exceedingly helpful when I asked him the best way I could get a good look at Wingfield Castle. His instructions were to continue along the road, past the driveway to the castle and the protective screen of trees, until I reached an open field. That was common land, and if I walked in a ways from the road a close, unobstructed view of the castle would present itself. I followed his instructions to the letter, tiptoeing warily past a couple of Holsteins grazing in the open field, and, when I had walked in about a hundred yards, suddenly there were no more trees on the right to block my view, and, seventy-five yards away, there was the castle, looming up as clear as a postcard. The water in the wide moat sparkled, as did the refurbished bridge leading over the moat to the front entrance and the massive twin towers framing it. (The drawbridge, at the rear of the castle, was out of my line of sight.) It was as magnificent a castle as I have ever seen. Near the base, the walls were of old gray, white, and black stone, but as they rose the stone gradually gave way to brownish brick, then to dull-red brick, and, finally to a dark-red brick that reminded me of the brick in some of the older colleges at Cambridge University, like Jesus. The crenellated central towers were of this deep-red brick. From where I stood, I could see only a small piece of the castle grounds. Not a soul was in view, but I could hear the clatter of a couple of power mowers, which were probably trimming the lawns along the driveway.

As I stood gazing at Wingfield Castle, an odd mélange of thoughts surged through my mind. If the Baron was so continually pestered by unwanted visitors, why didn't he simply shut the gates to the driveway? That would have solved his problem neatly and completely. For another thing, I really wished I had been able to visit the castle. I would have particularly liked to find out whether any traces remained of the court-tennis court described in Potter's book. This led me to the thought that overrode all the others. – Baron Ash's apparent ignorance that one of the Wingfields had invented lawn tennis a hundred years before, and his total lack of interest in the matter. When I got back to New York and looked up Graham Baron Ash in *Who's Who*, his attitude became a little less enigmatic. His entry was one of the shortest and tightest in the volume. Ash, it said, was born in 1889, was educated at Radley, and served in the Royal Air Force in both World Wars. From 1938 to 1939, he was High Sheriff of Warwickshire. Under 'Recreations' he had listed only one – shooting. Under 'Clubs' he had also listed only one – The Royal Automobile. That was it. It was ironic, considering how passionately Major Wingfield had longed for fame as well as for money, that the family castle had fallen into the hands of a shy introspective old man who had no taste for publicity and promotion and only wanted to be left alone.

THE OLD SCHOOL AND THE NEW

H. S. MAHONY

Widely divergent opinions are held as to the relative strength of past and present players, and everyone is naturally inclined to consider the various cracks encountered better than those of an earlier or later period. I shall endeavour as far as possible to give an impartial account of the various methods of playing the game, and the players who developed them.

There is no game in which there is so much variety of style, strokes and tactics, which causes many detractors of the game to say that it is 'unscientific' and can be played 'anyhow'! This view is to a measure encouraged by the attitude of mind of some players. At all ball games it is possible to play a strong game in bad style. Even at tennis and golf, where a certain stereotyped style is accepted as correct, and insisted on as the only road to success, many players will be found who, while their methods are anything but orthodox, are still very hard to beat. Yet no one supposes that good style is not a great advantage.

But a lawn tennis player who has been successful naturally resents adverse criticism of his methods, and if these differ widely from the classical, he must either admit them to be faulty, or deny that correct style exists. The fact that many different types of stroke are useful and effective, only shows of what development and variety the game is capable.

At first lawn tennis was entirely in the hands of tennis and racket players, who seemed to think that in cutting the ball heavily lay the road to success. As the object of cut at Tennis is to bring the ball down off the back wall, and as a lawn tennis court has none, such a method would seem to be lacking in common sense. The 'Badminton Library' on the game describes a practice match which took place at Wimbledon be-

28

tween H.F. Lawford and J.M. Heathcote, the Amateur Tennis Champion. Lawford is said to have been much puzzled by the cut stroke and service, losing game after game at the start. As he was rather a clumsy player, this can be readily understood, for off the low treacherous bound of a cut ball it is difficult to make a hard drive. But to expect him to go on misjudging the same stroke indefinitely was hoping for too much, and Lawford is subsequently said to have easily defeated his opponent. In modern days the cut stroke has been used very artistically by some players. Employing the usual top-cut ball on most occasions, they would undercut the ball when coming in to volley, the change of pace and bound considerably cramping their opponents' passing shots.

I do not propose to start with that early period when the game had not been exploited, but rather to begin with the Renshaw and Lawford era, when lawn tennis proper may be said to have begun. There can be no doubt that the game was made by the Renshaws. Before this, certainty of return was the chief and only important factor. With the soft and irregular bounding balls of that day it was very difficult to kill by driving, and as no one could volley properly, we are told that in a championship match there were over eighty returns in one rest. By introducing the volley, the Renshaws at once put an end to mere return, also to all the cuts and twists which had been considered effective, and now the base line player had to evolve some method of defence against the new attack.

H.F. Lawford is generally credited with being the originator of severe base line play, and was certainly at that time the leader in this department of the game. His forehand drive was by far his best stroke, the ball being struck with a horizontal racket and near the top of the bound, and an upward movement at the moment of striking imparting considerable top spin to the ball, causing it to drop very rapidly after crossing the net. The advantages of this method were that the ball could be struck much higher and harder without going out of court when a full-length stroke was played, and the 'duck' on the ball made it possible to play a much faster short cross when playing a volleyer.

This stroke has been so largely employed, and is so essentially a lawn tennis shot, that a further description of it may not be out of place. Nearly all the critics refer to this stroke as 'of low trajectory,' and as passing only inches over the net. I presume flat trajectory is what is meant. As a matter of fact, the trajectory is anything but flat. A rifle bullet is described as having a flat trajectory when the bullet drops but little. A projectile continuing indefinitely in a straight line would have an absolutely flat trajectory. But the 'drop stroke,' as it is called in America, has a very curved trajectory indeed, and to keep good length

29

must be struck feet over the net, it being easily seen that the greater the 'drop' the greater must be the elevation, supposing the velocity and length to remain constant.

This stroke has been at once the blessing and curse of lawn tennis players. Used by a Pim or a Larned it is a graceful and effective stroke, the ideal drive; although many of the best players have never employed it. But how many promising players have come to grief over it? Vainly endeavouring to get an unreasonable amount of top spin on the ball, all accuracy is thrown to the winds,* all other strokes neglected, and a good player spoiled. At the same time a reasonable employment of this stroke is most effective, and great credit is due to Lawford for evolving it.

William Renshaw has been called the father of lawn tennis and he certainly deserves the title, being also the strongest and most brilliant player of his day. His game was absolutely different from that of his great rival Lawford; he used no top on his stroke, rather a slight under-cut which caused the ball to skid on the ground, leaving it with a very low, fast hop. This was not done with a view to cutting the ball heavily, as at Tennis, but was rather incidental to his style of play. His main object seemed to be to hit the ball as soon as possible after it left the ground, giving his opponent little or no time to reach, much less to play the return. There has probably never been such a bustling player; his returns were a series of surprises; I am pretty sure his game would have held its own anywhere. To anticipate where the ball would next be placed was an impossibility. Instead of getting back to play a return off the ground, he would often dart in and volley a good-length stroke al-most from the back of the court, just as the striker was about to follow it up to the net, leaving the would-be volleyer helpless. No player who has not had personal experience of this stroke can imagine what it was like. How he had time to make up his mind to adopt this rapid change of position has always been a mystery to me, and only those who have tried to perform this manœuvre themselves can appreciate the quick-ness required for its execution.

Against Lawford, who was rather slow about the court, this style of play was most effective. Renshaw's service was properly delivered, which was by no means usual in those days; but in common with all players of that date, he never seemed to place it down the centre line. His first delivery was very fast, with a lot of kick and twist to the right in the righthand court, but the second would be considered weak ac-cording to modern standards. His backhand stroke down the line was

---

* If only Mr Mahony could have seen Bjorn Borg!

superb, and has served as a model to many. Delivered with startling suddenness and with considerable cut, it would skid and die away upon the ground before there was time to realise what had happened. As he could cross it with equal ease and the same action, it was not surprising that his opponent could often do nothing but look at it.

It can easily be imagined that such play was most fascinating to the crowd, more especially as it was executed with a graceful ease and rapidity of movement that was quite unique. He threw an amount of fire and dash into his game which could hardly fail to rouse the dullest spectator.

It has been the habit of many critics to deplore the want of brilliancy in more modern play when compared with the game of this period. One writer in particular, using a chess phrase, regretted the 'bits of Morphy.' The phrase is a very apt one. Many of Morphy's brilliant games have been shown to result in great part from weak moves on the part of his opponents, and would not be possible in modern chess. I shall endeavour to show that these very brilliant attacks must, as a rule, crumble before a steady and well-judged defence. But, indeed, counter attack would be a more correct term, as the chief object is never to play a weak short return, waiting till an opportunity offers to kill without undue risk.

It is just this undue risk which is the Achilles' heel of the very brilliant school; this was well illustrated in the encounters between W. Renshaw and W.J. Hamilton. These players met three times, and on each occasion the Irishman was victor.

He adopted the tactics which have always proved correct against a very hard hitter; speed of stroke was, to a large extent, sacrificed to length and pitch. To place the ball right in the corner, whether the stroke were fast or slow, was considered essential to success by the Irish players. I can distinctly remember, when competing in my first English Tournament, being much surprised at the short strokes that many of the competitors considered good enough to follow up to the net. Hamilton's drive was wonderfully safe and accurate, and, if the ball did not bound too high, a very fast stroke, but it was played mostly underhand, which prevented him taking the ball at or near the top of the bound, so that on a very fast court he had either to wait till the ball dropped or take it on the rise. The former method put him very far out of court, while the latter was so risky that to employ it persistently was not to his taste. In practice I have seen him make fancy strokes as well as anyone, but he always maintained that the most important quality for match play was reliability of execution, and that to attempt *tours de force* with the ball, except when necessary, was to court disaster. Those who

31

have had experience of match play can appreciate how sound is this advice.

But to return to the Renshaw-Hamilton matches. Off the very good length strokes of Hamilton, Renshaw now found that his winning shots could only be made at considerable risk, if they could be made at all. His opponent, by sacrificing some of his dash to method, and slogging to tactics, was content that the odds, on gaining the point, should be slightly in his favour, and his game, in consequence, a winning one.

From this description it must not be inferred that the Irishman played pat-ball, or that his game was one of mere return. His passing strokes were phenomenal, the ball pitching very near the side lines, and his lobbing of wonderful length. The moment Renshaw made a weak stroke he would instantly assume the offensive, but he hardly ever struck the ball right out of his opponent's reach at the beginning of a rest, which feat Renshaw performed several times during each set. Though the match was closely contested, the general impression left on many of the critics was that Renshaw's brilliant game had met its answer in Hamilton's equally effective but less risky tactics, an opinion which the results of the two subsequent matches would seem to justify.

But, sound as was Hamilton's game, there was a rod in pickle waiting for him in the shape of H.S. Barlow. For at Wimbledon, after defeating E.W. Lewis, he had to play Barlow in the semi-final. Barlow adopted his well-known volleying tactics, running in on the service. He would take no risk of any kind, save that of being passed at the net, and succeeded in winning after a very close match. Again strokes had to give way to method, and brilliancy to safer and more efficient system. Not that Barlow had not many good strokes; his overhead volleying was absolutely deadly, and he was most difficult to pass at the net, but his great strength lay in his generalship and iron nerve, enabling him to carry out at the critical moment what he saw to be the winning manœuvre. His general plan of campaign was, when serving, to place the ball down the middle of the court and follow it up to the net. His service had cut on it, which made it cling to the ground, and being placed down the centre, left the striker a very small space on either side in which to pass him. When his opponent served and did not follow it up to the net, he still played for the same position, playing a cut and twisted ball slightly to his adversary's backhand, and coming in close to volley on it. There was practically only one reply to such play – to rush in and volley everything; and even Pim and Baddeley were forced to adopt these tactics against him.

His form at Wimbledon was far in advance of his form at unimportant meetings. In one of the latter his love for losing the first two sets was freely indulged, and he has let matches slip through his fingers which he could easily have won but for this penchant. In consequence his powers have been largely underestimated. Wimbledon was the only meeting for which he ever trained in the least, and his form at the Championships in 1889 and 1890 would show him to be the equal of the Renshaws and Hamilton. I have not touched on his sensational match with W. Renshaw in 1889, in the final round of the Championship, as it has been so often described; it will suffice to say that Barlow was four times within a stroke of victory, which would certainly have been his but for a very bad decision.

I have given this rather extended description of Barlow's play because he represents the extreme type of stroke – play sacrificed to tactics. Why he should have cultivated this type of game is hard to say; probably cricket was responsible for his rather awkward grip of the racket. A lawn tennis player seldom gets any coaching when starting the game, so that his style will, to a great extent, be a matter of chance. This accounts mostly for the execrable style and feeble game played by the great majority of players. Every beginner grasping a racket for the first time will exhibit some peculiarity of grip and action; with this he will start playing, and by a process of experiment and failure evolve his own style. There is no friendly coach to tell him why he should break down so frequently over very simple strokes; he is thus thrown on his

33

own resources. If he be fortunate enough to have a strong player with good style to play against, or even to watch, he will often copy his methods largely. Barlow never acquired quite the correct grip of his racket, and though his wonderful activity, strength and sagacity enabled him to win, he could never have been a brilliant stroke player without changing his style.

E.W. Lewis's methods were the exact antithesis. Capable of making every stroke that can be made on a lawn tennis court, and also of many that would seem impossible, he always played what he considered the most effective return, regardless of the difficulty. The half volley was freely used, at which stroke he was *facile princeps*, and his cross backhand, both off the ground and on the volley, has left its mark on the Lawn Tennis world.

Ernest Renshaw had a style quite of his own, perfect grace of movement and ease of stroke being its most striking features. He kept his wrist quite flexible when striking the ball, allowing the momentum acquired by the racket during the preliminary swing to do the work of the stroke, the wrist and hand merely acting as guides to the direction. And though this method deprived his game of some severity (especially on the volley), it conduced to wonderful accuracy in strength and direction. He was very strong overhead, and was more successful against Hamilton than his brother. That he was as good a player hardly admits of dispute, though his record is not so fine.

W. Baddeley might fairly be described as the most successful player that ever was. Not that his record in the championship has been unsurpassed, but his successes were gained against stronger players than any other champion has had to meet. His method and generalship were unrivalled. This superiority lay in the type of game he cultivated, rather than in clever or tricky play in a match. Too often 'playing with your head' is taken to mean tricky, short drops, disguised directions or unexpected placing. To do this is comparatively easy for anyone possessing a little cunning and nerve; but to decide what is the winning 'play,' to use an Americanism, with a view to cultivating it in practice, requires no inconsiderable amount of sagacity.

It is here that so many players fail, though possessed of many good strokes, and it was just in this department of the game that W. Baddeley showed his superiority.

A very remarkable feature of his play was the considerable height at which some of his passing shots down the line would cross the net; this gave the strokes a high factor of safety, and as they were generally clean passes, to have played them lower would not have increased their efficiency, whilst he would have had to pay for additional risk in the shape of an increased number of balls placed in the net. His style approximated to a certain extent to tennis methods, as the head of the racket was generally kept well above the hand, and the stroke finished on the same side of the body, the secret of all straight hitting.

This latter characteristic was even more pronounced in his great rival, J. Pim. Possibly neither of these players were aware that this had been recognised as one of the first and essential principles of striking a ball at both tennis and rackets for many years, but the fact that they both carried it out in play testifies to their great natural aptitude. The general opinion of experts would seem to rank J. Pim as the finest player the world has ever seen. His game was of the very severe type, yet executed with such ease and nonchalance as to give the impression that he was taking no interest whatever in the proceedings.

A critic at Wimbledon once described his play as a combination of Lawford's drives and Lewis's volleys, and though his style was quite different from that of either of these players, the description is apt enough. His drive was a long, easy swing, combining little effort with great pace and accuracy. His extraordinary dislike to any hurried movement and his determination that the whole swing of his stroke should be carried through, often made him take the ball very late indeed. But the stroke was generally such a good one, and the direction so well disguised, that it was as effective as if he had played it sooner. If it suited him he could take the ball on the rise as well as anyone. I have seen him swing on to a big kicking first service, playing the ball on the top of the bound and right into the extreme corner, winning the point outright.

His volleying was remarkable for its great variety, combining great power and crispness with the softest and most delicate strokes. He could drop the hardest drives short over the net and well out to the sides, a most elegant and effective manner of dealing with them. His service was powerful and kicked considerably, the percentage of faults being very small, while the second delivery was nearly as severe as the first. His encounters with W. Baddeley produced the finest expositions of lawn tennis I have ever seen, and most lovers of the game who were present would seem to share this view.

Pim was badly handicapped in 1891 by an injury to his right hand caused by an outside car accident, and in 1892 he had only just recovered from typhoid fever. How he managed to beat Barlow in the Irish Championship, and gain a set from E. Renshaw the next day was a mystery to his friends, as he was totally unfit for hard match play. But in 1893 and 1894 he had matters all his own way, winning both Irish and English Championships.

Since this period I am inclined to think
that the game has not advanced; if
anything it has receded. The Doherty
brothers, however, form a brilliant exception
to the general stagnation. As their play is so
well known on both sides of the Atlantic,
I shall only touch on it briefly.
R.F. Doherty possesses the

severer strokes, his service
in particular being
unrivalled; the delivery is
so easy that he hardly
seems to put an
ounce of work into it;
yet the length and
pace are superb, and
he can place it right
out to the side or down
the centre line with perfect
precision. He only uses top-cut
occasionally on his forehand,
but it is freely employed
backhanded.

H.L. Doherty brings an amount of sagacity, activity and attention to bear on the game that renders him quite as formidable an antagonist as his brother. His extraordinary power of killing lobs from almost anywhere is a most striking feature of his play.

Charles Ambrose

Since American lawn tennis has been brought into prominence in this country by the visit of Messrs. Ward and Davis, and the various international contests, a short reference to American players may prove of interest. The first time J. Pim and the writer competed in America the general feature of the play in that country seemed to be a certain lack of method. Though the strokes were brilliant, no one seemed to play for position, rather simply to win the point. But my second visit found this all changed; everyone played for position, and that position was to get to the net first at any price. The general standard of play also had much improved, and we were treated to the twist service for the first time. The same evolution had taken place, the play was more effective and less risky.

Finally, to return to this country, I cannot help thinking that the play in the nineties was a considerable improvement on the form of the eighties. The chief features of this improvement lay in the following: The service was vastly improved, especially the second delivery; the cross backhand became much stronger, and lobs were dealt with more effectively. The value of position was more fully recognised, and undue risk avoided. Also the garden party idea that every good stroke must of necessity skim the net had, to a certain extent, been exploded; but there are even now many players who still cling to this fallacy.

As for the future of the game in this country, it seems to me to be merely a matter of time before the Championship passes into the hands of American players or foreigners. No young players of any ability are coming to the front, and as soon as the present exponents of first-class play retire, there would seem to be no one to take their place. Not that the number of players has not largely increased, but the numbers of the first-class are sadly shrunken. This should cause no surprise, as in the public schools in America the game is encouraged, whilst in this country it is not even permitted. This is all the more curious when it is remembered that rackets is freely encouraged and professionals hired to teach the game. Lawn Tennis is just as good exercise, possesses much greater variety of stroke, is played in the open-air and is much less expensive.

Until the game is permitted at some of the schools we can only expect to take a back seat in future, and this at a game which is played all the world over – the only really international game existing.

ANTHONY WILDING

AN APPRECIATION
A. Wallis Myers

Anthony Wilding, fighting for that Empire of which he was a unit, fell on May 9, 1915. Official intelligence of his death was conveyed to his father, Mr. Frederick Wilding, K.C., at Christchurch, New Zealand, through a report, dated May 14, addressed to the Director of Air Department, Admiralty, London:

> Sir, – It is with the deepest regret that I wired yesterday to report the death of Captain A.F. Wilding, R.M., who was attached to the Armoured Car Force.
>
> From information since received, his three-pounder lorry had been in action on the 9th inst., in the vicinity of Lestrem, up to 4.30 p.m., about which time the shell-fire became so intolerable that the gun's crew was sent to the trenches for shelter, Captain Wilding and three Army officers retiring to a dug-out close by. This was, however, shortly afterwards struck by a large shell, which killed the officers there, Captain Wilding dying in such a manner that his death must have been instantaneous.
>
> I beg to draw your attention to the fine work carried out by this officer. His loss will be greatly felt from a technical point of view, as he was carrying out experiments of great importance. On every occasion he had displayed the greatest bravery, exposing himself to every risk whilst working the armoured cars with the advanced forces of the Army. His loss is much regretted by the officers and men of the Armoured Car Division under my command.
>
> I have the honour to be, Sir, your obedient servant,
>
> REGINALD GREGORY,
> *Acting Commander, R.N.*

I begin this modest monograph of my friend with that report because it proves that Anthony Wilding, in the few months he had been on active service, had already made his mark. More, he had already impressed his personality upon his senior officers. They mourned him, not because in the tension and turmoil of battle there had been time for much intimacy, but because in their brief glimpse of him, in that transient communion of souls which is permitted in moments of mutual peril, some of his buoyancy, some of his great courage, and some of his philosophy of life had passed into their own consciousness. They had been the better for his coming.

Why were men in many countries attracted by Anthony Wilding? What was the talisman that enabled him to dispense with the ordinary passports of life? Why did he ingratiate himself so easily and so rapidly with people of distinction in all walks of life?

He was not a scholar. He cared nothing for politics; he hated war. Of books, music, and the fine arts he had but cursory knowledge. He never played nor dressed the part of a 'man about town.' He had no use for stimulants or narcotics; he neither smoked cigars nor drank whisky. The only form of scientific research in which he showed intelligent interest was mechanical traction. Wheels and petrol and quick motion he loved – loved them because, himself a perfect human machine designed for rapid propulsion, he was instinctively drawn to machines created by man for the same object; but very few who loved him had that passion. . . .

It may be that his physical vigour, the giant in Anthony Wilding, appealed to the æsthetic sense. He had won the highest renown at an amateur pastime. That renown had brought him prominently before the public; it had also brought him into contact with the royal and distinguished patrons of that pastime. But other champions had enjoyed the same prerogative; they had not created the same bonds. . . .

The physical factor, the reverence of the weak for the strong, is a partial but not a full answer. Anthony Wilding had more than his body to offer the world. The man was finer than his play. He possessed that rare, elusive quality called personal magnetism. Beneath his perfectly developed frame there beat the heart of a child. Like a child, he was pure and ingenuous. Like a child, he was unconscious of control and impatient of discipline. Like a child, using only the art of an unsophisticated nature, he claimed and won indulgence. Yet when the real test came – in sport or in war – Anthony Wilding revealed a steadfastness – a faculty for concentration, a self-reliance and a resourcefulness which made up a strong character. Physically and mentally he became a man; spiritually, he was a boy until the end.

ON THE COURT AND OFF
Anthony Wilding

By 'Championship' of course I refer to Wimbledon. Other arenas may draw larger and more demonstrative crowds – Melbourne, Sydney, Johannesburg, and Newport, for example – but there is no place so hallowed as the centre court of the All England Club, and no championship so worth striving for or so highly prized as the World's Championship at Wimbledon.

I recall very vividly the first match I ever saw on those famous lawns.* It was between poor H.S. Mahony and G.L. Orme in 1903. The friend who had taken me to Wimbledon, saying that he knew Mahony, offered me level money that he would be wearing odd socks, and made me a further bet that neither sock would belong to the genial Irishman. Just before play began my friend, evidently on intimate terms with the great man, called him up and said, 'Let me have a look at your socks, Harold.' To my surprise (that was before I knew Mahony) one sock was marked 'R.F.D.' and the other with less famous initials that were certainly not 'H.S.M.'

At the time I wondered if I would ever have the pluck to enter for Wimbledon, for the play seemed to me then nothing short of wonderful. Yet the following year I was battling on my own, and who should I meet in the second round but the man with the odd socks! To my great delight I captured a set and made Mahony talk to himself a great deal. I struggled along well the two following years until I met A.W. Gore, who carried too many guns and by mercilessly attacking my backhand from first to last wore down any attack I may have started with. I generally got away at first against him, and on two or three occasions had two sets to my credit, only to ultimately succumb. His pluck and pertinacity on these occasions always appealed to me.

The year that Gore beat me in the semi-final – 1906, I think – I played the longest single of my life. My opponent was W.J. Clothier, of America, a fine, loose-limbed man with the frame of a Guardsman. He had me two sets up and five games to two and 40-15 – a pretty tight corner for any man. However, I enjoyed a little luck, the tide began to turn, and altogether we played three hours and twenty-nine minutes. I won the final set at 12-10. I remember feeling at the finish that I could have gone on for another set.

* Wilding is writing of Worple Road, before the All England Club moved to its present site.

My next Wimbledon I met Beals Wright in the very first round. He had just arrived to take part in the Davis Cup matches, and, thanks to the fact that he was not properly acclimatized, I won by three sets to one. Beals did not go all out that day, I fancy. The following day I had an even stiffer proposition – my friend and colleague, Norman Brookes, who was ultimately to win the title. We played one of the fastest matches I have ever waged, the tennis being very fair. We got two sets all and three games all in the final set, when I dropped my service. That meant good-bye to any chance of the Championship in 1907. However, Brookes and I won the doubles comfortably, and, if my memory serves me rightly, we didn't drop a single set, beating the Americans, Beals Wright and Karl Behr, in the final.

Norman Brookes is, indeed, my favourite partner and the opponent by whom it gives me least pain to be defeated. He learnt all his tennis in Australia, and to Dr Eaves in large measure must be given the credit for bringing him up to his wonderfully high standard. The 'doctor' initiated him into the mysteries of the American service, and, as all the tennis world knows, Brookes made the ball 'talk' to such an extent that when he came home for the first time, in 1905, such prominent English players as Frank Riseley, Hillyard, Gore and Ball-Greene could make neither head nor tail of him. Brookes is probably the only instance of a player winning the World's Championship with local practice. In his early days at Melbourne virtually his only opponent was his brother, to whom he could easily give half-thirty and a beating. A more versatile games man I have seldom met. He can make his hundred break at billiards fairly regularly. He is on or near the plus mark at golf. He was one of the finest left-hand schoolboy bowlers in Australia, and if he had stuck to cricket his appearance in test matches must only have been a question of time. I remember staying with Brookes at his home in Melbourne when the Croquet Championship of Australia happened to be taking place. Brookes invited the winner to play him a match on Sunday, and a dreadful act of sacrilege was committed – the tennis court was marked out for croquet. The champion came, saw and was badly defeated. A keen motorist – though he always shuns my motor bikes as he would the devil – Brookes possesses two big F.I.A.T.'s, which he drives himself with consummate skill. But then the Brookes family is by way of being abnormal. One brother is nearly as strong as Sandow and Miss Brookes has a voice almost as fine and well trained as Melba's. A sister of Brookes, by the way, married Mr Deakin, ex-Prime Minister of Australia. As a partner Brookes is not always tranquil. He occasionally does those things you don't expect him to do and leaves undone others which you anticipate. But once understand him and no man can

42

wish for finer support. He invariably says what he thinks – a frankness
so often construed into conceit. He is married now and my one prayer
is that domesticity won't keep him off the court.

In 1908 I had a fairly smooth journey to the fifth round of the Championship, but at.that stage any further progress was peremptorily barred by the energetic figure and nimble brain of Roper Barrett. I won the first set with something to spare, but in the second I began to go to pieces, and by the time the fourth had arrived I wasn't worth a dog's chance. Roper Barrett is probably the cleverest player living. He is so quick about the court, so eager to seize the smallest opening, almost uncanny in his powers of anticipating. His volleying is versatile and sound, but I rate his generalship higher than I do his strokes.

Once more I had to console myself with the doubles. My partner on this occasion was Ritchie, to whose splendid spade work, rare tenacity and sound judgment, especially in a crisis, I, knowing his good qualities at first hand, can testify. We played together consistently for three years, twice winning the Championship at Wimbledon, and until last July in the challenge round at Wimbledon had never been beaten. I recall that we got the better of the Dohertys in the final at Nice – a match over the result of which a good many of the prophets, ignorant of the fact that R.F. Doherty was much below par, had their reputations shaken and their pockets drained.

I suppose the nearest shave Ritchie and I experienced was in the final at Wimbledon in 1908, when our opponents were Gore and Roper Barrett. It was an extraordinary match, for in the first two sets we only lost three games and in the next two we could only win two. The crowd were cheering the rally of the so-called veterans to the echo. Their applause was louder still when Barrett and Gore, moving forward gaily on the flowing tide, took the first two games in the final set. But both my partner and myself had a little kick left, and it was at this crisis more than any other that I appreciated Ritchie's supreme steadiness. His lobs were so well timed and so judiciously placed that Barrett was continuously seeing a balloon go over his head, while Gore was forced to run from corner to corner on the base-line. Those tosses, at such a time – and, I am almost ashamed to add, in such a sun – were of priceless value and one of them, perhaps the best of all, won the match in the sixteenth game, after our opponents, fighting grimly to the end, twice held the 'vantage game.

In 1909 I was being called to the New Zealand bar, but in 1910 I came home again. My father was quite keen for me to have another shot at the Wimbledon target.

Thus it came about that in January I left my native shores. South Africa was *en route* for England so I stopped at Durban and ran up to Johannesburg for the South African championship. My voyage took over eight weeks, a coal strike in Australia making us five weeks overdue. I thoroughly enjoyed myself in South Africa and just managed to win. But I was not at all confident about the result. Straight from a voyage of eight weeks to the glare of a Johannesburg tennis court and the whirligig of life on the Rand is a change difficult to imagine. It had been a long and tedious voyage with very few passengers to enliven the trip, and more from the need of keeping myself occupied I trained hard. Punch ball, skipping and, before breakfast, a pyjama gymnasium class, of which I was honorary instructor, all served to keep me fit. I also gazed at the sun for a fixed period every day to accustom myself to its hot rays and, in order to keep my grip 'green,' I waved a tennis racket about on the top deck. Yes, I think I deserved to win that South African championship.

My stay in Johannesburg was absolutely delightful and I never wish to meet a finer school of sportsmen than those with whom I came in contact. The Motor Cycle Club escorted me over to Pretoria, where we all lunched together and made motor bike speeches to celebrate the occasion. Then we adjourned to the tennis courts and had some good doubles. To finish a fine day we raced back on our machines to Johannesburg. Dreadful to relate, all this happened on a Sunday.

On the way to the Cape I stayed a day and a night at Kimberley. Local experts combined with the weather to make me excessively hot, the tennis there being medium. But of course the 'draw' at Kimberley are the diamonds. The boardroom of the De Beers office, round which I was taken, is a veritable diamond museum. Yet I confess I was very disappointed with the unpolished diamond. For all the world it looks like a dull pebble picked up haphazard from the seashore. Judging from the size of some of the diamonds rescued from the insides of adventurous kaffirs, the thieves deserved a happier fate than that which actually befell them. The system of catching the diamonds is at once novel and simple. Some genius discovered that water and stones will run over grease without sticking but that a diamond gets caught every time. This simple principle is now universally adopted. The stones are all crushed to a workable size and then mixed with water and run over large open shifting trays. The net result is that the water and stones run away and the diamonds remain on the grease. But the largest diamonds rarely reach the crushing machines. They are either captured in the mine or picked up on the flow by natives, to whom liberal commission is paid. More interesting even than diamonds is the De Beers stud farm – the best in South Africa. At Cape Town I had some more tennis and immensely enjoyed motoring round the mountains and to other places which really are intensely interesting. I formed a very high opinion of the beauties of Cape Town.

The voyage home on the *Saxon* was uneventful except for a catastrophe which occurred near the Canary Isles: my punch ball responded to an extra hard smack by flying over the life-boats and so into the sea. In vain I tried to improvise another. The sports proved a veritable triumph for Father Kelly of Bloemfontein. He was travelling in the second saloon, and as both classes combined for these sports a little friendly rivalry existed. But no one on our side could stand up to Kelly, who towered head and shoulders above everyone at all these games. He swung the monkey farther than anyone else. None of our heroes could sit on the bar for thirty seconds without Father Kelly dealing him a blow with the pillow that sent him spinning. Some months later I was playing the final of the London Covered Court Championship and who should I see up in the gallery but the hero of the pillow fights. He had taken the trouble to come all the way up to Queen's to see me play.

But to come to the Wimbledon meeting of 1910. Any luck the draw could bestow did not come my way. Indeed, I was fated to draw Roper Barrett in the very first round – one of my most dangerous opponents, and the man who had last beaten me, two years ago, in England. Moreover, the centre court, especially after its extensive alterations, was a most demoralizing arena in which to play a first match. The background, light and general atmosphere, were all changed. In this particular match conditions were made more difficult than usual, for it was sunny and windy. I was very much disconcerted at first. Playing from the town end I was forced by the rays of the sun to keep back. Directly rushing tactics were adopted, my opponent would cleverly lob, and, as everyone knows, it is quite impossible to smash accurately and well with the sun shining straight into one's eyes, especially as air pockets (to borrow an aeroplane term) kept issuing from the passage between the two stands. However, fortune was on my side. After losing the first set I became more accustomed to the strange conditions, and won the match 4-6, 6-4, 6-1, 6-4. And very pleased I was!

My next opponent was my friend, J.B. Ward, who only bothered to win one game in the three sets. The third round put me against an old opponent, M.J.G. Ritchie. At first all went well, but in the third set Ritchie pulled himself together and, playing very well, won it at 7-5. The last set I won at 6-2. The fourth round was not so difficult and I managed to win all three sets against McNair without losing a game. Keen is hardly a strong enough word to describe my enthusiasm at the time, and if straining every nerve and making every effort to win I could have defeated my opponent by more than 6-0, 6-0, 6-0, I would have done so. When well trained and in good form I'm sure it is policy to go in and play every stroke as if your very life depended upon it.

In the fifth round I met Froitzheim and I believe many judges prophesied a close match. But playing tennis interposed with too many dinners and dances at Homburg is a very different matter to playing for the championship at Wimbledon. Froitzheim no doubt found me a very different player to the man he had beaten in Germany a year before. The match does not call for much mention except that I only came to the net on something good and studiously avoided giving my opponent angles from which to make his wonderfully accurate passing shots. If you intend to volley a player like the German champion you must keep him in the centre of the court. The match ended 6-1, 6-2, 6-1.

In the semi-final my opponent was J.C. Parke, the Irish champion. He is a good lawn tennis player but an even better footballer and was the treasured possession of all representative Irish fifteens. In fact, his lawn tennis is reminiscent of Rugby football. On this occasion he fairly took my breath away for the first few games, and before I fully realized what was happening was leading by four games to one. Luckily I was able to make a recovery and to win the set at 7-5. The last two sets were not so close and I took them 6-2, 6-1. Parke tries a little too much and feels the want of a really reliable backhand; but he is wonderfully active and executes brilliant strokes from all quarters.

My final against Beals Wright proved a long and very interesting match to play – whatever it may have been to watch. I lost the first two sets 6-4, 6-4. Both were very close and might have been won by either of us. I was forty love in the tenth game of the first set and lost it. During this early stage of the match I stayed at the back of the court more than usual and as far as possible saved myself. I had proved before to my own satisfaction that it was possible to get the better of my good friend Beals by hustling up to the net, thereby depriving him of his only really dangerous weapon of attack – his volleying. But I had also come to the conclusion that it was nearly impossible to start hustling a man like Wright and to keep it up to the end. When I had last met Wright in Australia I hustled at first and paid the penalty. At Wimbledon I kept the hustle for the end. My tactics may have been right or they may have been wrong; they were, at all events, profitable in this particular match. Throughout the entire contest, I felt fairly confident. I knew that Wright's close quarter attack, maintained at such a high pressure, must weaken in the third set if I could only give him enough to do. Once I forced him to drop back, as drop back he did, I felt my chance would come. Several spectators of this match seemed to think – judging by their subsequent remarks – that I won solely on condition. Perhaps I may be allowed to quote the special correspondent of *The Daily Telegraph*, who, writing on the morrow of the final, said:

The secret of Wilding's victory was, I think, the husbanding of his strength, the 'holding himself in' during the first two sets. He discovered it in Australia pitted against Wright himself in 1908 and Brookes in 1909. It is a secret that H.L. Doherty found out and employed with great success in the past. Applied to American and Colonial volleyers who follow their service to the net, but plainly, it is this – give them enough rope and they will hang themselves. In other words, let them drain their resources in the first two sets, encourage them by a stout resistance to go all out; but keep a little something in reserve for the third set, when the hustling campaign is bound to exact its penalty. You may say Wilding won on condition. That is only partly true. He won because, like a sagacious commissariat officer, he apportioned his resources over five sets instead of three. He stood his ground in the thick of the American bombardment and when the ammunition of his antagonist had run dry he had enough strength and powder left to capture the fort.

Let me add here that I consider Beals Wright one of the finest sportsmen it has ever been my good fortune to be defeated by and in turn defeat. A tryer from first to last, invariably keen, he takes victory and defeat with the same smiling grace. If his ground strokes were equal to his wonderful volleying and his service, there is not a player born who could beat him.

In the challenge round I met A.W. Gore. It was freely proclaimed by Gore's friends, and even hinted at by Gore himself, that he was right 'out of form.' Fortunately I took no notice of these remarks, so was not at all surprised to find him the same tough proposition I had been up against on countless previous occasions. The most pertinacious player living, he goes hard all the time – you have never got him. I may not admire his style, but I have always admired his pluck. Only once have I partnered him in doubles, at Leicester in 1906, and then we came within a point of beating the Doherty brothers.

Gore started well, getting in his forehand drive with alarming frequency. In fact, he played as finely as he had ever done before against me. He led in the first set by four games to one; but the Fates were kind and I managed to win that bout at 6-4. The second set was very close and I just won it at 7-5. In the third set Gore tired a little and no doubt profiting by the declining vigour of his drives, I got going much better and led by four games to two. At that point one of those heavy rainstorms for which Wimbledon is famous suddenly descended. A quarter of an hour's halt was called; we had to wait and shiver in the wings. You may imagine what that pause meant to one who felt he had the Championship in his grasp. When we resumed the court had a greasy surface. Gore got to work well and won the next six games off

48

A.W. Gore

the reel – that is, the set at 6-4.
The court was very much
against me. Weighing thirteen
stone two, it was impossible
to skip about a greasy
court, shod in light rubber shoes,
with the same degree of activity that
ought to be displayed by
a man of ten stone. However,
the court improved, and
fortunately I did not get unduly
cast down. I won the last
set by six games to two.

Needless to say, I was relieved when the last stroke was won. I had
experienced considerable mental strain, enhanced by the fact that I had
come all the way from New Zealand for this one event. My chief delight
was in knowing the joy it would give my father and mother in New Zealand. Such a result had always been their ambition. I fondly believe that

if I had been elected Prime Minister of England it could not have given them more pleasure. In large communities that prevail in England one can hardly realize the wonderful *esprit de corps* existing in a little country like New Zealand. Winning a lawn tennis championship is really a very small performance, but every friend in that country, from the Prime Minister downwards, cabled me his delight.

Any success I have enjoyed at Wimbledon has been due to my kind hostess, Mrs Horn, of Wimbledon Park House. She would never permit me to go near the beloved motor cycle. Long before I developed any symptoms of a cold my head was pushed into a eucalyptus bath. All the good things to eat and drink were 'tăpu,' as the Maoris say. Nor was I ever allowed to forget bed-time or seven A.M. Little wonder therefore that I have never been so fit before or since. I had a difficult draw, but, being fit, I rather liked it than otherwise. The final against Beals Wright was the only match over which I had any anxious moments, but even then I felt fairly happy.

The less said the better about the challenge round of 1911. The heat was abnormal – the thermometer stood at 88°F. – and the play very bad in consequence. The match was a great disappointment alike to players and spectators. Roper Barrett had had enough after four sets – so had I – but he 'chucked it' first. The court, entirely shut in, and surrounded by people, closely resembled a baker's oven. Personally I had done everything in my power to enter the lists fit, but I candidly confess to being more or less a victim to the heat. At no time during this match could I follow a single service up to the net. Tactics hardly existed. Get the ball back somewhere and somehow was almost the height of our ambitions. Barrett's success lies in placing and dropping balls short and he played his usual game, only minus about 80 per cent of his usual agility. During the match I probably ran some five miles farther than he did, conditions favouring rather than otherwise his style of game. I occasionally marvelled at Barrett's wonderful endurance under those altogether normal conditions, but had little mind for reflection. Davis Cup matches in the tropical heat of Australia (96°F. in the shade, to be precise) were to my mind not nearly so trying as last year's challenge round at Wimbledon. Probably under normal conditions Mr Barrett and I would last equally well, but what is entirely beyond my comprehension is that, suffering from illness, he could go on as he did. His scratching came as a great surprise to me, as I hardly thought it was possible for him to be more 'baked' than I myself felt during the entire course of the match. I attribute the very mediocre tennis displayed by both of us entirely to the conditions. To affirm that the heat only affected one party is unfair and untrue.

So many diverse opinions have been advanced on the question of 'playing through' at Wimbledon that I should like to express my views regarding it. I may emphasize one point, which in my opinion is the keynote to the whole affair. The holder and the challenger are not confronted with equal risks of defeat. I presume the object of the Championship is to decide which is the best player of the year. That being so, surely all players should start under the same conditions, and, as nearly as practical in a knock-out event, run equal chances of being 'quitted.' But how can the conditions be called fair when the challenger has eight matches to win and the holder one to gain the same end – *i.e.* the Championship for the year? It is for this reason, and not because of the physical strain, about which so much exaggerated twaddle has been written, that I give my vote for the holder playing through. Physical strain there undoubtedly is, but not so much as critics and so-called judges would have us suppose.

An all-important fact on which sufficient stress has never been laid is that no player can be called upon to play more than one match during a day. From personal experience, and from observation of others, I am convinced it is a succession of matches on the one day that brings on staleness, physical exhaustion and other tennis ills. One hard match a day, with an occasional double thrown in, and this only when the player feels inclined, ought never to affect a trained man, mentally or physically. But give a man one match in the morning and two in the afternoon for a couple of weeks; then staleness, accompanied by all the other tennis maladies, will very quickly result. Up to the present, the average first-class lawn tennis player has hardly given a thought to training. If players who desire to gain the highest laurels at Wimbledon would embark upon a scientific course of preparation less would be heard of their physical collapse. A collapse brought about by what? By playing one match a day for two weeks, with a complete no-play rest on Sundays and on the day before the challenge round? I honestly believe, provided a little trouble and care are exercised, that the average player can come up for the challenge round better for a really hard struggle than he was on the opening day. But the time has come when a player, if he wishes to be successful, must train, and train systematically. It is too ridiculous to picture a prizefighter entering the ring trained in a like manner to some of our Wimbledon stars. The modern tendency in lawn tennis is to make the game faster; it may not be such an accurate style as that adopted by the giants of yesterday, but strenuous it is, without a doubt. The essence of the game as played by the rising Continental and American players is to attack – not attack as fancy calls, but to attack hard from the first stroke to the last and never slack off for an instant. Here it is that the trained athlete has an incalculable advantage. A possible explanation of the unpopularity of training among tennis players may be that a vast majority of matches are decided on skill alone. Physical attributes only become apparent when players of equal, or nearly equal, calibre are opposed. During the progress of the All-Comers at Wimbledon neither of the ultimate finalists is likely to be thoroughly extended in more than two or three matches at the very utmost.

What about the mental aspect? Here temperament is everything, but I don't think many players handicap themselves much on this score. Certainly one man will sleep like a top on the eve of meeting a dreaded rival on the centre court, while another, under similar conditions, will spend the whole night tossing among the bedclothes, missing easy smashes and making double faults in his dreams. But here again the thoughtful and careful man who has taken the trouble to fit himself for his task comes out on top. If players will get themselves into perfect health and training they will probably sleep as soundly before a match as at any other time. The worry of playing day after day what, for length and anxiety, is the equivalent of an ordinary final, must naturally jag the nerves of the challenger a little. But to counterbalance this, a player meeting with success day after day on the same court and under the same conditions plays himself in, and gains great confidence. It is unnecessary to point out what a wonderful asset confidence is. Further, the challenger also gets thoroughly acclimatized to his surroundings.

Now let us turn to the holder, and briefly summarize his preparation. It is only fair and just that the authorities should allow the holder to practise in the morning on the almost sacred centre court. But play is only permitted when the court is absolutely dry, and then only for a limited time. These rules are quite fair and I agree with them. Practice, however, no matter what its severity, is not the same thing as a match. The morning and afternoon lights are absolutely different. During a match the people in the stands and the puzzling position of the sun (a blemish which really spoils the centre court in sunny weather) make the atmosphere, light and surroundings those of another sphere from the serene and quiet morning.

It will be apparent from what I have endeavoured to say that in my view (1) Far too much importance is attached to the supposed advantage held by the holder who waits for a challenge, and (2) that in normal circumstances it may more often be found that it is the challenger who is really favoured by the present conditions. While these are my views yet I must say that I am strongly in favour of all conditions being equal for everyone.

Having given expression to such an opinion I am anxious to go further. If the All England Club will bring about this altogether desirable change, I, as champion for 1911, am willing to assist them in every possible way that lies in my power. If resigning the championship would facilitate matters nothing would give me greater pleasure.

Wilding's generous offer was not taken up. He had been dead seven years before the challenge round was abolished in 1922. And it was not until 1983 that another New Zealander reached the Wimbledon final. Wilding would have applauded Chris Lewis, not merely for his spirit and sportsmanship, but also for his strict adherence to the systematic physical training Wilding advocated so strongly all those years before.

If you look up the old draw sheets of the Wimbledon Championships, those prior to 1914 especially, and for other British tournaments of the period, you will find here and there the identity of a player discreetly hidden by the use of a pseudonym.

'Dagger', 'J. Verne', 'Pollux', 'Castor' – all these and many more are to be found. One of the great users of such anonymity was H. Roper Barrett, one of the most famous of old British players who, having been a Davis Cup player himself, became British Davis Cup captain in the days when it was not only possible for Great Britain to win the trophy but actually did so in the 1930s.

Doubtless such discretion of printed anonymity was the habit in the U.S. also. I am here more particularly concerned with the British experience because of what was concealed for many years – murder, no less.

The use of the pseudonym in Britain persisted more or less up to 1939. It was a well recognized and officially permitted way of keeping one's identity reasonably secret. In Britain there was a regulation that while a different pseudonym could be used by a player, he or she had to stick to the same one for the duration of the season.

Why a pseudonym anyway? Well, in the good old amateur days – and even in the shamateur ones – a fellow might be quietly taking time off from his office to enjoy the delights of a tournament. He did not want his boss, or maybe a customer, to know he was not attending to his business by having his name in the paper.

Certainly in Britain in the old days it was the habit of the press to respect such anonymity. Of course if the pseudonymous hero got to the final of a tournament the chances were that his identity would be disclosed. Though not always, as the following cautionary tale will reveal.

V. 'St. Leger' was the man. When I first began to dabble in lawn tennis history I used to ponder about 'St. Leger'. Who and what was he?

The St. Leger is, as all Englishmen know, a famous horse race. But what has that got to do with the Wimbledon Championships of 1879?

It was in that year, the third in line of the historic meetings, that the pseudonym V. 'St. Leger' appeared. In the first round he won 6-1, 6-2, 6-3 against F. Durant. Then he beat A.J. Mullholland 6-4, 2-6, 6-1, 6-4. The third round saw matters getting tougher. 'St. Leger' got by G.E. Tabor 6-2, 6-5, 5-6, 6-3 (advantage sets in those days were played only in the final). That took our hero into the semi-final and there he had a bye through to the final. Byes in those days were not restricted to the first round. The final was not of the championship itself but of the All-Comers' event.

But as it happened in 1879 the title holder, Frank Hadow was not able to defend his championship. He had gone back to his coffee plantation in Ceylon. That meant that the All-Comers' Final would decide the championship. V. 'St. Leger' played against the Reverend John Hartley, whose game was in every respect a product of the vicarage lawn.

'St. Leger', it seemed, volleyed like mad but rather wildly. Hartley, an Anglican vicar from the north of Yorkshire, returned every ball with maddening consistency. He beat his man 6-2, 6-4, 6-2 and so became Wimbledon Champion.

So, who was 'St. Leger'? He never played at Wimbledon again. Actually he won the second prize in 1879 because, having had a bye through the semi-final, he had to play against C.F. Parr to settle the 2nd and 3rd prizes. He won 4-6, 6-2, 5-6, 6-4, 6-4.

'St. Leger' was, it seems, quite a lad and quite well known. He had, it was said, a fine backhand. Prior to Wimbledon 1879 he had taken part in the inaugural Irish Championships in Dublin. That meeting that year was famous for initiating the first women's singles championship in the history of the game.

And 'St. Leger' was the first men's singles champion. It was not an easy championship to win because it rained a lot. It always has tended to rain a lot in the Irish Championships and the start in 1879 was no exception.

There was an entry of 15 for the men's singles and all four rounds had to be played in the one day. 'St. Leger' was up to the effort and he beat C.D. Barry in the final by 8-6, 8-6. I suspect, too, that he and other competitors had a jar or two to cheer themselves up and keep the damp out.

'St. Leger' did keep his Irish title the following year. In 1880 he was, it seems, unfit. At any rate he lost, 6-1, 6-4, 6-3 in the Challenge Round to William Renshaw, who was then taking his first steps to become the greatest player of the decade.

Well, who was 'St. Leger'?

He was an Irishman and one of a distinguished family. He was born in 1853, the younger brother of Sir James Stephen Goold, 4th Baronet in the County of Cork. He was Vere Thomas St. Leger Goold.

Such a name, such a lineage, was enough to get a man a lot of credit anywhere. But one should not over-estimate Vere's good fortune. I know nothing about this brother, to whom the baronetcy descended, only that he can hardly have prospered in accord with the nobility of his background since he had emigrated to Australia in 1863 and was employed as a railway ganger. From what I know of Australians he must have had to take a lot of leg pulling if his fellow workers got to know that Jimmy Goold was really 'Sir James'.

Nor is much known about Vere. When his later troubles descended on his head it was stated he had been in the public service in both Dublin and London.

In 1891 Vere got married in Bayswater, London. Both he and his wife were then 38. She was French, born Marie Girodin in the department of Isere, France. On the marriage certificate she was described as Violet Wilkinson, rather mysteriously. It seems she had had an earlier husband. Vere's lawn tennis must have been a thing of the past, at least at a competitive level.

One gets the impression, though there are few hard facts to support anything, that Vere was an impoverished son of an impoverished Irish family living the best he could on his wits. It seems that Mr. and Mrs. Goold lived for a time in Montreal. Then they opened a laundry at Waterloo, near Liverpool, England.

It is certain that in August 1907 they were living in Monte Carlo. A great place, Monte Carlo – with just a little capital to start you can live in the sun and consume nectar and ambrosia and never think of sordid things like work, always provided the right numbers come up at roulette or the right cards at Baccarat or chemmy.

The Goolds had a flat in the Villa Menesini. They also had acquaintance with a Danish widow, Emma Livey, a woman of some means.

Such was the background to 'St. Leger's' most famous contest.

In the early evening of 6th August Mr and Mrs Goold arrived in Marseilles on the train from Monte Carlo. With them was a trunk and a large suitcase. They attempted to deposit the article in the cloakroom, talking of having them sent to London.

The attendant was neither helpful nor cordial. Rather he wrinkled his nose and called for the police.

They in turn, having opened the luggage, invited explanation from Monsieur and Madame Goold. How do you explain the dismembered portions of a woman?

The subsequent trial took place in Monte Carlo, starting on 2nd December and lasting three days. There were 30 witnesses called.

So far as it was possible to get credit from such a sordid affair Vere Goold seems to have earned it. At least he played out the final moments of his match sportingly. He confessed to killing Madame Livey following a violent quarrel when she pressed for the return of a loan. His wife, he claimed, was guiltless.

The prosecution called evidence to show that such a murder and the subsequent dismemberment of the body could not have been by one person. A black picture was painted of the Goolds living from hand to mouth, of falling from borrowing to stealing and, finally, to murder.

The court took the view that Mrs Goold was the more guilty. She was sentenced to death, Vere to penal servitude for life. That was on 5th December 1907. Their appeals were rejected, though the sentence of Mrs Goold was commuted to life imprisonment.

There were no advantage sets to be played by either. The unlucky Vere was dispatched to Devil's Island, the notorious penal settlement in French Guiana, where he died of the inevitable fever in September 1909. His wife was incarcerated in Montpelier Prison and died there in 1914.

They did not have penalty points in the days when poor 'St. Leger' came so near to being the champion of Wimbledon. I doubt, though, whether any top player was made to pay so harsh a penalty.

BIG BILL TILDEN
FRANK DEFORD

With any artist who attains the ultimate in his craft, there must be one moment, an instant, when genius is first realized, when a confluence of God's natural gifts at last swirl together with the full powers of endeavor and devotion in the man to bear him to greatness. Virtually always, of course, that moment cannot be perceived, and it passes unnoticed, but with Big Bill Tilden it was isolated, forever frozen in time.

He knew precisely when he had arrived, and, thoughtfully, he revealed it.

This happened on Centre Court at Wimbledon in 1920. Tilden was already twenty-seven, and although he had never won a major championship, he had reached the finals. It was his first trip abroad, and to his delight the British, unlike his own countrymen, had taken to him right away. Americans always only grudgingly granted Tilden recognition, never mind respect, largely because they were emotionally hung up on Big Bill's main rival, Bill Johnston, who was affectionately known as Little Bill, or even, in the soupiest moments, Wee Willie Winkie. Johnston was five feet eight, a wonderful cute doll-person from the California middle class, and all Americans (Tilden prominently included) were absolutely nuts about him: the little underdog with the big heart who cut larger fellows down to size.

By contrast, at six feet one and a half inches tall, 155 pounds, angular and overbearing, a Philadelphia patrician of intellectual pretension, Big Bill was the perfect foil for Little Bill, and the great American villain. Until 1920 he had also cooperated by remaining a loser with a healthy reputation for choking in important matches. The year before, in the finals at Forest Hills, Johnston had defeated Tilden in straight sets, and so it was assumed that Wimbledon would serve as the stage where Johnston, the American champion, would duel Gerald Patterson, the Wimbledon defender, for the undisputed championship of the world.

Unfortunately for hopes for this classic confrontation, Johnston was waylaid in an early round by a steady English player named J.C. Parke. Not until the next day, when Tilden routed Parke, avenging Little Bill's defeat, did Big Bill move front and center as Patterson's most conspicuous challenger. Of course, from the moment Tilden strode upon their grass that summer, the British had been enchanted with him – his game, his manner, his idiosyncrasies: 'this smiling youth, so different from other Americans.' A woolly blue sweater Tilden wore seems to have positively enthralled the entire nation, and the London *Times* exclaimed that 'his jumpers are the topic of the tea-table.'

While little Johnston struck the British as just that, a pleasant little sort, the lean giant caused them admiration and wonder: 'Of great stature, he is loosely built with slender hips and very broad shoulders . . . in figure, an ideal lawn tennis player.' His game they found so arresting – 'There is no stroke Mr Tilden cannot do at full speed, and his is undoubtedly the fastest serve seen' – that one of the more poetic observers even rhapsodized, 'His silhouette as he prepares to serve suggests an Egyptian pyramid king about to administer punishment.'

Seeing Tilden for the first time, unprepared for that sight, was obviously a striking experience. Not so much in what exactly they said but in their evident astonishment and determined hyperbolic reach do the British of 1920 best intimate what an extraordinary presence Big Bill Tilden must have been. Yet perhaps even more important, the British understood immediately that here was a different sort of athletic temperament. The Americans were not to fathom this in Tilden for years, if indeed many of them ever did. But Tilden had played only a handful of matches in England that summer before he was assessed perfectly in the sporting press: 'He gives the impression that he regards lawn tennis as a game – a game which enables him to do fascinating things, but still a game. . . . When he has something in hand he indulges his taste for the varied at the expense of the commercial.'

Pleased at the attention given him, even more gratified that his playing philosophy was appreciated, Tilden grew assured, and, boldly and not without some conceit, he began to enunciate his theories of the game. When not at the courts or attending the theater, he spent all his time writing in his hotel room, and within three weeks he had completed his first book, *The Art of Tennis*. 'The primary object in match tennis is to break up the other man's game' was, significantly, the point he most emphasized.

Patterson, meanwhile, remained quite confident. An Australian, the nephew of the great opera star Nellie Melba, he was not only the defending Wimbledon champion but star of the team which held the Davis Cup. He was at his peak and generally recognized above Johnston as the ranking player in the world. At Wimbledon Patterson had only to bide his time scouting the opposition and practice at his leisure, for in those days the defender did not play in the regular tournament but was obliged only to meet the 'all-comers' winner in a special challenge round.

Patterson's supremacy seemed all the more obvious after Tilden appeared to struggle in the all-comers final against the Japanese, Zenzo, Shimizu. In each set Tilden fell far behind: 1-4 in the first, 2-4 in the second, 2-5 in the third. He won 6-4, 6-4, 13-11. Nobody realized it at the time, but it was one of Tilden's amusements, a favor to the crowd, to give lesser opponents a head start. Tilden had whipped Shimizu 6-1, 6-1 in a preliminary tournament the week before Wimbledon, and he certainly had no intention of cheating his Centre Court fans with that same sort of lopsided display. In the final set Big Bill tested himself and kept things going, largely just by hitting backhands and nothing much else.

'The player owes the gallery as much as an actor owes the audience,' he wrote once; and Paul Gallico summed it up: 'To his opponents it was a contest; with Tilden it was an expression of his own tremendous and overwhelming ego, coupled with feminine vanity.' Big Bill never really creamed anybody unless he hated them or was in a particular hurry to get somewhere else.

Certainly he was not ever anxious to hastily depart Centre Court at Wimbledon, and he returned for the championship against Patterson on Saturday, July 3. Big Bill found this date especially felicitous; an obsessive patriot, he noted that, for an American, July 3 was the next best thing to July 4. He further buttressed this omen by somehow obtaining a four-leaf clover that he was assured had once grown under the chair that Abraham Lincoln used to sit in on the White House lawn. And so, with that talisman safely ensconced in his pocket, he set out to become the first American ever to win the Wimbledon men's championship.

Patterson had a strong serve and forehand, but his weakness was an odd corkscrew backhand that he hit sort of inside out. And so, curiously it seemed, Tilden began by playing to Patterson's powerful forehand. The champion ran off the first four games with dispatch and won the set 6-2. But then, as Tilden changed sides for the first time in the second set, he spotted a good friend, the actress Peggy Wood, sitting in the first row with a ticket he had provided her, and he looked straight at Miss Wood, and with a reassuring nod, that kind delivered with lips screwed up in smug confidence, he signaled to her that all was quite well, that it was in the bag, that finally, at the age of twenty-seven, he was about to become the champion of the world.

Miss Wood, of course, had no notion that she would be used as a conduit for history; nor, for that matter, could she understand Tilden's cockiness. He had lost the first set 6-2; he was getting clobbered by the best player in the world. But down the five full decades, and more, that have passed, she cannot forget that expression of his, nor what followed. 'Immediately,' she says, as if magic were involved, 'Bill proceeded to play.'

In that instant he had solved Patterson's forehand, and the champion, his strength ravaged, had nothing but his weakness to fall back upon. *The primary object in match tennis is to break up the other man's game.* 'A subtle change came over Patterson's game,' the *Guardian* correspondent wrote in some evident confusion. 'Things that looked easy went out, volleys that ought to have been crisply negotiated ended up in the net.'

Tilden swept the next three sets at his convenience, losing only nine games, and toward the end it was noted for the record that 'the Philadelphian made rather an exhibition of his opponent.'

Big Bill did not lose another match of any significance anywhere in the world until a knee injury cost him a victory more than six years later. Playing for himself, for his country, for posterity, he was invincible. No man ever bestrode his sport as Tilden did for those years. It was not just that he could not be beaten, it was nearly as if he had invented the sport he conquered. Babe Ruth, Jack Dempsey, Red Grange and the other fabled American sweat lords of the times stood at the head of more popular games, but Tilden simply was tennis in the public mind: *Tilden and tennis*, it was said, in that order. He ruled the game as much by force of his curious, contradictory, often abrasive personality as by his proficiency. But he was not merely eccentric. He was the greatest irony in sport: to a game that then suffered a 'fairy' reputation,

Tilden gave a lithe, swashbuckling, athletic image – although he was in fact a homosexual, the only great male athlete we know to have been one.

Alone in the world of athletics, nearly friendless and, it seems, even ashamed of himself, there was seldom any joy for the man, even amidst his greatest tennis triumphs. It's quite likely that in his whole life Tilden never spent a night alone with an adult, man or woman. And his every day was shadowed by the bizarre and melancholy circumstances surrounding a childhood he tried to forget; certainly it is no coincidence that he did not blossom as a champion until just after he discarded the name of his youth.

He had been born on February 10, 1893, and christened William Tatem Tilden Jr., which he came to hate because everyone called him Junior or June. Finally, arbitrarily, around the time of his twenty-fifth birthday, he changed the Junior to the Second, II. That onus officially disposed of, June became Bill and then, even better, Big Bill.

He had been introduced to tennis early. It was an upper class game, and the family he was born into was rich, of ascending social prominence, and even greater civic presence. The family mansion, Overleigh, was located in the wealthy Germantown section of Philadelphia, only a block or so from the Germantown Cricket Club. The Tildens belonged, of course, and the club was indeed to be the site of many Big Bill triumphs, but the family summered at a fashionable Catskill resort, Onteora, and it was there that young June learned the game of tennis, in the last year of the nineteenth century.

The first clear vision of him as a player does not arise, however, until about a decade later, when Tilden was playing, with little distinction, for the team at his small private school, Germantown Academy. This day he was struggling on the court, slugging everything, all cannonballs, when Frank Deacon, one of his younger friends, came by. Even then, as a schoolboy, Tilden was always closest to children years younger than he. At the end of a point, which, typically, Tilden had violently overplayed, hitting way out, Deacon hollered to him in encouragement, 'Hey, June, take it easy.'

Tilden stopped dead, and with what became a characteristic gesture, he swirled to face the boy, placing his hands on his hips and glaring at him. 'Deacon,' he snapped, 'I'll play my own sweet game.'

And so he did, every day of his life. He was the proudest of men and the saddest, pitifully alone and shy, but never so happy as when he brought his armful of rackets into the limelight or walked into a crowded room and contentiously took it over. George Lott, a Davis Cup colleague and a man who actively disliked Tilden, was nonetheless this mesmerized by him: 'When he came into the room it was like a bolt of electricity hit the place. Immediately, there was a feeling of awe, as though you were in the presence of royalty. You knew you were in contact with greatness, even if only remotely. The atmosphere became charged, and there was almost a sensation of lightness when he left. You felt completely dominated and breathed a sigh of relief for not having ventured an opinion of any sort.'

Tilden himself said, 'I can stand crowds only when I am working in front of them, but then I love them.' Obviously the crowds and the game were his sex. For a large part of his life, the glory years, all the evidence suggests that he was primarily asexual; it was not until he began to fade as a player and there were not enough crowds to play to that his homosexual proclivities really took over. But ahh, when he was king, he would often appear to trap himself in defeat, as he had against Shimizu, so that he could play the better role, prolonging his afternoons as the cynosure in the sun, prancing and stalking upon his chalked stage, staring at officials, fuming at the crowd, now toying with his opponent, then saluting him grandly, spinning, floating, jumping, playing his own sweet game, reveling in the game.

And yet, for all these excesses of drama and melodrama, his passion for competition was itself even superseded by another higher sense: sportsmanship. Tilden was utterly scrupulous, obsessed with honor, and he would throw points (albeit with grandeur, Pharisee more than Samaritan) if he felt that a linesman had cheated his opponent. Big Bill was the magistrate of every match he played, and the critic as well. 'Peach!' he would cry in delight, landing any opponent who beat him with a good shot. And, if inspired or mad enough at the crowd or at his rival, he would serve out the match by somehow holding five balls in one huge hand and then tossing four of them up, one after another, and pounding out four cannonball aces – bam, bam, bam, bam; 15-30-40-game – then throwing the fifth ball away with disdain. That was the style to it. Only the consummate showman would think of the extra ball as the closing fillip to the act.

'He is an artist,' Franklin P. Adams wrote at Bill Bill's peak. He is more of an artist than nine-tenths of the artists I know. It is the beauty of the game that Tilden loves; it is the chase always, rather than the quarry.'

Further, even more unlike almost all great champions in every sport, whose brilliance is early recognized, early achieved, Tilden was required to make himself great. Very nearly he created himself. Only a few years before he became champion of the world, he could not make the college varsity at the University of Pennsylvania. He taught himself, inspired himself, fashioning a whole new level for the game in the bargain.

Withal, it is probable that the very fact that he was homosexual was largely responsible for the real success he achieved in tennis; he had none elsewhere. Urbane, well-read, a master bridge player, a connoisseur of fine music, he held pretensions to writing and acting as well as tennis, but these gossamer vanities only cost him great amounts of stature and money, and even held him up to mockery. For all his intelligence, tennis was the only venture that June Tilden could ever succeed at, until the day he died in his cramped walk-up room near Hollywood and Vine, where he lived out his tragedy, a penniless ex-con, scorned or forgotten, alone as always, and desperately in need of love from a world that had tolerated him only for its amusement. 'He felt things so very deeply,' Peggy Wood says. 'He was not a frivolous person, and yet, I never saw him with anybody who could have been his confidant. How must it be like that? There must have been so many things deep within him that he could never talk about. I suppose he died of a broken heart.' It seems he did.

To the end, in the good times and the bad, he searched for one thing above all: a son. He could not have one, and so he would find one for himself, make one, as he made himself a great player to honor the dead mother he worshipped. But the boys he found, whom he loved and taught, would grow up and put away childish things, which is what any game is, what tennis is, and ultimately, what Big Bill Tilden was. He was the child of his own dreams, always, until the day he died, age sixty, his bags packed, ready once again to leave for a tennis tournament.

GOLDEN JUBILEE

NORAH CLEATHER

It was in 1926, the last year of Suzanne's sensational reign at Wimbledon, that the All England Club celebrated its Golden Jubilee, the fiftieth anniversary of the first lawn tennis championships; but to recall the French girl's final appearance there brings back a host of other recollections of that historic gathering.

'Commemorative medals will be presented to the champions by Their Majesties King George and Queen Mary' announced the papers just before the meeting. Wimbledon was to be Royal indeed, with Royalty in the Committee Box and Royalty actually due to appear on the courts, for in addition to the presentation ceremony, our present King, then Duke of York, was to compete in the men's doubles.

The curtain rose on the impressive scene of the presentation when, at three o'clock on the opening day, all the champions and ex-champions were lined up on the centre court, waiting to make their bow or curtsy to Their Majesties.

I can see them now, thirty-three of them; masters of the game who for half a century had helped to make Wimbledon one of the foremost sporting events in the world. The men were grouped in front and behind the lady players; only one familiar figure was missing, Jean Borotra of the many berets, while for their part the huge crowds of spectators looked up affectionately at the Royal Standard, fluttering high above the marquees and stands, saluting it with many thousand eyes as they filed into the Club to pay tribute to their favourite players, the stars of the past and present.

At the ends of the centre court stood all the other competitors of the meeting, watching their more illustrious colleagues with a very natural mixture of envy and respect upon their faces.

None, from that friendly, admiring throng, had as yet qualified for any of the coveted titles, and though none could say that his neighbour might not one day be the lady champion, or carry off the men's singles, no one guessed that the beautiful Spanish newcomer, Lili de Alvarez, would emerge from their ranks that very year to reach the final round and come so close to winning the ladies' singles at her first attempt.

As the presentation ceremony progressed, the attention of the crowd was soon divided between the Royal party and two slight figures waiting at the tail-end of the main procession. One, Suzanne Lenglen, stood like a dancer, on tip-toe, hand on hip, nervous, excited, acutely conscious of the crowd's interest in her, for she was at the very zenith of her fame. The other, Kathleen McKane, or more correctly Mrs Godfree, for she had recently married her mixed doubles partner, one of our leading men players, stood smiling, cool, quietly confident, the epitome of the English sports girl.

With Helen Wills unable to take her place at Wimbledon that year owing to her recent operation for appendicitis, it seemed that still another Lenglen-Godfree clash would be inevitable and the crowds looked down with keen interest at the contrasting personalities of these rival stars as they waited together, chatting; Mrs Godfree so composed and placid, while Suzanne was in such a state of nerves that she never seemed to put her heels to the ground for a single moment.

Farther down the court, the men champions were being presented to Their Majesties, but while this ceremony was going on with apparently perfect smoothness, there were frantic scurryings and worrying behind the scenes, for Borotra had not yet reached the Club.

'Borotra!' 'Where's Borotra!' The whispering and astonishment communciated itself to the remainder of the players. Jean Borotra always flew to England at the last minute for the championships and this time it seemed that he had badly miscalculated the time of his arrival. Sensing the drama of the occasion, Suzanne, his country-woman and partner, danced a little more excitedly and glanced repeatedly towards the entrance.

Slowly the procession moved forward. The last of the men had filed past the King and Queen and Miss Maud Watson, the first woman ever to win at Wimbledon, was approaching Queen Mary and was preparing to make her curtsy. Borotra had missed his turn. Everyone was wondering what could possibly have caused him not to appear on such a memorable occasion when suddenly the Basque himself bounded into view. Borotra, at the last minute as usual, but this time he had almost left his entrance too late!

Delayed over the channel by fog, he had changed into his tennis kit in his car on the way from the landing-ground and he carried two rackets under his arm. 'Am I too late?' he exclaimed, as he leapt from the still moving limousine. 'Hurry up, hurry up, you need not have changed!' I answered frantically. Realising the cause of the commotion

near the doorway, Miss Watson quietly stepped back to her place at the head of the waiting ladies, and someone snatched Borotra's rackets from his hand as I pushed him, breathless, on to the court to receive his medal.

Miss Watson, Mrs Hillyard, Miss Dodd, Mrs Sterry, winners of the last century; Mrs Lambert Chambers, Mrs Geen and Mrs Larcombe, winners of the nineteen-hundreds: one after the other the lady champions of the past followed behind the Bounding Basque to receive the Royal congratulations.

When at last Suzanne had passed the Royal pair and, with Mrs Godfree's curtsy, the ceremony ended, everyone claimed that their own particular favourite had received the most applause, but the consensus of opinion gave the vote to the reigning champion, Suzanne Lenglen.

Six times Suzanne had been queen of Wimbledon and there seemed no doubt that she would retain her crown.

Who could have told, on that sunny afternoon, that the great Lenglen had already played her last final on the centre court the year before? What spectator would have been bold enough to predict that the two slim girls, standing at the end of the long line of champions, would never again meet in single combat – that this year, it would be the unknown Senorita who would contest the final round with Mrs Godfree, the predestined successor to the Lenglen throne.

The unknown Senorita turned out to be one of the most glamorous figures ever seen on a lawn tennis court. She had beauty, grace and style to a most unusual degree, and in addition to the knack of making the most difficult shots look easy, when she played she had also that elusive gift of showmanship which often calls for the easy to be made to look difficult.

Though Lili de Alvarez was of Spanish nationality, she was born in Italy and she had spent most of her youth touring the fashionable resorts of Europe with her parents, starting to take part in winter sports and to play tennis at a very early age.

Lili had made her first appearances in big tennis on the Riviera at a time when both good looks and talent adorned the game to an extent that may never be surpassed. Even so, her dark and fiery beauty, and the extraordinary grace with which she executed all her shots, made a deep impression on everyone who saw her; so much so that after her first appearances at Wimbledon in 1926, she was described by the Press as a 'goddess' and with innumerable other superlatives which had hitherto been reserved exclusively for Suzanne herself.

On the court, Lili's game certainly necessitated a miracle of co-ordination between eye and racket. Critics wrote that whereas Suzanne had always been content to win her points by the smallest margin that sufficed, Lili seemed bent on winning each of hers by the largest margin possible.

This naturally led to a higher proportion of errors in her matches than was usual with players of her class, but the daring of her conception was ample compensation, if any was required, for her shortcomings, and every time she appeared it was to give a glorious exhibition of skilled grace that delighted the fans who soon followed all her matches with devotion.

Moreover, it was soon apparent that Lili's outward fascination was no mere façade and that here, indeed, was a person of many other accomplishments. Her English, like her equally perfect French, German and Italian, betrayed no trace of a Spanish accent, and though in talking any of these languages Lili made full use of that languorous drawl that speaks so eloquently of Southern sunshine, this was just another part of the battery of charms that she exercised at will, and usually with devastating effect.

Fittingly, Wimbledon's fiftieth anniversary seemed fated to be outstanding in nearly every respect, for following closely after the presentation ceremony, two British men players, both destined to become famous in the tennis world, made their first appearances there, and almost as if the ladies were determined not to be outdone, they in turn

produced two more
newcomers, both of
whom were to make big
names for themselves and
were to play a leading
part in many subsequent
championships.

'Bunny' Austin, Pat
Hughes, then Simone
Mathieu and Betty Nuthall.
This was a really remarkable
array of young talent. Normally,
one could count on the fingers of one hand the years when one, or
perhaps two, new and important figures made their initial bows to the
Wimbledon spectators. Lili de Alvarez *and* four other future stars within a single week was certainly a record well worthy of even this memorable occasion.

Unfortunately, the pleasure and excitement aroused by the appearance of so many new faces in so short a time was quickly marred by
the regrettable incident which caused Suzanne's withdrawal from the
championships; though, as a happier climax to this week of sensations,
on the first Friday, came the occasion when our present King appeared
in a first-round doubles match partnered by Sir Louis Greig.

For many years, players on the centre court had become accustomed
to frequent Royal patronage. To have a Royal competitor playing
among them on the outside courts was an experience not to be treated
lightly, and they, as well as the crowds who thronged the No.2 court
stands to see the match, were greatly disappointed to see Sir Louis and
his Royal partner quickly defeated, in straight sets, by that long-experi-
enced pair of ex-title-holders, Gore and Roper Barrett.

The first Saturday saw Lili's début on the centre court. In a few short days she had already endeared herself to the crowds, but this was her first appearance inside the main arena and she celebrated it in typical style with a flashing victory over Phoebe Watson.

The other newcomers had to wait till later years to take their true place in the story of the centre court. The Jubilee Championships were like that. Day by day, fresh excitements and disappointments followed each other in quick succession until the very last shot of this moment-ous meeting which saw Mrs. Godfree and her husband on the winning side in the mixed doubles final.

But perhaps the greatest excitement of all came when Mrs. Godfree beat the glamorous Alvarez and thus recaptured the title which she had first won in 1924 against Helen Wills, the previous invader who reached the last round at Wimbledon at her first attempt only to suc-cumb to tenacious Biddy Godfree when apparently within sight of vic-tory.

This was Mrs. Godfree's third singles final at the All England Club, but it was just as exciting and as packed with thrills as the second, two years previously, for after two sets of hard and accurate hitting, when both opponents seemed almost to have run each other to a standstill, Lili went ahead to within a point of leading 4-1 in the deciding set only to find that Mrs. Godfree's extraordinary determination was not to be denied.

In 1924 the English girl had faced young Helen Wills in similar cir-cumstances. This time, regaining the initiative in a crescendo of applause, she overtook a less experienced opponent, and ended the long struggle with such a fine burst of confident hitting that Lili did not even attempt to return three out of her last four shots. Biddy Godfree was once again the lady champion of Wimbledon. For the second time in her career she had succeeded where Suzanne had failed.

In the men's Jubilee events, the tide of French supremacy was at its height, and even in the absence of her most redoubtable Musketeer, Lacoste, France made short shrift of America when Borotra defeated Howard Kinsey in an astonishingly quick-fire final, and Brugnon, part-nered this time by Cochet, won the first of his many titles at the expense of Kinsey and Vincent Richards.

But the Lenglen Era was over. That dazzling spell of meteoric bril-liance was gone from Wimbledon for ever.

Mrs. Mallory was already fading from the ever-changing scene and Mrs. Godfree's star waned, too, soon after Lili began her succession of dashing challenges and Helen Wills' long heralded supremacy be-came a reality at last.

HELEN MOODY'S HOPE OF COMEBACK

PAUL GALLICO

San Francisco 1934

We stood on top of Telegraph Hill, the girl and the reporter, and looked out over one of the loveliest sights in all the world – the blue hills and blue waters of San Francisco Bay and the golden gate, Alcatraz the grim, lying like a steel stud on the ultra-marine surfaces, the black hulls and gay funnels of the Orient steamers tucked in their berths below.

Behind us the gray towers of San Francisco, to the left the Presidio and white flat buildings shining in the afternoon sun, buildings that

somehow remind you of Havana of the Antilles. Across the bay, Berkeley gleamed dim and distant. A gray tramp steamer stole out from under a bluff, and moaned a wistful homecoming with its siren, a white plume of steam at the throat of the rusty stack. From behind us came the roar of the city. In the air was the smell of peat smoke and salt air and fish and spices and waterfront things.

Drawing by Mac

The girl had gleaming light blue eyes, a straight nose and the pure Greek profile. She wore a simple black frock, with white lace at the neck and shoulders, a small close fitting black hat and a silver fox. She motioned toward the town and said: 'See how all those buildings merge into a sort of a gray wash – no detail, but just the feeling of a great city.'

71

May I present to you, Mrs. Helen Wills Moody at home. Now, if you are looking for a sensational story or inside information on what happened at Forest Hills last fall when the most famous woman tennis player in the world walked off the courts and left victory and the championship to her deadliest rival, Miss Helen Jacobs, we part company here, because this is just the story of two people who went sightseeing, who fell under the spell of San Francisco and who talked of things that interested them.

This much I can tell you: In all probability, and if it's humanly possible, you will see Helen Wills Moody on the No. 1 court at Forest Hills next August fighting for the championship which for so many years had been hers. Something is driving her on to it.

She spoke wistfully and with a faraway look in her eyes when she said: 'I want to play in the nationals – very much – if I possibly can.' Her expression changed. She left the rest unspoken. But I thought that her nostrils dilated a little and that she was scenting battle. Rest, until March, or until the pain leaves her spine; practice – and then a date at Forest Hills. For many reasons, or perhaps for no particular reason, it is hard to tell, she is a strange, introspective girl.

We lunched in the mural room of the St. Francis. She sipped sherry from a tiny thin-stemmed glass, one glass. She told how desperately she missed the exercise of tennis and the fun of playing it. She found that she had to have a substitute and so she swam – and loved it. There was a constant ache at the base of her spine. Only rest would help. Until that disappeared she was not to touch a racket. It was hard. She loved to play with her friends around Frisco and Berkeley. Did I know whether athletes who were injured ever went to osteopaths?

She hadn't given up her painting – had two canvases finished and was working on a third. With a spoon, she drew on the tablecloth a makeshift skeleton and showed me where the doctors said the trouble lies – but the doctors weren't sure. They said rest was the best doctor. I asked her to sign the tablecloth sketch and she laughed, showing even white teeth.

It had been a strange physical experience for her, she said, that adventure back East. 'I'm not used to feeling tired, you know,' she said. 'I've never been tired. Playing with a drag took all the fun out of it. I love tennis. I miss it dreadfully now, I know if I start to play before this injury clears up, I'll just start it all over. But it is a terrible temptation.'

After lunch we walked for a while and poked into curio shops and looked at ancient jades and silks and crystals. There were still two hours before my ship returned to Los Angeles. We stopped at the garage for her car and, with pride and excitement, Helen Wills Moody showed me the city she loves. We drove to the waterfront that smells of hemp and tar and tea and spices, where the great liners head west to the Orient, and passed the fish wharf where hundreds of little fishing boats are tied in orderly rows, where Eyetalians with gallant black mustaches fish gigantic gleaming pink crabs out of steaming cauldrons on the sidewalks and sell them, hot and glistening; where the gray gulls perch bright-eyed on the roofs of the fish stalls and the parked cars. We laughed at the indignant look on a gull that was sitting on a car that was backing out and that refused to get off.

We climbed hills so steep that it seemed the car must drop over backward. We went to see Mrs. Moody's own little joke – the indoor tennis courts in the palace of fine arts, an enormous semicircular building, pillared and colonnaded in front, bare in back. The roof is of glass, the floor of asphalt. Mrs. Moody persuaded the city fathers it would be a perfect place for indoor tennis courts when the building was not in use for exhibitions. They put them in. They are the finest indoor courts in the world now.

We drove through the Presidio and saw ancient abandoned gun emplacements where the mortars once roared and we came out at a high point and saw far below at our feet the Pacific Ocean battering white froth at the black crags of the cliffs. On the way back to town we fell to talking again about people and newspapers, and I asked her whether the reams of publicity meant anything to her, whether she had been disturbed by the many columns of criticism of the past year. She said gravely and quietly, 'I bear no grudges. Everyone is entitled to his opinion. I read only a few of the sports writers, those whose writing I like. I read Tunis and Danzig and Hawthorne and Rice, and some of the things that you write. Whatever is written, is written. I love peace more than anything.'

We finished the drive, threading down through the once bold, bad Pacific Street, the Barbary Coast, past Spider Kelly's and the beautiful bas reliefs outside the wicked Thalia, then up to the top of Nob Hill, the old residential section, and back to the St. Francis. The most famous girl tennis player in the world waved good-bye. Something tells me the next time I see her will be in Forest Hills in August, and I wouldn't miss that one for millions.

In fact Helen Wills never played at Forest Hills again, not because of her back but because of differences with the USTA. She did however add to her Wimbledon titles, winning in 1935 and 1938.

AMERICAN TAKE-OVER 1946-50

MAX ROBERTSON

1946 Wimbledon emerged from the war slightly bruised – there had been the odd bomb about – but all was very quickly put so nearly to rights that the 1939 fans coming back to their Mecca might well have thought that from a tennis point of view no Second World War had existed.

All this was largely due to the organization for which Wimbledon has ever been justly famous. The Secretary, Lt-Col. Duncan Macaulay, who had been an assistant referee up until 1939, soon got a firm grip on the running of the Championships. Duncan Macaulay put his stamp on Wimbledon and he ran it all by what he called his black book. This was a harvesting of experience set out in one loose-leaf book, to which he constantly referred and added in the light of experience. Self-analysis has long been a characteristic of the All England Club which for fifty weeks a year is a private club, but which devotes ninety per cent of its effort and administration throughout the year to making the Championships the nearest thing to perfection in international sport.

There was evidence of the war in the 1946 programmes, still very much utility efforts with only eight pages and practically no advertisements. A notice on the inside of the back cover and outlined in black, headed 'Bomb Damage to Centre Court' told of the night of Friday 11 October 1940 when a 'stick' of five 500 lb bombs straddled the Club grounds. The first bomb demolished the tool-house. The second bomb of the 'stick' fell on the roof of the Centre Court, the third fell in Church Road at the northeast entrance and the last two produced bunkers in the Wimbledon Park golf course.

The damage to the Centre Court meant a loss of approximately 1200 seats.

After a gap of seven years the known form of the various entrants in many cases scarcely existed, and the Referee must have had an extremely hard job working out acceptances and seeding. However, some of the old guard needed no introduction. Among the men Tony Mottram, who was to serve Britain so well in the Davis Cup, had played as a youngster in 1939, since when the RAF had claimed him with so many others, including John Bromwich of Australia, who had lost their best years and their best chances. Jaroslav Drobny, a name unfamiliar to most people then, but who was to become a Wimbledon heart-throb, had surprised everybody in 1938 with a victory over his famous fellow Czech, Menzel.

But the name on everyone's lips as the seemingly inevitable winner was Jack Kramer (seeded No. 2) of America. He and his compatriot Tom Brown were also favourites for the Doubles. Kramer was a tennis machine, superbly built with the big American serve–volley game and, although seeded No.2, he was most people's favourite.

Kramer's fourth round match with Drobny soon had Number 1 Court bursting at the seams. Kramer took the first set 6-2. The second, a titanic struggle, eventually went to Drobny 17-15. This battle killed Kramer's hopes. He had aggravated during earlier matches a blister on his racket hand. This was further inflamed during the gruelling struggle with Drobny. Drobny took the third set for a 2-1 lead. Kramer equalized in the fourth. But the effort with his blister had been too much and, with the crowd by now firmly supporting Drobny, the Czech won the deciding set.

Drobny went on to beat Pellizza of France in straight sets in his quarter-final. In the semi-finals he himself was beaten in three by Geoff Brown of Australia. Brown had previously beaten the graceful Lennart Bergelin (8) of Sweden 13-11, 11-9, 6-4. Bergelin, like Cochet before him and Krishnan a little after, was a marvellous player of the unorthodox shot – especially the half-volley which he would pick up and turn into an attacking stroke as he wandered seemingly quite casually to the net. Today Bergelin is the man who brought Bjorn Borg to his pinnacle as Wimbledon Champion and Swedish tennis therefore has a double debt to him.

Dinny Pails (1) of Australia floated comfortably through the quarter-finals. There he met Yvon Petra (5), of France, who put out Pails in four sets. Poor Dinny. On the way to Wimbledon that day he missed a train on the London underground. What made things worse is that he was playing on the Centre Court. He finally got on court twenty minutes late. Having kept everybody waiting, including Queen Mary, he was sweating with nerves and at a tremendous psychological disadvantage when he faced up to the big serve game of Yvon Petra.

Petra did not so much play tennis as perform. He was something of a mixture of Tilden and Nastase. The effect was that of a one-man whirlwind. Nor did it help Pails that each time he was at the Roller end he could see the familiar sight of Queen Mary, straight-backed, awe-inspiring in her familiar toque hat. She was flanked by the Chairman of the All England Club, Sir Louis Greig – who had partnered her son on his Wimbledon appearance – and Lady Greig, who took it in turns to hold her Majesty's sunshade, relieving each other when an anguished look indicated that the arm was tiring.

After disposing of Pails, Petra beat Tom Brown in five hard-hitting sets. Came the Final and Petra rushed to a two-set lead against Geoff Brown (3) and most of those present thought he was on his way to quick victory. Brown did not think so. There then unfolded a memorable David versus Goliath battle with Brown conceding at least seven inches to his giant opponent.

Petra used his full height to unleash cannonball serves and thundering forehands. But Geoff Brown, small as he was by comparison, yielded nothing to Petra for power. The wind-up and the arc of his right-handed service swing were short, but the resulting delivery was so fast that he reminded one of a spring, tightly coiled, being suddenly released. And, like David with his sling, Brown served with such accuracy that, despite a low trajectory which allowed little margin of error, he served many aces. He had a left-handed forehand and an explosive two-handed shot on his backhand.

Brown came back at Petra just as furiously as Petra had come at him and he rallied to win the third set. Petra seemed to have got clear again when he made it 5-3 in the fourth set and at 40-15 was serving for the match. Whereupon Brown hit two devastating two-handed returns of service straight through the incoming Frenchman, followed by yet a third which left the crowd – and Petra – stunned. Brown won the game and took the set. Petra hit back in the final set which he won 6-4 for the match and the title.

Petra had many distinctions. To start with he was born in Vietnam, then the French colonial possession Indo-China, learned to play tennis in his bare feet and also became a soccer goalkeeper of some repute. After his family returned to France, Yvon became a barman and spare-time tennis player. During the last war he was badly wounded in the leg and taken prisoner. By one of the ironies of war, when it seemed that the leg would have to be amputated, it was saved by the skills of a German surgeon who operated on prisoner Petra.

The Ladies' Singles in 1946 produced more evidence of the old guard. Names like 'Jed' Jedrzejowska, who had conquered Centre Court hearts as a girl of sixteen, Kay Menzies (4) – Kay Stammers that was – one of the most beautiful stylists who must surely have won during the war years, the Woodgate sisters, Mme Mathieu, that persistent French Champion who was a Wimbledon semi-finalist in the years 1930-2 and again in 1937, Mrs Jean Bostock (6), Mrs Uber (winner of the All England Badminton title in 1935), Mrs Strawson, one of the leading pre-war players, Joan Curry, Mrs Betty Hilton, and Betty Nuthall.

However, the favourites were clearly the Americans who had come with a tremendous reputation which was fully justified when they provided all the semi-finalists. The No.1 seed was Pauline Betz. She played like a ballerina. Her grace was matched with power and she never had a qualm in taking the title without dropping a set. Her opponent in the Final was Louise Brough (5), who had had a big semi-final battle with her great friend and doubles partner, Margaret Osborne (2) (later du Pont). These two were to dominate the women's game for some years to come in company with Doris Hart (7). What had been hinted at by the masculine effectiveness of Alice Marble's winning game in 1939 was now an established fact. Top American women played like men. They produced big serves and they could volley.

1947 Jack Kramer (1) had come to Wimbledon in 1946 to win. He failed, probably because of his blistered hand (although he himself refused to use that as an excuse). Kramer simply became more determined, if that were possible, when he came back in 1947. For it meant that he was now a year behind schedule. The Kramer plan was that he would win Wimbledon, turn professional and make his living from tennis. He had decided that to make good in the world he would do it through what he was best at – playing tennis. So, from being an excellent player he turned himself through unrelenting practice into a great one.

With his crew-cut hairstyle and lean, keen looks, Jack Kramer appeared to have come straight from the Harvard Business School. That was how he played. He brought to tennis the percentage game. His tennis was intelligent. It was powerful, it was ruthless. His victory in the Final against fellow American, Tom Brown (3), saw him drop a mere six games and throughout the whole Men's Singles tournament he lost only thirty-seven games. He must figure in any list of Greats.

Kramer, majestic and efficient on court, was to prove to be a businessman with the same flair, allied to shrewdness. After winning Wimbledon, which opened the golden door to professionalism as a player, he quickly became a promoter running an international 'circus', signing big cheques as readily as he had served and volleyed, but as ever with great thought behind the flourish.

In the absence of Pauline Betz, who had left the amateur scene, Margaret Osborne (1) took the Women's title with a good win over Doris Hart (3). To get to the Final Doris had beaten Louise Brough (2) in a great three-setter while Margaret Osborne had outgunned the graceful South African, Sheila Summers (7). Many more battles royal were to be fought between these queens of the court.

1948 In 1948 John Bromwich (2) of Australia looked destined to achieve the crown which all who saw him knew he deserved. He was seeded No.2 to America's Frankie Parker (1), a rather mechanical player who relied more on length and percentage shots than inspiration. Matters seemed set all the more fair for Bromwich when Parker was beaten in the fourth round by the graceful Swede Lennart Bergelin. Bergelin was then blasted out by Bob Falkenburg (7), the gangling American with a cannonball serve, very reminiscent of Vines. Bromwich, with his soft wiles, bringing delicacy to the two-handed stroke, got through to the Final without dropping a set and must have felt in form enough to handle anything that Falkenburg would throw at him. But neither he, nor anybody else, knew what was in store.

Many names were being applied to the lanky Falkenburg – Daddy Longlegs or, when he sank to his knees, the Praying Mantis. Bromwich had set-points for the first set but lost them to his own nerves and fine passing shots by Falkenburg. The American then appeared wantonly to throw away the second to love and was already taking time out lying on the ground or stalling before service. Bromwich's concentration and confidence were disturbed, and his habit of shaking his head from side to side in a slow, rueful manner became even more noticeable. His game disintegrated in the third set which Falkenburg won 6-2. However, more 'throw-aways' by Falkenburg helped Bromwich to square the match at 2-all and the Australian got to 5-3 in the final set. At this point Falkenburg repeatedly held up play, sinking to his knees in Praying Mantis fashion. Clearly these delays took toll of Bromwich's nerves when he was at the brink of his ambition. He led 5-3 and 40-15 on his own service. Falkenburg saved the first match-point and a missed volley cost Bromwich the second. A brave passing shot by Falkenburg saved yet a third. Bromwich was clearly over-anxious and, having missed these chances, he scarcely won another point.

After the match, Fred Perry said to 'Buzzer' Hadingham, now Chairman of Slazengers who always provide the equipment for the Championships, 'Well, I'd say Falkenburg won by thirty-four falls to thirty-one headshakes.' There was much controversy over Falkenburg's 'stalling' tactics. It did emerge subsequently that he suffered from a thyroid deficiency.

Tony Mottram had the Centre Court crowd roaring for him in his fine third round win over Cucelli of Italy. It was a most exciting and exhausting match, the score being 6-8, 6-3, 10-12, 9-7, 6-2. When at the Roller end, where the Groundsmen's friends have privileged seats on and in front of the roller itself, they heard Cucelli several times say 'Basta! Basta!' meaning 'Enough! Enough!' To English ears it sounded rather different. The roller is the pony roller with long shafts that was brought from Old Wimbledon to prepare the new Centre Court. The stands were built round it before anyone realized that it could never be got out.

There was no question mark against the winner of the Ladies' Singles. The year 1948 saw the inauguration of a conspicuous reign by a tennis queen. After a Final in which points were fluently and fiercely contested, Louise Brough (2) beat Doris Hart (4) 6-3, 8-6 to win the first of her four singles titles. By her record alone Louise Brough has earned a special place in lawn tennis history. In all she was to win thirteen Wimbledon singles and doubles titles and in the Wightman Cup, playing for America between 1946 and 1957, she was unbeaten in twenty-two rubbers.

1949 Wimbledon 1949 was a vintage year. It provided Drobny's first final; it saw the one appearance in his heyday of one of the all-time greats, Ricardo 'Pancho' Gonzales (2); and the year also marked the only appearance ever in the singles of F.R. 'Ted' Schroeder, the No.1 seed who quickly became known as 'Lucky' Ted.

A second round match between Van Swol of Holland and Abdessalam of France provided the only occasion on which a squirrel has invaded and left its mark on the Centre Court, helping to change the course of at least a minor piece of tennis history. Van Swol, a big blond Dutchman, was 5-3 down in the final set and seemed to be sinking fast to the little Algerian Robert Abdessalam. Suddenly the Centre Court was engulfed in roars of laughter. A squirrel was sitting pertly in possession of the court. Van Swol, quick to seek any relief, turned his racket head upwards and had a sit-down. A linesman made heroic but unavailing efforts to catch the offender. After an enthralling chase in which the squirrel jinked like a rugby three-quarter it was caught by a ball-boy, who promptly got bitten for his pains.

The squirrel was removed, chattering unrepentant while the ball-boy received attention from the St. John Ambulance men. It was then back to the tennis. Van Swol, who had been able to enjoy a respite of some three minutes, rallied to win the set and the match 13-11.

After his great win over Kramer in 1946, Jaroslav Drobny (6) had become the Wimbledon crowd's 'favourite' favourite. So there was relief when the American champion, Gonzales (2), was removed from Drobny's path by little Geoff Brown of Australia. None of the tennis lovers who later came to idolize Gonzales could know that he would not be seen again at Wimbledon until the arrival of Open Tennis in 1968 – when he was still a giant but no longer a Colossus. It was a further tribute to Gonzales' ability and drawing power that he did not need the glamour of a Wimbledon title to be the No.1 target for Jack Kramer to sign for his professional circus.

In the semi-finals Drobny beat John Bromwich (5), losing only six games. Bromwich had previously got some revenge over his Final conqueror of the previous year, Bob Falkenburg (4). It had been another astonishing display. Falkenburg, when leading 2-0, threw twelve games to take a rest and Bromwich won the final set 6-4.

Lucky Ted Schroeder had almost gone out in the first round to unseeded Gardnar Mulloy, who took the first two sets. Schroeder with his chunky appearance and sailor's gait was just like Popeye and he did have a corn-cob pipe. You almost expected him to take a handful of spinach to sustain him through the next crisis. Not that he ever seemed to need sustaining. He was as cool as the refrigerators he sold – even in the tightest of situations. In the quarter-finals, against the speed and power of twenty-one-year-old Frank Sedgman, he found himself trailing two sets to love. He squared the match. In the final set he was called upon to save several match-points. On one of these he was foot-faulted on his first service. His nerve held and he went for a good and not just safe second serve, rushed the net to take the vital point and eventually the set at 9-7. In the semi-final he came from 2-1 behind to beat South African Eric Sturgess (7), who brought all the delights of the pre-war baseline game to his graceful stroke play.

In the Final against Drobny, Schroeder dropped the first set, won an inspired second set to love, took the third but lost the fourth. He got to 5-4 in the final set and then clinched the title in the grand manner by serving out the last game to love.

The line-up for the Women's Final was Louise Brough (1) against Margaret du Pont (2). It produced a memorable three-set battle which went to forty-three games. Louise won the first four games and Margaret the next five, and it was not until the third break of service that the set went eventually to Louise at 10-8. Margaret, ever the fighter, came right back to take the second set 6-1. The final set was a survival battle. The first six games saw four service breaks. At 8-all Louise found herself 0-40 on her own service, only to serve her way out of trouble and then hold on to win the match 10-8, 1-6, 10-8.

It was not only serves, volleys and a squirrel which caught the eye that year. The lace around Gussie Moran's panties gave fashion designer Ted Tinling his first real imprint and brought an added alertness to many a male eye.

A MEMORABLE MATCH
FRED TUPPER

The sixth of July, 1957 was a red letter day at Wimbledon. The combination of extraordinary events on that afternoon remains rooted in the memories of all who were there. It was the first time that Queen Elizabeth had graced the All England Lawn Tennis Club. It was the first time that a Negro had won Wimbledon (Althea Gibson beat Darlene Hard in an All-American final). It was the day that Centre Court tradition was violated when a woman stepped on the sacred turf carrying a banner proclaiming peace. It was the day that the best amateur of his time, Lew Hoad, made the decision to turn professional. And it was the day that provided one of the sensational doubles upsets in the history of tennis, a result so astonishing and so moving that long after the match was over players and spectators alike were milling around the lawns discussing it with awe and wiping their eyes with emotion.

The finalists on that memorable afternoon were Lew Hoad and Neale Fraser of Australia against Budge Patty and Gardnar Mulloy of America. The day before the moody, magnificent Hoad had trounced Ashley Cooper in straight sets for his second Wimbledon crown running and proved that he was in a class by himself. Fraser's great days were near at hand. He was to win Forest Hills in 1959 and both Forest Hills and Wimbledon in 1960.

It seemed almost a miracle that Patty and Mulloy were there at all. The elegant Patty, an expatriate who was the idol of post-war Paris, had won his Wimbledon way back in 1950 and had played the finest match of his career four years before in a 93 game, five setter over 4 hours and 15 minutes against Jaroslav Drobny that is ranked among the tennis classics of all time. By now Budge was 33 years old, his best years behind him and at Wimbledon purely for the fun of it.

Mulloy was going on 44, a ridiculous age for topflight tennis. That is, for anybody but Mulloy, a physical marvel. His frustrations at Wimbledon were legion. Twice before, in 1948 with Tom Brown and in 1949 with Ted Schroeder, he had reached the doubles final only to lose it. The odds were prohibitive that he would lose it again. For Hoad and Fraser were top-seeded; Patty and Mulloy were not seeded at all. In fact, the two Americans had played together for the first time, more or less as a social occasion, that spring at Gloria Butler's annual invitation tourney in the South of France.

Yet they had done surprisingly well at Wimbledon, almost unnoticed. In a first round match they had won from Alex Olmedo and Hugh Stewart in four close sets. They had upset the Swedes, Sven Davidson and Ulf Schmidt (who were to win it in 1958), in another furious four-setter to enter the quarters, then reached the semis with a fantastic 6-3, 6-3, 6-0 decision over the third seeds, Mal Anderson and Ashley Cooper of Australia. When the freakish result came into the press room there were queries. Must have been the other way round, said the British writers. One dazed man from the Paris Herald Tribune said it was true. 'I saw it but I can't believe it,' he mumbled, looking at his notes. 'Mulloy missed only four returns of service in the entire match. Incredible.'

By now Wimbledon was agog. The girls in the tennis office who had rooted for Mulloy over 11 long years sneaked into the stands on Thursday to see the Americans beat Roger Becker of Britain and Bob Howe of Australia 9-7, 7-5, 6-3. The old boys had done jolly well, everybody admitted. They had returned service beautifully. It would be good to see them in the final. But it was insane to give them a chance against Hoad and Fraser. Earlier on, out of sentiment, the man from the Trib had placed a pound at 10-1 odds and was protesting it was possible. That win over Anderson and Cooper still had him mesmerized.

Miss Gibson and Miss Hard had now exited from Centre Court that hot, humid Saturday and the doubles finalists marched in, turning abruptly to bow to the Queen.

The first set went to the Australians as everybody thought it would. The Aussies were holding their service easily, the Americans were struggling under pressure. Mulloy saved a set point at 4-5 when he and Patty tangled rackets, but in the 18th game Patty was broken at love as he popped a series of volleys into the net. Then Mulloy took command. It had long been his axiom that when you lose a service game, you try that much harder to break through on the next. Gar hit four wonderful shots, deeply angled to awkward places, that broke Fraser's serve in the first game of the second set. The Americans had found their rhythm. The tennis clock had turned backward. And then Mulloy pulled the psychological ploy of the match. Hoad had bludgeoned an overhead that bounced high into the stands. Mulloy charged after it.

83

He had no hope but he kept on, leaping into the lower deck and falling into the lap of a lady spectator. He asked her to move over and then he sat down beside her watching the court. The crowd exploded in laughter and Hoad's concentration snapped. Returning, Mulloy won the point that mattered most, a breakthrough on Lew's service for the vital first game of the third set. Soon the Americans were leading two sets to one.

There were murmurings around the ivied crater now. Teatime had come and gone, yet nobody moved. Patty's touch of genius was back on the volley, Mulloy was still rifling the service returns into tiny holes. There was a sustained roar as the artful ancient caught Hoad off balance for the service break in the seventh game. People were punching each other with delight.

Mulloy to serve for the match at 5-4 in the fourth. He hadn't lost his service all afternoon. And he didn't lose it now. Majestically he won that game at love as the applause rolled round court, like good brandy on the tongue. It was a tribute reserved only for old friends. Match to the Americans 8-10, 6-4, 6-4, 6-4. It broke an Australian dominance in doubles that had run for seven years. It made Mulloy the oldest man ever to win a title at Wimbledon. And it so moved the Queen that she came down out of the Royal Box onto court to present the trophies.

Years earlier Mulloy had met the then Princess Elizabeth at a garden party. He had asked her why she never came to Wimbledon. It was explained that royalty had many duties. 'I thought maybe you couldn't get tickets,' said Mulloy, brasher then, 'I can get them for you.'

The Queen shook hands with Mulloy. 'It's nice to see you again,' she said, passing over the silver tray. 'Today I'm glad I had tickets.'

Up in the stands the girls from the tennis office were weeping unashamed. The man from the Paris Trib took them into the bar. There was no paper on Sunday and he had a tenner he wanted to spend.

CITADELS OF THE GAME

ROME, PARIS AND WIMBLEDON:
THEN AND NOW
Richard Evans

Those of us whose memories stretch back to the pre-Borg era are always talking about how the game has changed. And indeed it has. In mood and in substance it is a different kind of sport now. More competitive at the amateur level; harsher, more demanding and less fun for the pros on the world court.

But not all the change has been bad. Far from it. Heaven knows how long it would have taken to bring the game up to date had not Wimbledon thrown open its doors to the pros in 1968 – a move which finally jolted the International Federation out of its moribund stupor – nor does one like to speculate how many wars would have been fought had the Association of Tennis Professionals not taken that unpopular stand at Wimbledon in 1973 when they boycotted the Championships.

All that created deep and lasting changes in the structure of the game. But, as in any walk of life, the great institutions can absorb change without losing their basic character.

In America, of course, the necessary decision to move the US Open from the cozy tradition of the West Side to the end of an airport runway did indeed alter the character of the event because its very roots were torn up. Given the circumstances, that was probably inevitable and, despite the planes, Flushing isn't that bad.

But in Europe three great Championships have remained, in essence, the same. The changes have been numerous and some of the surgery considerable. Yet no visitor returning after a ten or even fifteen year gap could fail to recognize the Italian, French and Wimbledon Championships for what they were and what they still are – citadels of the game, then and now.

ROME: *Then*

It was the smell that I remember best although smell is too strong, too vulgar a word. The scent of it, perhaps – a special mingled fragrance of pine and cedar and that tart fragrance that hangs inside buildings where marble and mortar are shielded from the sun; a cool, clean scent, unmistakable, unforgettable. And the clay, too. You could sniff those courts as the red dust lay dampened by the groundsman's hose.

Away from the mad, honking bedlam of the city center, the Foro Italico offered an oasis of serenity when you arrived each spring for first round matches played before a handful of spectators.

The crowds would build as the week progressed, bringing with them the odd movie star from the Roman studios that were still enjoying La Dolce Vita, and with them, of course, came the noise and the excitement. There were moments of passion, too, generated mostly by that imperious Roman Nicola Pietrangeli whose stroke play on court was always as immaculate as his dress was off it. But if Nikki lost, as he sometimes did, there was usually another hero – an adopted one if necessary like the exiled Australian they quickly dubbed Martino Mulligano. Marty did them proud, winning the Italian title three times in the face of such formidable opponents as Manuel Santana and Tony Roche.

So the noise was always part of the Foro Italico even in those pre-Open days of the mid-sixties. But somehow it never seemed intrusive. There was always time for a caffe latte and ice cream (and what ice cream! Dennis Ralston used to lap it up, scoop after scoop, all day long) or, better still, a leisurely lunch of mozzarella and tomato salad, fettucine and a half bottle of chilled white wine on the balcony of the players' restaurant.

Court Two lay directly beneath the balcony (the whole area has been enclosed rather claustrophobically with glass now) so between mouthfuls one could gaze down to watch Lea Pericoli hoist lobs to eye-level before they descended again in a lazy arc of maddening accuracy behind some poor exhausted opponent.

The organization in those days was always chaotic.

Ball boys, tiny chaps decked out in sponsors' T-shirts and sun hats, were a law unto themselves and a source of great entertainment to everyone except the players. I remember the British Davis Cup player Tony Pickard freezing in mid-serve as he caught sight of this little fellow scampering across his court, coke bottle in hand. Pickard, too weary and too surprised to be angry, asked what on earth was going on. 'My friend,' explained the ball boy, shrugging off the incident as a minor disruption of play, 'my friend over there work scoreboard – he need drink!'

After dusk had settled and the last tired body had dragged itself up the long flight of stairs from the locker rooms, the players, writers, mothers, girl-friends and wives would return to a selection of small hotels across the Tiber to congregate later in restaurants like Otello near the Spanish Steps before taking a late-night stroll down the Via Veneto. It was a small family then, the tennis circuit. Agents, coaches and clothing company reps were almost unknown. It didn't stay that way for long.

ROME: *Now*
Open Tennis arrived in 1968 but the explosion did not really hit Rome until 1971 when, briefly, the Italian Championships became a WCT event. Lamar Hunt's pros flew into a veritable clay court ambush that year. With little or no time to practise on that demanding surface after a long tour indoors, they found themselves being ground into dust by a bunch of unknown Italians who had been practising on those courts for weeks.

Everyone was in trouble in the early rounds – even John Newcombe, who found himself scrambling away from match point on Court Three as hordes of screaming Italians climbed the trees, hung over the railings, and jostled each other on the terracing for a better view of the drama. A man called Franchitti, who eventually rose to the dizzy heights of Number 10 in Italy was Newk's opponent that day and, to give him his due, he certainly made the reigning Wimbledon Champion fight for his life.

Tennis became big news in Italy after that year of surprise and drama, and the Italian Open was never the same again. Today it is noisier, bigger and more disciplined. Frightened by ugly crowd scenes (they threw coins at Borg one year in a wholly unsuccessful attempt to ruffle the impassive Swede), the Italian Federation went overboard with security. In 1979 it got so bad you couldn't move from one area of the club to another without being accosted by some over-eager guard. Mussolini, who built the arena in the thirties as a monument to the future of Italian youth, would have loved it. Most of us loved it less.

But somehow Rome is still Rome for the tennis caravan. Most of us have opted for the convenience and comfort of the Holiday Inn with its huge pool and two clay courts rather than the quaint and cramped alberghi downtown. Parties, often organized by Cino Marchese, IMG's man in Rome, tend to be brash disco affairs at Jacky O's or the Piper Club. One futuristic shindig at the Piper a couple of years ago when everyone – especially the girls – turned up looking like the inhabitants of Gommorrah in 2001 was adjudged by Vitas Gerulaitis to be one of the best parties he had ever attended. Coming from Vitas I suppose that is something of an accolade.

But although he surprised everyone, not least himself, by winning the title in 1977 and repeating the triumph two years later, Vitas is only a supporting act in Rome. Adriano Panatta is the current Caesar – revered and acclaimed to a point that far transcends his actual accomplishments.

'It does not matter what else is happening,' Paolo Bertolucci told me one day. 'All the papers want to write about is Adriano. And if they can't find anything to say about Adriano they write about his dog. A few weeks ago many of us were playing in Hamburg. Borg was being carried off court with a leg injury. Many things were happening. But did you see the headlines in the Italian papers?'

Bertolucci, a player of enormous talent who has rested contentedly in Panatta's shadow throughout his career, pauses for effect. 'Adriano's dog is ill – is in hospital for operation. Is true – I swear to you is true!'

Bertolucci's ample frame shakes with laughter as he settles back underneath the canopy that links the clubhouse with that famous Center Court where the huge marble statues gaze down impassively every year at the impassioned antics below them. Like some senator in ancient Rome Bertolucci is approached by fans, friends and acquaintances in endless waves; a handshake; a word of advice; a quick deal to play an exhibition.

Like the statues Bertolucci has become a fixture – a figure of permanence in a tournament that has grown and prospered and changed – not always for the better but, equally, never enough to lose its vivid, distinctive flavor. Even now if I get there early enough, before the hordes descend and the guards start telling me where I can and cannot go, I get a whiff of that special fragrance. For that alone I shall always return to Rome.

PARIS: *Then*
You have to go back before my time to catch the beginning of Stade Roland Garros, the now legendary stadium on the outskirts of Paris that has housed the French Championships for so long. But not before Ted Tinling's time. The man who put lace panties on Gussie Moran, who dressed every woman player of note in the modern age and who now designs exclusively for Tracy Austin was an umpire when Roland Garros first opened in 1928. The stadium was named after a French aviator of World War I fame and built as a showcase for the talents of

the four Musketeers: Henri Cochet, René Lacoste, Jean Borotra and Jacques Brugnon.

While the members of that quartet were at the height of their powers the crowds were huge. The original Center Court held 14,000 spectators and it was often packed.

But after the Second War when French tennis went into temporary decline, Roland Garros, like the Foro Italico in those pre-Open days, was a peaceful sort of place to while away a Parisian spring.

I have the dimmest childhood memories of being taken to Stade Roland Garros by my sister. It must have been 1946, when our family had returned to Paris after the war. There wasn't much to eat, unless you paid exorbitant prices through the black market, but that didn't seem to stop anyone from playing tennis.

I remember a large, leafy place near the Bois de Boulogne with lots of people in white hitting balls on red courts. We sat under the trees on what must have been Court Three, licking ice-cream (of a rather watery kind) and watching God knows who. Marcel Bernard? Benny Berthet? The names would have meant nothing to me then although many of the players there that year must have become friends later.

It was fifteen years before I returned, pen in hand this time, to witness one of the most emotional finals the French Championships has ever seen. Nicola Pietrangeli, champion for the previous two years, reached the 1961 final as obvious favorite to make it three in a row – something no one had achieved since World War I. (Bjorn Borg finally managed it in 1980.) But we were underestimating the determination of a toothy ex-ball boy from Madrid called Manuel Santana. His talent had been obvious during the hot days preceding the final when the sun had blazed down on that old concrete stadium, with its rows of permanently cemented concrete benches – a gray place until people filled it with color and players graced it with their skill.

Few have ever graced it with quite such artistry and charm as did Pietrangeli and Santana on that memorable Sunday in May 1961. In a match that resembled nothing so much as a physical game of chess, Santana finally prevailed over five long and enchanting sets. Quite overcome with exhaustion and joy and disbelief, the winner collapsed into the arms of the loser and wept copiously on Nikki's understanding shoulder. It was one of those pure, special moments in sport that give true meaning to the games we play.

PARIS: *Now*
Two decades later, the French Championships and indeed Stade Roland Garros itself are both very different. France is experiencing the

kind of tennis boom we saw in America in the mid-seventies and many of the causes for that sudden upsurge in interest can be traced directly to what Philippe Chatrier and his team have achieved at what is now one of the world's great tennis centers – Roland Garros.

Chatrier is chairman of the Pro Council – the nine man body that attempts to administer the complex world-wide professional game. The bespectacled Frenchman is also founder of the magazine *Tennis de France*, president of both the French and International Tennis Federations and one of the game's great visionaries. Philippe dreamt of what Roland Garros and the world's premier clay court championships could become and, unlike most dreamers, proceeded to do something about it.

Leaning on such good tennis friends as Jacques Chaban-Delmas, a former Prime Minister of France, Chatrier persuaded the Government to underwrite a rebuilding program that has changed the face of the old 11-court complex that lies just past the Porte d'Auteuil.

The work began five years ago when the locker-rooms were completely rebuilt. The press area was enlarged with an old basement storeroom being turned into a restaurant and writing area. And underneath the stand at the opposite end of the stadium to the official tribune, two-story offices have been created for the French Federation.

But most dramatically of all, a brand new 5,000 seat secondary stadium has risen on the spot where an old house used to stand. The two covered courts have been demolished and replaced with two new clay courts with seating for several hundred people. Winter training is now conducted in the considerable comfort of three courts that lie just below ground level in a corner area of the property that was never properly utilized. Above them, a flat roof can be used as tarmac courts most of the year or, during the Championships, as the commercial village where colorful tents are rented by leading international companies to entertain their clients in true Parisian style. And most importantly for the revenue of the Big Event, the Center Court has been enlarged to a capacity of 17,000.

With Yannick Noah, Henri Leconte and Thierry Tulasne all beginning to make their mark at the top international level there seems to be no shortage of local talent to justify this expensive modernization program. But one must remember that Chatrier put it all on the drawing board when his current trio of stars were still in short pants. So the man is a gambler as well as a visionary.

Considering the extent of the face lift it has received, Roland Garros has remained remarkably familiar during the Championships. Madame Durr, mother of the former French No.1 Françoise, still sits in her little booth by the entrance to the players enclosure, writing out tickets for cars that will take the players back to their hotel. The difference is that the drivers are now professional chauffeurs driving a sleek fleet of Citröens.

It is the professionalism that is the most striking hallmark of everything that happens at the French Open now – and the crowds. Quiet days in Auteuil vanished when the fans started arriving in droves from the moment the first ball was hit. Even in the dead of night there is no peace for poor old Roland Garros, for as soon as the garbage trucks have cleaned the side-walks of torn tickets, crumpled copies of L'Equipe and coke cans, the whores arrive to take up their beat. Wearing little and revealing all for the curb-crawlers who cruise the block, they make an eye-popping contrast to the activities of the day.

For the players, nocturnal activities are spread out far across town to various little restaurants near the Champs Elysées or on the Left Bank. Bob Lutz and his wife Sharon have a whole list of favorite haunts as do Ray and Rose Moore but, over the years, only Castels, a chic restaurant-discotheque on the Rue Princess, has remained a permanent meeting place for the tennis crowd. Jean Castel's right hand man Jacques Renevand has made sure of that. Renevand, who has come to know 'Tout Paris' since he began working for Castel some 15 years ago, was a former French Davis Cup player. With an introduction from Jacques, Monique, who guards the door and never forgets a face, might let you in. But as she has been known to refuse Lord Soames when he was the British Ambassador in town, don't count on it.

With its overflow crowds and saturation coverage on radio and television, the French Open is now one of Europe's major sporting spectacles; a two week festival of tennis that provides a superb showcase for the game. And that, of course, is precisely what Philippe Chatrier, the dreamer who made his dreams come true, always intended.

WIMBLEDON: *Then*

It was smaller than I had expected, the first time I saw it. The stage on which Sedgman and Patty and Drobny had aired their rapier skills had loomed very large indeed in my schoolboy imagination, deprived as it was of television's all-seeing eye.

So when I first walked up those stone steps that lead to the press box one day in the late fifties to peer expectantly onto a deserted Centre Court, I was struck not only by its smallness but by the intimacy of the place. The low, sloping roof is responsible for that, I think; shielding so many of the seats in darkened shadow so that, even without sunshine, the brilliant greeness of the court stands out as if illuminated from above like a billiard table.

91

It is one of the few stadiums I know that lives and breathes a life of its own; that oozes personality when completely empty. It does, of course, exude a quite different atmosphere when 15,000 people fill it with colour and noise as they react to the feats of two figures in white playing a game that, for more than a century, has become virtually synonymous with a single word – Wimbledon.

But if you go there in the weeks before the Championships are due to begin when the grass is still unscarred and the place is resonant merely with memory, you can beckon into action any giant of the past that leaps to mind and let he or she replay great moments and great deeds in the eerie silence. I never saw the copperheaded Budge or the crew-cut Kramer play there in person nor Perry in his long flannels or even Gussie Moran in Ted Tinling's daringly designed lace panties. But with the bare stage before you and still photographs to fuel the imagination, all can be summoned to life.

Now, after 22 Wimbledons, my own memory has stored away enough vignettes to fill an afternoon of vivid reminiscing should I ever find the time to choose my seat in an empty press box and let play commence.

Roy Emerson crashing into the umpire's chair and injuring his shoulder against Owen Davidson one damp and slippery day in 1966 – a mishap that effectively deprived Emmo of what surely would have been a third consecutive crown. The late Rafael Osuna quick-stepping his way through matches of dazzling brilliance against Rod Laver and Manuel Santana. One of the fastest and most cunning players of his era was Osuna, a delightful man whose only reaction to a shot good or bad was to tug on the gold cross that hung from his neck; turn on his heel and march rapidly back to the base-line. You got breathless just watching him.

In comparison Ramanathan Krishnan, father of Ramesh, was a heavy-footed plodder until the wand he called a racket conjured up strokes of magic. He produced enough of them to twice reach the semi-final. Santana, too, was a player of special skills with a first serve of sufficient power and penetration to carry him to the title his good friend Emmo so conveniently vacated in 1966.

But Santana could volley, too, of course – you had to in those days because the Slanzenger balls were lighter and faster than the ones used today; a factor that is often overlooked when old-timers wonder how Bjorn Borg, with a volley that is still barely more than adequate when judged by the highest standards, could win five Wimbledons. Heavier balls have given Borg and Jimmy Connors at least the option of staying back – an unthinkable alternative for Laver, Emerson, Chuck McKinley or the first man I personally saw win the title, Neale Fraser.

The famous Centre Court with its unique atmosphere is the Cathedral of the game, and even the most fiery personalities seem to realize that there is nothing they can do to upstage it. Of all the potentially rambunctious players I have seen perform there only the great Pancho Gonzales has had the grandeur and arrogance to dominate the place through the sheer power of his personality. That evening when the light was fading and Charlie Pasarell was blitzing him with huge serves, Gonzales prowled the base-line like a caged lion. 'Get the referee!' he roared. 'How can I play when I can't see?' To hell with history, tradition and the way things are supposed to be done. Wimbledon or not, Gonzales was still just trying to win a tennis match and he knew that if he were forced to play much longer in that kind of light, his 40-year-old eyes would give out on him.

Even when the light rain began falling from leaden skies, the referee, Capt. Mike Gibson, stood stony-faced at court side, his military moustache twitching occasionally as if the conditions were to be gauged by the occasional sniff, and, for what seemed an eternity, did nothing. Gonzales continued to rant and rave, saving match points one minute and throwing his racquets at the base of the umpire's chair the next. On television he came through like some great green Aztec god – an awesome, fearsome sight. That proud Centre Court stage had at last found an actor to match its stature.

But at Wimbledon the rules are the rules and only when Capt. Gibson's moustache told him that it would be dangerous to continue was play called off for the night. The next day Gonzales came back from two sets to one down to beat poor Pasarell in one of the most dramatic matches Wimbledon had ever seen.

WIMBLEDON: *Now*

All that took place in the early days of the Open era which the All England Club and its late chairman Herman David had precipitated by announcing, in 1968, that the Championships would be open to all categories of player no matter what the International Federation had to say about it.

That move, as radical a step as any the game has known, spotlights the curious mixture of ancient and modern thinking that gives Wimbledon its split personality. The creeping ivy (the horticulturists keep telling me it isn't ivy but it sure looks like it), the strawberries and cream which manage to remain identifiable despite the Wimbledon caterers who produce so much other unrecognizable food, and the dear old things who stand for hours on outside courts, loving every moment of matches between players no one else has ever heard of – all this was and is Wimbledon in all its traditional eccentricity.

But the changes are also evident – not quite so obviously evident because nothing is allowed that will impair the overall image of a gentlemanly game played in white on superbly manicured lawns. But the All England Club Committee was the first to realize that the Championships had to move with the times or get swept aside as big dollars poured into the game.

Wimbledon changes while managing to remain the same – an admirable sleight of hand which those of us who find the place enchanting and exasperating in almost equal measure are forced to admire.

For the players Wimbledon is a serious period in the year because careers can be made or destroyed at a tournament which is still treated more seriously than any other by the world's press. So nocturnal frivolity is muted although it was overpopularity that forced American exile Ken Lieberman to give up his annual fancy dress party at his Pelham Crescent home. The cost of keeping people out was getting a bit much even for Ken.

So it is to Tramps in Jermyn Street or Stringfellows that players – usually the losers – go to disco the night away, often after a candlelight dinner at Alexander's, a hospitable Chelsea restaurant that has been feeding tennis players for the past two decades.

London itself has an unchanging aspect to it which gives a sort of reassuring continuity to the never ending merry-go-round. Not quite so merry these days, perhaps, but somehow life would be very strange if Paris did not follow Rome with the promise of Wimbledon ahead.

SO LONG FOREST HILLS
Bud Collins

The voice on the radio whispered that he was Lev Richards at a place called Forest Hills. I took his word for it. The puh. . .puh. . .puh of smitten tennis balls accompanied his soft tones, and applause signaled the end of a point, when he said something like '. . . Schroeder scores with a backhand volley!'

In those days – before TV, before prize money, even before Kenny Rosewall – Lev Richards came on the air for a few hours every year to describe the climactic matches of the U.S. Championships at the West Side Tennis Club in the Forest Hills neighborhood of the New York borough of Queens. I listened only because I listened to any kind of sports event on the radio, not out of any urge to know what was going on at Forest Hills. But I was fascinated and puzzled, too. I couldn't quite picture it. Baseball, football, basketball, boxing – those I could visualize. Forest Hills gave me trouble. Hills and a forest in New York City? Maybe surrounding the courts? Were people sitting on the hill-side, watching?

I knew what tennis was, all right, though kids didn't play much in my town. Deuce was a mystery. Courts, the four of them, were dirt. When Lev Richards spoke of grass courts, it was beyond comprehension. In my town the courts had been constructed simply by stripping the grass from a vacant lot, rolling, and lining. Any persistent blades that poked through were considered intruders.

Years afterward, I got the picture. I was hacking away now for the high school team, and I was determined to see Forest Hills. Fired by the image of a god named Jack Kramer on the cover of *Time* magazine, three of us (team mates Gus Gehring, Al English, and I) boarded Al's geriatric Ford and set out on a pilgrimage. Twenty-four hours of non-stop driving and nonsensical navigation later, we arrived from Ohio at the shrine. Queens Boulevard, then as now, was garish, unfriendly, tumultuous. Yet at the gates of West Side we found tranquillity. It was dusk, the best time at Forest Hills. Play was just about over for the day. A man leaving the grounds handed us his ticket stubs. We hurried in, sprinted up the steep concrete stairs, burst through the portal, and stood above a gorgeous meadow.

Yes, it was grass. Two men in white were still playing, although few remained in the stadium. The minarets of the Forest Hills Inn and the groves of the Forest Hills Gardens stood confidently in the gloaming, sturdy defenders of the faith, gray against an azure evening. Forest Hills.

It seemed Mecca to the pilgrims.

There is no romance to Forest Hills now. Smog and Queens press in. The Inn, no longer a stylish hotel, wobbles toward collapse, a decaying sentry. But I remember the first encounter romantically. I remember a lot of first encounters that way.

Sam Match, a college kid, was playing Elwood Cooke, an ex-top tenner, that evening in the stadium. First round. Match one. Cooke had been Wimbledon finalist to Bobby Riggs eight years before. Twenty-nine years after, I asked Match if he, too recalled that meaningless match that took on considerable importance to me. Sam, a genial peddler of securities in Los Angeles and a tennis tutor to such as Dan Rowan, of course remembered. 'That was my first match at Forest Hills, too. I remember thinking Cooke was one of those old guys – in his 30s,' Match laughed. 'But it's funny how fast you become one of those old guys.' Sam currently ranks No.5 nationally among the 45s.

My pals and I stayed two days, living in a hotel for retired fleas out on Long Island, until the money and the week-end ran out. We got to see Kramer, but not much of him, in a first-round shuffle past one Ed McGrath. Four other players stuck in my brain. Aussie Geoff Brown and an American, Bill Vogt, served harder and faster than I believed possible, stacking up ace after ace. John Newcombe and I were talking about big servers one day, and he wondered, 'Ever hear of a guy named Geoff Brown?' I told Newk of my Forest Hills pilgrimage. 'Damned if he doesn't serve just about as fast now,' Newcombe said, 'and he's over 50. Just a skinny little guy, but what coordination – just whips that ball! Sheer strength isn't necessarily the clue to big serving.'

Then there were a couple of nonentities, an American, Charlie Mattman, and an Indian, Man Mohan. They played a long, exhausting match that neither appeared capable of winning. It was on a field court so we could stand next to them, get the feel of the caprices of grass – the skidding, low bounces, the uncertainty, the wild spins and caroms. A totally different game, altogether new and intriguing to us dirt-kickers.

Used balls were for sale at the club, authentically and distinctively smudged in green. I bought one to show the guys back home. A grass-stained tennis ball. A wonder. A curiosity, something like bringing back a chunk from the White Cliffs of Dover.

That ball rested on a shelf in our dining room, to be talked about and admired, a symbol of the journey to another realm. Like a koala outside its native habitat, however, the ball didn't survive. Chlorophyll faded, vanished. Its soul was gone, and the ball lay white and dead on the shelf until I had to dispose of it.

When the chlorophyll went out of the U.S. Championships in 1975, transforming Forest Hills from a pretty pasture to a dustbin, the last of the romance went with it. We should have known then, that with the rape of the grassblades, and their replacement by clay courts, Forest Hills was doomed as the site of the U.S. Open. The place was clearly outgrown by the event, no longer the place to relax for an afternoon, wandering casually among the courts outside the stadium and grandstand, or even spreading out over several seats in the stadium itself, which was seldom crowded until the final weekend. The tennis epidemic had enveloped the West Side Club; times had changed, but the club was in no mood to change at the same pace and update.

Abruptly, the U.S. Tennis Association, piloted by the deceptive cornpone slicker, W.E. 'Slew' Hester, pulled a Carpetbag Reverse.

Hester, the southerner, came North and lifted the goodies out of Forest Hills, transferring the Open across town to a public park called Flushing Meadow. Business opens at Flushing Meadow on hard courts next year. Thus, this Open of 1977 is hail and farewell to Forest Hills, where U.S. champs have been anointed since Little Bill Johnston (1915) and Molla Mallory (1921, when the women's nationals moved from Philadelphia).*

But Slew Hester has worked out a 15-year deal with the City of New York for the U.S. Open and is considering renaming the new site Forest Hills Racquet Park. After all, the West Side Club did move several times during the last century, from the West Side of Manhattan en route to Queens, without changing its identity. But West Side and Forest Hills aren't moving; they're staying put. I suggest to the USTA that Flushing Meadow is a fine name, and in time will take its place among prominent sports addresses. A fresh start, a fresh name: as in the move in 1916 from the narrowness of the Newport Casino to the invigorating atmosphere of New York and Forest Hills, when the tournament game in America began to come out of a closet hung with blue-stockings. No need to confuse the public by setting up another Forest Hills.

Bill Riordan, the Svengali of Salisbury (Md.), strolling about Forest Hills on that epochal first day of 1975, when the athletes began testing themselves on the pea-soup-green grit, sighed, 'It just doesn't smell like Forest Hills any more. Grass is class.'

So it is. But Riordan, as much as anyone else, realized that grass is also passé (except for fleeting instances such as Wimbledon and the Australian Open). Demands of pro tennis are too much for American grass. Tennis is more interesting and entertaining, usually, on slower ground. Cheering the change, I still mourned the passing of the gay blades of Ownie Sheridan's lawn.

The abandonment of grass was just another indication that tennis had outstripped a conservative, even reactionary past, and gone beyond a leisurely, more glamorous day when the late grass-court circuit stretched between private clubs of the East like a three-months-long scene out of F. Scott Fitzgerald. The Open got too big for West Side. Although a day at Forest Hills was fun, customers could sense the club's disdain for the general public.

So it is time to move on to a bigger, and maybe better, place. Growth of a game means you lose some of the niceties – the tradition, drinks

---

* The men's championships of 1921, '22, '23 were played in Philadelphia at the Germantown Cricket Club while the Stadium was under construction.

on the clubhouse porch, strolls through the quiet streets of Forest Hills. Gardens, the waitresses and bartenders, club members and committee people you got to know through the years, and who were by and large helpful and friendly. Forest Hills meant grass – not mean-looking grit – and when that ended, the party was really over, although it took three years to wind down completely. Flushing Meadow will offer a 20,000-seat stadium and smaller stadia to properly accommodate anybody who wants to see the Open, as well as sufficient parking and greater care for the customers. It won't be Forest Hills, but you can't maintain a first affair forever can you?

The tennis epidemic was bound to kill off the customary watering spots. Pro tennis has gone indoors and necessitated the construction of bigger stadia indoors, predominantly in public places. When Forest Hills has been kissed good-bye, only four of the old, entrenched playgrounds will continue to present major tennis in the U.S.; Longwood Cricket Club in Boston (the U.S. Pro); the Casino at Newport, Rhode Island (the Hall of Fame tourney); River Oaks Country Club in Houston (a WCT circuit tourney); Orange Lawn Tennis Club at South orange, New Jersey (a Grand Prix event).

Turmoil has been a sometime mark of Forest Hills. The barbaric response of the crowd to the boorishness of Ilie Nastase during his struggle against Hans Pohmann – and everybody else – last year was one occasion.

Another was the boisterous, one-sided demonstration for Pancho Gonzales in 1968 as the customers shouted and cheered him through a jolting of Wimbledon finalist Tony Roche. Silence is more the rule, and frequently more powerful, as during the Jimmy Connors–Bjorn Borg third-set tiebreaker a year ago, an excruciating passage that went to Connors, 11 points to 9, after he had canceled four set points.

'God, the place gets so quiet.' Arthur Ashe recognized the dramatic force of the tiebreaker, which dawned, in Sudden Death form, in 1970. 'I was never so nervous.' That was the idea. Bill Talbert, the tournament director, had the foresight and *chutzpah* to put inventor Jimmy Van Alen's hallucination into practice at Forest Hills. The world followed, even though the male players (never noted for promotional instincts) had, prior to the Open, presented Talbert with a petition demanding that he drop the idea. Tiebreakers had been used elsewhere previously, but the Forest Hills imprimateur gave the game new life through Sudden Death. Nevertheless the male pros continue in trying to kill that off, preferring the less nerve-jangling Lingering Death method.

We all have our memories of Forest Hills, the place where hundreds of thousands of us first saw fine tennis. We will be nostalgic, and it will seem better than it actually was. Long after my first visit, I returned with a typewriter: to get in free to watch tennis, and write about it, which really beats working for a living.

For a while, each match stayed with me clearly, but . . . then they multiplied to hundreds . . . numerous forgotten altogether . . . yet fragments of most sticking. So many tremendous matches: Newcombe's overcoming Wimbledon champ Jan Kodes in five sets in 1973 was the best played by two finalists; Billie Jean King's resurgence to beat Evonne Goolagong in the 1974 final the most thrilling; Chrissie Evert's resuscitation from six match points at the hand of Mary Ann Eisel in 1971 perhaps the most memorable because a great player-to-be (then only 16) was nervelessly overturning an internationalist and suddenly imprinting herself on the public consciousness. Rod Laver's Grand Slam wind-ups in 1962 and 1969 seemed the most pleasurable, allowing us to look over a master's gargantuan shoulder and watch him apply the finishing strokes to very rare creations. Arthur Ashe's success in 1968, as an amateur, was the most stirring because he was conquering more than a game.

None of the winners rolling through Forest Hills caused greater jubilation or notice than Ashe. The triumph of a black man held so many implications and ironies, one being that Arthur, champion or not, couldn't have joined the host club at that time. But more than his subduing of Tom Okker in the title round, I remember his father, Arthur Ashe, Sr., whom I noticed beneath the stadium after the match. He was off in a corner, alone, unrecognized, crying – in relief, gratitude, happiness. He looked up from his handkerchief, saw me: 'Excuse me . . . but . . . that boy of mine . . . that boy . . . nearly died as a baby . . . now this . . . it's too much . . . too good . . . but, excuse me . . . .' I shook my head, quickly took his hand, said congratulations, and moved away. It was his moment.

I think also of two losers. Carole Caldwell Graebner made her way painfully to the 1964 final. Her right arm was bandaged; she wore a gauze glove on her racket hand to cover terrible burns received through an allergic reaction to the sun and some medication she'd been taking. Carole nerved her way to the pinnacle where her reward was a dismal 40 minutes with Maria Bueno. Bueno was brilliant, belting Carole 6-1, 6-0, the worst beating ever at Forest Hills. Carole never complained.

Tony Roche in the 1969 and 1970 finals was up against history-makers. He won the first set against Laver, wound up a statistic in the Rocket's Slam. The next year Tony won the first set again, but Ken Rosewall, on the verge of 36, was in one of his trances, delighting the customers, many of whom had sat in on his win over Lew Hoad 14 years before. Roche was forlorn, but he was also young and blooming. Nobody felt too badly for Roche then. He was just the opponent, the foil for his countrymen to score popular victories. Obviously, Tony was the heir-apparent to Laver as No.1, and would have his chance in the winner's circle. Who could foresee the injuries and know that Rochie would never again come closer?

The departure from Forest Hills is a loss for all of us. Momentarily. We'll recover. So will the U.S. Open, to be continued next year at Flushing Meadow on slow hard courts. That's an improvement surely, the ideal flooring for both men and women, and making the U.S. Championship courts unique among the Big Four.

At twilight Sunday, September 11, three decades after initially climbing the stadium steps, I will make it one more time, carrying a glass of champagne. Forest Hills will be over. I will peer across the West Side grounds, at the minarets of the Forest Hills Inn and the groves of Forest Hills Gardens, and I will drink to Sam Match, Elwood Cooke, Man Mohan, Geoff Brown and all the others who came after. A final toast to Forest Hills and what was. And to Lev Richards, who whispered to me from a radio about a place called Forest Hills.

Filled with forebodings I walked moodily through the fading light of a
Hamburg dusk. A thin drizzle had been falling down since dawn. There
were pools on the concrete apron, shining coldly under the blue-white
glare of the arc-lights. Ahead, emerging from the mist, stood the Pan-
Am jet, stark and sombre.

I huddled deeper into my great-coat, and let my mind return to the
events of the previous evening. The note, enclosed in a plain white en-
velope, had been thrust under the door of my room at the Hauptbah-
nhof.

'Imperative that I see you. I will wait in the lounge at 8 precisely.' It
was signed, simply, 'Lister'.

I met him there. He wasted no time in getting to the point.

'It's a new assignment for you, old lad,' he said quietly. 'America.'
He paused then and waited.

In spite of my months of training, I started imperceptibly.

'Yes,' he said, with a thin smile. 'It will be no picnic. We both realise
that. But it must be done and you're the man to do it.'

'What about Segal?' I asked in a flat voice.

'We're afraid he might crack,' said Lister. 'Besides, he talks too much.
No, Forbes, there's nothing for it. It must be you and you only.'

I smiled briefly, and met Lister's eyes.

Air Vice Marshall Sir Claude Lister, now seconded to Intelligence. I'd
been through a lot with Lister, but never anything like this. The American mission was suicidal – a desperately slender hundred-to-one long
shot. He knew it and I knew it, and he knew that I knew it, so there
was little doubt in my mind that we both knew it.

'Depend on me, sir,' I said firmly, with a confidence that I was far
from feeling.

He took my hand warmly then, his fingers trembling impeceptibly in
spite of their steely grip. 'This will be the last one, Forbes,' he said
quietly. 'Complete this thing and you're in from the cold. Nice warm
desk in Whitehall for you, old lad.'

I smiled again. Lister, I noticed, had carefully avoided mentioning the
alternative. Instead he was talking of the mission. 'You'll have Drysdale,

of course,' he said, 'not much experience in crisis, but he'll be there, notwithstanding.'

'Drysdale!' I laughed inwardly at that. At nineteen he was barely out of diapers. 'Drysdale!' Good God! But I said nothing. What, after all, was there to say?

For five hours Lister briefed me, and then we retired, exhausted, for a few precious hours of sleep. At dawn. America. There could be no turning back.

I reached the great jet at last, and hurried up the stairway, settling myself into the window seat to which the stewardess directed me.

America: I shivered slightly, and, ordering a double Scotch-on-the-rocks, I went over my instructions for the umpteenth time.

I had obviously been reading Alistair MacLean a good deal about that time. Nevertheless, the entry, although tongue-in-cheek, reveals the impact that my first tennis trip to America made upon me.

You could either play the middle-eastern circuit in those days or venture across the Atlantic to play the American East Coast tournaments which lead up to the United States National Doubles event in Boston and then Forest Hills – the fourth leg of the four major tournaments, known as the 'Grand Slam', namely, Australia, the French and Wimbledon. At that time only one man in the history of tennis had ever won all four of these tournaments. The man was Donald Budge. Of the other players who had tried, Lew Hoad had come closest in 1956, losing Forest Hills to Rosewall with the other three titles in hand. Other great players might have done it, could have done it, had planned to do it, or had dreamed of doing it. But only Budge *had* done it. And now, in 1962, with three titles already won, Rod Laver was poised to make his attempt.

In 1962 I received an invitation from the USLTA to participate in tennis events in the United States. I had never before been to America, for the reason that the USLTA were particularly thrifty with their invitations and I could not afford the cost of a private trip. Such was the state of tennis in those days that, although I was rated in the first twenty players in the world, I rarely saved more than one hundred dollars a week, some of which had to be saved to pay the bills for my little family at home.

The American invitation offered me travel, accommodation, and two hundred dollars per week for five weeks – good by any standard then, and for America, excellent. I played the German championships at Hamburg and boarded my flight to New York with a certain amount of apprehension. The very thought of America had always diminished me somewhat, and the tales of hordes of huge American college boys with mighty serves on bad grass courts gave me tennis elbow in anticipation, as well as a mild case of the dreaded sinking feeling.

In addition, I had been playing indifferent singles for some weeks, and for the American stint I had lost my doubles partner, Abe Segal, and was to play with Cliff Drysdale, whom I still regarded as an irresponsible minor, with no idea at all of the gravity of my situation.

I landed at Idlewild, which it was then called and which name I loved, and by a series of what I could only explain as miracles in that vast place, I found my luggage, cleared customs without a hitch, and suddenly fond myself taken by the arm with a voice saying: 'Mr Forbes! We've been expecting you. We have a car ready to drive you to Southampton.'

I gave a sigh of relief. I am one of those people who worry secretly (but not obsessively) about being forgotten and left to wander the streets of New York alone, holding my suitcase and tennis racket. We drove down the Long Island peninsula that hot afternoon and the journey became for me one of those moments in life that remain forever in the mind – sharp little nudges of the memory simultaneously happy and sad.

The car radio gave frequent weather, temperature and time checks in the best American style, played Errol Garner recordings, a song called, *It's my party and I'll cry if I want to* over and over, and suddenly announced that Marilyn Monroe had died, while the endless landscape of roadhouses, gas stations and flashing signs floated by. The driver of the car deposited me and my baggage at the entrance to the Meadow Club. There, on a motley of grass courts, were my huge Americans with their enormous services. It was a Monday afternoon, matches were in progress everywhere, and I had the strange feeling that I might at any minute be called upon to *play a match*!

The whole scene, in fact, looked singularly uninviting. The courts, or most of them, were literally laid out upon a meadow. On the back courts one fully expected domestic animals to be grazing, or at the very least, a few stools of fresh dung into which the huge services might fly on big points. Daisies grew in fair profusion and the grass, though not actually waving, quivered in the breeze. Against this pastoral scene the athletic abilities of the sweaty players and their American profanity seemed particularly ominous.

I presented myself at the players desk and they said:

'Gordon Forbes! We sure have been expecting you. Why don't we just show you to your quarters where you can freshen up. You have a match at four!'

103

A match at four! I felt as though I'd been travelling for days and had the vague idea that for me, with the time change, it was about three in the morning. With enormous relief, I saw Fred and Pat Stolle and Cliff Drysdale approaching. Things began to brighten considerably. Fred was the eternal optimist and Cliff, although alarmingly confident at all times, presented a welcome return to a world which I knew. After cheerful greetings, I told them that I was feeling tired and was scheduled to play someone called Roger Werksman in the first round.

'Roger Werksman,' said Cliff.

'Roger Werksman,' said Fred.

'Yes,' I said, 'Roger Werksman.'

'Can't mess about with Werksman,' said Fred. 'Got to get in and play it tight. You'll beat him, of course, but you'll have to play it really tight.'

'Oh, you'll beat Werksman all right,' said Cliff in a very positive way. Except that he'd said the same thing when I played Lundquist in our Davis Cup matches against Sweden, and against Martin Mulligan in Hilversum.

'Only don't pay any attention to what he says,' Cliff had continued. 'He talks a lot.'

I'd long ago decided that it was useless to ask one's fellow competitors about players whom you didn't know, but against whom you found you had to play. Because if one's fellow competitors *did* know them, they usually scared you badly by saying ambiguous things like:

'He hits a lot of balls. Boy, does he hit a lot of balls! But you really shouldn't have any serious trouble!'

Or: 'He has a hell of a serve, but if you can get that back, you're home and dry.' Then add: 'Big forehand, though. Must keep away from the forehand. Bloody frightening forehand!'

If they had not heard of them, one found alarming thoughts about 'Dark Horses' flashing through one's mind. There is little fun to be found in the early round matches in America. The population there is generally of very athletic bent – and Americans are taught from birth to display an air of terrific confidence at all times. They *never* hide their lights under bushels. Cliff accompanied me back to the large wooden beach house where we were staying – one of those summer houses for which Southampton is famous. Not as fabulous as Gatsby's house, but well established, expensive enough, and smelling of holidays, canvas chairs and surf boards. What was more, there was a French maid, whose name, inevitably, turned out to be Françoise. She met us at the front door and carried my racket and coat. She was unbelievably French, with wide-set eyes, wider mouth, still wider hips and strong calves, and possessed the kind of looks which spent their time balanced on the knife edge, between 'very ugly' and 'very beautiful'. I could see that Cliff had already summed her up completely. When it came to girls, Cliff was a lightning mover.

'She has a friend,' he told me in a matter-of-fact way, as I unpacked my gear, 'also French.'

'Good Lord!' I said. Two French maids sounded twice as promising as one, and in a distracted sort of way I made a mental note to find out more about her when the time was right. But the four o'clock Werksman encounter loomed large. I was sharply aware that William Clothier had persuaded the United States authorities to issue my invitation and I didn't want to let him down. To make matters worse, Cliff told me that our host had backed us to the tune of five hundred dollars as the likely winners of the men's doubles event.

The dressing-room, when I entered, seemed to be full of towels. Americans have a thing about towels and aren't really happy unless there are dozens close at hand. One towel to an American is the same, basically, as one glass of wine to a Frenchman, or one cup of tea to a Briton. Hopelessly inadequate.

I changed and made my way to the referee's desk. It was just four o'clock – Werksman hadn't arrived. By five past I began to hope fervently that he'd been let down by some form of transport. There are few feelings so good as those evoked by the news that one's opponent hasn't arrived for a match which one has been secretly dreading. At four-fifteen, just as the term 'default' was being bandied about, Werksman arrived – or rather, exploded upon the scene.

My first impression was one of relief – he wasn't a huge American – in fact, he looked a little weedy. A closer look, however, revealed that he'd definitely played the game before. His racket grips had that well worn look about them, his shoes were streaked with grass stains which seemed to creep upwards onto his socks and towards his knees; and he carried a tennis racket headcover full of stuff – salt tablets, glucolin, elastoplast, sweatlets, a few dollar bills and so forth. He also had the type of short, sturdy legs which should be slow but which are, in fact, as fast as the devil. Besides, he'd just come off a practice court, and stood hopping about from one foot to the other and telling a friend that his game had 'come good just at the right time!'

We made our way to our allotted court, with Werksman followed by a little knot of supporters. One hears a lot of snippets on the way to one's court. '– Great serve and volley,' someone was saying to Werksman, 'but a nothing backhand. Can't break eggs', referring of course to me. And someone else said, '. . . South African. Supposed

105

to be good on grass, but doesn't really look as though . . .' And: 'Forbes and Werksman. This I've got to see. . .'. By the time we'd reached the court, I had heard several bits of information about myself which I had not heard before.

The warm-up was enough to let me know that I had a problem. There is a solid, compact way some smaller players go about their games that spells trouble. It didn't look to me as though Werksman missed too many balls. I was even less impressed by his service (on which, like most Americans, he took about fifty practices) – one of those low, flat affairs which come off the grass at ankle height and curl round at you. So I clenched my teeth and set about the business of becoming accustomed to grass again in three minutes, and getting my backhand to break eggs.

Tennis balls fly off grass faster and lower than off hard surfaces and the curved balls keep going – never kicking back. I liked to play on grass, especially true grass, as it suited my game and levelled things out to a certain extent. But, nonetheless, it took quite a bit of getting used to. And I wasn't used to having to cope with daisies in the grass.

We held serve in a conventional sort of way until about five or six all in the first set, at which stage I broke his service in a way which I considered to be quite conventional – one backhand passing shot aimed crosscourt which went off the wood up the line, and a neat net cord at 30-40. Werksman, however, seemed of the opinion that my efforts had been tinged with a dose of good fortune. He had the habit of muttering things to himself and not quite under his breath, so that one caught snatches of things like: '– a foreigner! A thin man from Africa! and you're struggling Werksman!' Or: '– if you weren't such a big, deep asshole, Werksman, you'd be towelling off by now, *having won!*'

The monologue which took place as we changed ends after that set was far more extensive.

'You are losing,' he muttered fiercely, 'to a man who has arms and legs like pretzels! If you weren't paralysed, you would be able to *break* them off and serve them with beer! He *cannot* play, and you *can* play, and he's winning and you're losing – so get your tail out onto the grass and *play!*'

I was tired and irritable and not amused, and secretly began to wonder if there was any truth in what my opponent said. I lost the second set after a bitter struggle, but broke his service in the second game of the final set and quickly took a 4-1 lead. At this point he muttered something about my having a head like a pineapple and that he should be chopping it up and serving it with cocktails. He then proceeded to play superbly, restricting his utterances to things like – 'Now! You've got him!' or 'One more break and his backhand's got to fold!'

I found myself leaving the court having lost 7-5, feeling utterly dejected, but surprised by the many sympathetic remarks from even casual tennis acquaintances. So I drank three beers with Drysdale and Stolle, slept for eighteen hours then awoke and found myself left only in the men's doubles, but with a week to get some grass court practice, and to investigate the talents of the two French maids.

The beaches at Southampton are long and sandy and the weather that year was particularly warm. Françoise obediently produced her friend, a tall languid girl with a straight sheaf of dark hair which half obscured an eye and fell to an angular point beneath the line of her chin, like a Vidal Sassoon sketch. Where Françoise was big-boned and happy, Nicci was introspective, had a semitic profile, a slightly grainy skin and smiled instead of laughing out loud. She smelt of France – peppery perfume and a hint of garlic and everything about her was lanky – legs, waist, hands and throat – like a newly-born giraffe. Her legs wobbled at the knees. I find girls with long legs that wobble at the knees very attractive in an oblique sort of way. To my surprise, I found that she liked beer.

And so, on most evenings, we watched television and drank beer, eating the hamburgers which Françoise created in the kitchen. Afterwards, with a white Long Island moon at full strength, we would walk down to the sea and hit the water with mighty leaps and shouts.

The beach, the shining sea with its mild waves, and the moonlight, reminded me of the famous love scene played by Burt Lancaster and Deborah Kerr in *From Here to Eternity*, a film which had left a great impression on me when I had first seen it. With this in mind, I tried a long shot, and tentatively told Nicole that she looked a little like Deborah Kerr. She gave one of her rare chuckles and said, ' Ah, mon chéri, but no more than you look like Burt Lancastaire!' Unromantic fare, but nonetheless, the seed had been sown. We walked arm in arm, wading ankle deep in the surf and talking in whispers and at a suitable spot, fell to our knees with the waves breaking around our thighs. True to form, we finally achieved a horizontal position on the sand, locked in a tender embrace.

Fate can play savage tricks on amateur romantics. Disaster struck in the form of a freak wave. We were suddenly overwhelmed by roaring water which rolled us over several times towards the shore, shook us briefly, then hauled us seawards in a swirl of liquid sand, before leaving us lying there like two pieces of driftwood. Both my ears were filled with sand, Nicole, who finished up underneath, was in a far worse plight, with almost all her orifices silted up. We struggled to our feet.

'You and your romantic notion,' she cried, half laughing, half sobbing, 'such a thing would never 'ave 'appened to Lancastaire!'

She was probably right, although if it had, I suppose they would have done another take. We would never have *seen* Burt Lancaster rolled over and have *his* ears filled with sand! It took some considerable sluicing off in the water to clear ourselves of sand and seaweed and, in retrospect, we both agreed that the whole business of embracing on the water's edge by moonlight, was overdone and best left lying in the mind!

French maids' company must be good therapy for men's doubles. Cliff and I formed an unlikely, but effective, combination and reached the final round without undue desperation. On finals afternoon, Bill Clothier arrived and I was determined that we win the tournament. I had even spent some time the previous evening persuading Cliff to have an early night, and also to *knock off the sitters* – as he had a nasty habit of trying clever and Larsen-like shots off the easy ones, which caused flurries of activity at a moment when I felt the umpire should be calling the score in our favour. There is nothing as bad as being in a tight match, getting an easy one, not quite killing it and having your opponent recover it and send up a high lob, which you suddenly realise is going to drop in, and saying to yourself, 'Oh Jesus Christ, now I have to do the whole thing over again, and I should be towelling off and sipping coke!'

Our final was scheduled at four in the afternoon, against some couple like Whitney Reed and Eugene Scott. Chuck McKinley and Dennis Ralston, the current United States doubles champions, were not playing at Southampton that year, leaving a mixed bag of American teams, all good, but not *that* good.

Cliff and I hit some practice balls at about two thirty, and then he announced that he had to return to the house for some or other reason. I watched the singles finals for a while, then remembered that I had forgotten to bring my spare rackets. I returned to the house and opened the front door in time to see Françoise and Cliff disappearing furtively into our suite. I ran up the stairs and opened the door.

'Oh no, you bloody well don't,' I cried and for once Cliff looked sheepish.

'It's quite good before doubles,' he said. 'It clears your eyes. Before singles, it's a bit ambitious.'

'Your eyes are clear enough for doubles,' I said grimly, 'and I am not interested in your theories about singles. I am not leaving for the courts without you!'

We won the finals and received silver water pitchers and the congratulations of Clothier. I was delighted with Cliff as a doubles partner – he had excellent reflexes and particularly damaging service returns, and he obviously enjoyed playing with me.

I made the journey across the Sound to Newport in a light aircraft, feeling far happier about playing in the United Sates. The tournament, held at the Newport Casino, was run by the great American innovator and enthusiast James van Alen.

As mentor, founder and general factotum of the Newport tournament, van Alen insisted even then that the nine point sudden death tie-breaker be used in all matches, if the games' score reached five-all. In the first round there I came within a hair's breadth of being done in by Clark Graebner who led me one set, five-all, and four points to love in the tie-breaker. To win five consecutive points, two of which were on his service, against Graebner on grass, was a miracle by any standards and so rattled him that I won the third set quite easily.

There has always been a great depth of competent players in the United States. You could be sure that even number thirty-four on the National Grading List could play well enough to add a few grey hairs to visiting foreigners. Even if they weren't the standard big serve and volleyers, they were always other things – diabolical forehand hitters, lightning net rushers or neggety devils who dug in on the baseline and hit heavy groundshots; and all of them behaved as though it was simply a matter of time before they would become the world's best tennis players.

To breeze through the early rounds of any big American tournament, one had to be an almighty player, fully equipped with everything, including a sense of humour. After Graebner, I beat Larry Nagler in another third set tie-breaker, and after him, someone else whom I can't remember.

Chuck McKinley in the semi-final was too hard to handle. On court he behaved like a rubber cannon-ball which had been fired into a walled enclosure, bounding about and hitting everything at a hundred miles an hour. Against him I kept feeling that he was about one point ahead of me, so that by the time I had completed my point, he was already half way through the following one. By the end of our match, which he won in three sets, he had begun towelling off and I was still busy playing the last point or two when I heard the umpire call the score. It was very disconcerting. Cliff and I lost to McKinley and Dennis Ralston in the semi-final, also in three sets.

The United States men's doubles championship took place in Boston in those days, during the week preceding Forest Hills. The doubles combination which Cliff and I had drummed-up made the event far

more interesting and I arrived at the tournament filled with enthusiasm.

'You'll be staying,' they told me on arrival, 'with the Furcolos. Rod Laver will also be there and you will be sharing the guest suite.'

I was excited. Foster Furcolo was the ex-governor of Massachusetts and lived with his family in a superb old house not far from the club. Besides, Rod, tremendously famous always, was at that time at the height of his fame, as he was about to compete at Forest Hills for the last leg of his grand slam. We were firm friends by then, and I knew we would have an interesting time. My faithful friend, Clifford Drysdale, was consulted and relegated to more modest digs, while I made ready to move into the luxury and culture of Bostonian society.

The house was beautiful. It had a hall with a wide and elegant stairway which divided into two on the landing, before giving way to the suites above. On the wall above this landing hung a great sail-fish, a trophy, I think from some heraldic deep sea fishing trip of days past. After climbing the section of stairway beneath the sail-fish, one reached the upper floor and turned immediately left into the suite which Rod and I were to occupy. This elaborate description all seems irrelevant now, just as then it did to me. Only later, after that night, had I cause to examine the topography of the place more carefully.

Rod had already arrived. He was sitting in the bedroom upon one of the beds, surrounded by piles of new tennis equipment. Most of the better players of the circuits were well provided with tennis gear, but I never got used to the quantities and varieties showered upon Laver. He looked up as I entered, with typical Laver-like casualness.

'Hello bastard,' he said, although I hadn't see him since Hamburg. 'Look at all this bloody gear. Enough gear here to start a store. And that's only half of it. There's no way I'll ever be able to wear all this lot, unless I change my bloody shirt after every game!'

I felt happy and at home with Rod – he had a mild manner with a sense of humour which often played on understatement. He'd understate almost everything, especially his remarkable successes and superb tennis ability; like the unbelievable, impossible shots he sometimes pulled out of a hat when they were least expected and badly needed. These he would scrutinize soberly, before remarking:

'Not a bad little bit of an old nudge, would you say?' or: 'Rare bit of old arse, that one, don't you think?'

When Governor Furcolo gave us a Cadillac for the week, Rod gave it an appreciative look. ' Thanks Governor,' he said, 'now we've got transport!'

Now, sitting on his bed, busy lacing up a tennis shoe, he waved a hand at the extravagant surroundings and said. ' Choose a bed. It's not much, but it's home!'

There was only one other bed apart from the one upon which he was sitting, so I established myself upon it and began unpacking. Rodney told me that he and Fred were top seeds for the tournament, and that Cliff and I would meet them in the quarters.

'Who do we play on the way to the quarters?' I asked him warily. He had a bad habit of judging other people's abilities on the strength of his own, thus carving away the mere possibility of losing before the quarters, at least.

'Oh, teams,' he said vaguely. ' Dell and Bond. Hoogs and McManus. Eugene Scott and somebody. People like that. Just got to keep the ball in play and give the loose ones a bit of a nudge.'

'I see,' I said. 'You mean just coast through the early rounds.'

He nodded, not even recognising my slight sarcasm. Competitive tennis, I realised, was a very simple matter for Rodney George.

I began unpacking and as I did so, an uneasy thought struck me. Rodney was, as far as I knew, unaware of my erratic nocturnal behaviour. It was true that Abe Segal had frequently raved about, 'Forbsey belonging in a strait-jacket at night,' or other such remarks, in various lounges and dressing rooms, but it was equally true that Abie himself was considered highly unreliable as a source of factual information and, in fact, an imminently eligible strait-jacket case himself – moreover, not only at night.

I conducted a quick consultation with myself about the wisdom of even broaching the subject with Rodney. I'd hardly done anything unusual for weeks, discounting the odd outburst or two and the fact that Cliff informed me one morning that I had pulled him out of bed the previous night and coldly instructed him to get on with the match, as play had to be continuous – an accusation which I felt to be groundless, as I usually had some vague memory of my more positive actions, whereas, on this occasion, I'd had none. Still, Laver was Laver, and I baulked at the idea of taking him completely by surprise, so I decided to mention the thing very casually.

'In case you hear me moving about the room in the dark,' I said, idly examining one of the racket grips at which he continually scraped and whittled, 'don't worry. Just put on the light.' He looked at me thoughtfully.

'What might you be doing?' he asked.

'I, er, sometimes, very occasionally, well, you know, I, er –.'

'Start a revolution,' he interrupted. 'Don't tell me big Abie wasn't just raving on?'

'Abie exaggerates enormously,' I said. ' At worst I usually walk quietly round my bed, or give one or two instructions.'

He said no more, besides giving me a penetrating look and muttering, 'My bloody oath,' under his breath once or twice, in a very Australian way.

The Furcolos were a great family, epitomising the warm, but casual hospitality, the lack of pompousness, yet the proper dignity of the true American. We had dinner and a game or two of table tennis before turning in. It was as well that I had warned Rodney. Sometime during that first night, in the light of the moon which poured in through the window, I saw a thin, smallish and vicious-looking animal leap onto my bed and run up the covers towards my face at an alarming rate. Laver or no Laver, action had to be taken. In the nick of time I leapt up, rolled the creature up in the bed covers and, kneeling on my bed, I was busy squeezing the rolled bed cover violently in order to throttle the creature, when Rodney awoke. He sat up immediately.

' What's happening?' he asked, not unreasonably.

'I've got the little devil in here,' I cried.

' Who is he?' asked Rodney.

'A thin little bastard,' I replied.

Suddenly I threw the rolled up cover on Rodney's bed.

'Have a look if he's dead yet,' I commanded.

Rodney backed way. 'You have a look,' he said.

I began to realise then that something passing strange was going on, but was still in the grip of the dream. Gingerly I unrolled the cover and by the time it was open, I had fully awoken.

'I warned you that I sometimes did things in the night,' I said sheepishly. 'You should have switched the light on.'

'Sorry about that,' said Rodney, typically. ' Came as a bit of a shock though. Didn't know what you had rolled up in there. Wasn't sure whether you'd managed to kill it. Thought it might jump out. For a moment there I really thought you had something!'

'So did I,' I said fervently and quietly thanked my stars that the incident was over and that it had not been worse. Also, to my great relief, I began sleeping like a log, so that it seemed that my night-time performance had been a flash-in-the-pan.

I practised each morning with Rodney – rigidly effective Hopman type practice which forced you to make every shot with a purpose in mind – not the comfortable, free swinging hit-ups which were so tempting and which made you imagine that you were beautifully in form, and playing like a sort of improved version of Donald Budge.

Ten minutes of forehand cross courts – ten of forehand to backhand, up the line, ten of backhand to forehand, ten of cross court backhands; then all four repeated twice over with alternate players volleying. All that added up to two hours, leaving thirty minutes for practising overheads, services or any special weaknesses. A half-hour practice set completed the three hour session which Rodney insisted we follow. By the end of the week I had never played better, and often in retrospect, I have thought of those far off sessions and said to myself wistfully, 'If only! Forbes, if only!'

Cliff and I continued our efficient combination, edging out the American teams by the odd service break – all that is needed in grass court doubles. In the quarters we found ourselves faced by Laver and Stolle, having beaten Donald Dell and Billy Bond in the sixteens. It was strange that, having begun my doubles link-up with Cliff in a state of some uncertainty, we now found ourselves in the quarters of the United States National Doubles, actually discussing positively the possibility of beating the first seeded team.

The evening before the encounter, the four of us drank a few beers together in a mood of good-natured banter. Fred Stolle warned Cliff against hitting, 'Those arsey shots off that crappy double hander', and Cliff in turn said that Fred should, 'Watch his tramline and not serve too many doubles.'

This remark carried a slight edge to it, as Fred never pandered to caution on his second ball, serving it virtually as hard as his first. This resulted in a restless time for the receiver, but also, on Fred's off days, a good many double faults. Rodney said very little except that he thought the four of us should be able to, 'Move the ball about a bit out there on fast grass!'

Rodney and I turned in early that night. And I remember clearly that the thought of any unforeseen activity did not even enter my head. I was tired and fell asleep almost at once. Our room was so arranged that the wall which backed up against the stairwell consisted of a long built-in cupboard which Rod and I shared. As Rodney had chosen the bed furthest from the cupboard, my bed was adjacent to it, at a distance of perhaps ten to twelve feet.

Some time late that night, I opened my eyes to find the room full of moonlight. Standing in the cupboard, quite still, was a man whom I could see clearly through the open door. My heart froze as my mind raced through the possible reasons for his presence, finally fastening onto the obvious one. He was there to 'get' Rodney. There was no doubt about it. Rodney was a celebrity and this man, hiding in our cupboard, was an American psychopath, out to do him in. But my bed was between him and Rodney and the thought that he may not be sure which was Rod and which was me, made the situation even more desperate. The headline, 'Laver saved when Assassin strikes Thin South African,' flashed through my mind. Action had to be taken at once.

Suddenly a daring and subtle plan occurred to me. The cupboard had heavy doors with keys which turned easily. All I had to do, I decided, was to brace myself, leap up, slam the door and lock him in. There was no time to lose so, tensing myself for the deed, I began the countdown. In a state of nervous tension, one moves like lightning. I counted to three, hurled aside the bed clothes, gave a mighty leap, landed beside the cupboard, closed the door with a slam, and turned the key. As the noise died away, I heard an answering rumbling from somewhere in the house, then silence. I leaned for a moment against the cupboard door, weak with relief and overwhelmed suddenly by tiredness. Such was the depth of the nightmare that I was still tightly in its grip. It was then that I noticed Rodney, standing bolt-upright on the far side of his bed.

'Bit of a hell of a bang,' he said shakily, ' What's happening?'

'There was a guy in the cupboard,' I replied, 'who was going to get you. I locked him in.'

'Oh really?' said Rodney.

'We'll get him out in the morning,' I said.

I was desperately tired and climbed back into bed. The incident was closed, my mind was blank, yet at that moment as I lay back and closed my eyes, the first nudges of reality occurred.

'It's not possible,' I remember thinking to myself. 'I *couldn't* have actually done *that*. Not again. Not tonight, of all nights!'

But then there was a knocking sound and I opened my eyes. Rodney was standing next to the cupboard, tapping on the door with his knuckles and holding an ear to it.

'Anyone in there?' he said in an urgent whisper. 'Who in the hell are you?'

'It's OK, Rodney,' I said loudly and he jumped about three inches off the floor, 'there's no one in there.'

'You just told me there was,' he said. 'Could have believed you too.'

'It's one of my dreams,' I said. 'I'm terribly sorry. You should have put the light on.'

'No time for that,' he said. 'Just a bloody great bang. A man doesn't think about switching lights on when he thinks he's in a raid. Anyway, I'm opening this cupboard, just to make sure!'

We both watched in silence as he gingerly unlocked the door and opened it. Immediately inside it hung my raincoat on a hanger. Rodney gave it a contemptuous punch.

115

'Fooled you, you bastard,' he said to the coat. 'Thought you were going to get us, hey? Hadn't counted on my friend here, had you?'

Now, thirteen years later, the unreality of that particular situation still occasionally strikes me – Rodney Laver, chatting to a raincoat in the middle of a far-off night in Boston!

We slept, eventually. So badly did I want to disassociate myself from the incident that, when I awoke, I found myself still with the faint hope that the whole thing might yet prove to be a dream within a dream.

'I dreamt I had a dream last night,' I said to Rod when he finally awoke.

'Your dream couldn't have been as bad as *my* dream,' he said with deep conviction.

'Bad, hey?' I asked.

'Nearly crapped myself,' he said cryptically. 'Going to pay a lot more attention to what Abe Segal says from now on. Now I realise why he sometimes behaves as though he's got someone after him! Always looking over his shoulder, these days, is big Abie. Now I'm beginning to understand why!'

We went down to breakfast after I had made Rodney promise not to tell of the incident. Governor Furcolo looked up as we entered.

'Morning,' he said cheerfully. 'Quite a night wasn't it?'

I was speechless, but Rodney found words.

'Something happen in the night?' he enquired carefully.

'God-darned sail-fish,' said the Governor.

'Sail-fish?' Rodney looked puzzled.

'Been hanging on that wall for nearly eight years now and last night – down he came. Made a mighty bang, too. We kinda thought you might have heard it.'

'You hear a bang in the night, Gordon?' he said.

'Can't say I did,' I muttered.

'Broke a piece off his tail,' said the Governor. 'I'll have to get it glued up.'

My private theory was that the banging of the heavy cupboard door had dislodged the sail-fish, but it could never be proven. I consoled myself with the thought that there was just a chance that by some remarkable coincidence, the fish had chosen that particular moment to drop from the wall. Just a very small chance. But we never found out.

Our match was scheduled for about three that afternoon on one of the centre courts. The weather was sunny, the grass fast and from the very outset I had the feeling that Cliff and I might just play very well.

We held firm until four games all in the first set, then dropped service and lost 6-4 in a very conventional sort of way. At about six all in the second set it occurred to me that we were containing the game – that it was not, as I had been afraid, running away with us. If anything, Rodney was perhaps too much the individual to ever be as great at doubles as he was at singles. While he made some shots so quick and stunning that he left everyone, including his partners, with severe cases of dropped jaw, he also sometimes confused things by playing unconventional shots – things like drive volleys, or topspin lobs for service returns or colossal ground shots from the back of the court when he should have been at net. He also sometimes advanced to net behind his own lobs, quite confident apparently of volleying back his opponent's smashes, which he sometimes did.

Men's doubles is a game where certain rules should always be stuck to, and these rules seldom allow for the spectacular, usually demanding firm, if sometimes tedious, positional play, while openings are looked for. Rodney, being a law unto himself, firmly believed in making his own openings by sheer weight of shot. The result was hair-raising for his opponents. If he happened to be on form they spent a good part of the match collecting balls and protecting their persons. If not, he was vulnerable to solid resistance. Fred Stolle was a great doubles player, orthodox, intelligent and hard to penetrate. We became locked in mortal combat that day, and played for hours. I remember that Cliff and I won the second set at 12-10 and then, as though annoyed by our effrontery, Rodney and Fred snatched the third out of our hands at 6-2. Rodney's pre-match prediction was perfectly accurate. The ball *was* moving about like lightning. Fred's service led me to believe that he was conducting some fresh experiments in rocketry; Cliff hit tremendous two-handers and Rodney startled all three of us in his usual mercurial way by flashing about in tight circles and pulling every conceivable shot out of his hat. At two sets to one down, it seemed likely that Cliff and I were about to suffer one of our gallant defeats, but to our surprise we latched onto the fourth set and stuck like limpets. At 10-9 for us we found ourselves with points for the set, won a hand-to-hand volley exchange, and heard the score called at two sets all.

By the time the fifth set began, we'd been playing for close to three hours and still the match hung in the balance. With the score at twelve-all in that set, dusk was coming on and a heavy dew had begun to settle, making the court surface very slippery. At fifteen games all in the fifth, with the light fading fast, I held my service after several deuces and we changed ends leading 16-15. As we towelled off, the umpire turned to us and announced that we were to play only one more game, a decision which, I remember thinking, was decidedly strange as it put a lot of pressure on Fred, whose turn it was to serve. On the other hand, to return Fred's service on a greasy grass court in fading light was also not the easiest thing imaginable. We took up our positions in silence. It was one of those occasions when a match catches the imagination of the public. The stands were packed with players and spectators, excited by the fact that the top-seeded pair were in trouble.

Fred opened proceedings with a clean ace to Cliff on the right hand court. He then served a huge double fault to me, the first ball hitting the tape of the net and the second narrowly missing my heel.

As I moved to take my position for the next point, Rodney caught my eye and murmured something about Fred giving his second ball too much of a nudge. At fifteen-all Fred served a flat bullet of a first ball down the middle to Cliff, who apparently anticipated it, for he stepped into it and hit a two-hander down Rodney's tramlines so hard that the point was over before Fred had recovered from his service swing. This time Rodney's murmur was drowned by the roar of applause, but I saw his lips moving and guessed that he was discussing Cliff's 'nudge' with himself. At 15-30 Fred served an ace to me. At thirty-all Cliff mis-timed his two-hander so that instead of a clean return the ball went off the throat of his racket with a wooden clunk, hit the tape in front of the oncoming Fred, ran along the top of it for about a yard, then fell over on his side and disappeared into the grass. Fred rolled his eyes upwards. The crowd roared, the umpire called out the score at 30-40, and Cliff and I found ourselves with a match point against Laver and Stolle at 16-15 in the fifth set, on a wet grass court and in the dark to boot. In absolute silence I got ready to receive.

Fred's first ball narrowly missed Rodney's head and someone in the crowd laughed nervously. His second was so deep that for a fleeting moment I thought he had served a double. But the ball hit the line and presented me with an awkward skidding backhand which I managed to dig out of the corner with a late slice like a nine iron in golf. My shot drifted slowly towards the net, climbing slightly as it went, like a tired bi-plane trying to get airborne, with me closing in behind, while Fred approached the net from his side with a worried look. With a final surprising spurt, the ball cleared the net and settled into the grass at Fred's feet, leaving him an appallingly difficult half-volley. He got it back, but not well enough, and Cliff pounced with his two-hander down the middle and knocked it off. Game, set and match to Drysdale and Forbes – 4-6, 12-10, 2-6, 11-9, 17-15.

FOREST HILLS
All the visiting players were accommodated at the Vanderbilt Hotel on about Thirty-fourth Street. I was relegated to sharing a room with Cliff

Drysdale again, while Rodney was ensconced in the suite of honour where he immediately became inundated again with tennis gear and, in fact, apparel of all kinds, to the extent that, at one stage, it was almost impossible to get into his room. Cliff made a facetious remark about my 'rejoining the common people' as I entered our room, but I shut him up immediately by reminding him that I, by being billeted with Laver, had made a decisive contribution to our best-ever doubles win by scaring the wits out of him the night before. Roy Emerson also turned up at the Vanderbilt, having just completed the Middle Eastern circuit. He was as cheerful as ever, spilling grins and greetings all over the place. And so we all gathered for the United States Nationals, at Forest Hills.

It was hot and rainy for nearly a week, at first, and practice courts were at a premium. Besides, officialdom at Forest Hills at that time was about as bad as I had ever known. Players were treated as intruders, necessary evils, and people of low culture and little brain. Lunches, served in a damp marquee were hardly edible, and service at the main clubhouse was haughty and reluctant. Only the faithful white towels were plentiful. The official in charge of allocating practice courts was about a hundred and two years old, half blind, and with a memory which latched only onto odd and random pieces of information. His immediate reaction to any request for practice facilities was that there were either no courts available, or no balls, or neither. The only person whom he could remember was Roy Emerson. The name Emerson, for some obscure reason, had irrevocably lodged itself in his mind, and I soon discovered that the only sure way of getting a practice court was to arrange to play with Roy and then have him ask for the balls. He would walk up to the old fossil, pat him on the back, and with a huge grin ask him for a court.

'Name?' the old fellow would grunt.

'Emerson,' Roy would say.

'Ah, Emerson, take court nine. Here are the balls,' and off we'd go. When I mentioned this to Roy, he looked at me sceptically.

'He'd give you a court,' he said.

'Not a hope,' I replied, 'I've tried.'

'Bet you a dollar he will, bastard,' said Roy.

'OK,' I said. 'We'll go up to him, you ask for a court and tell him you're Forbes and see what happens.'

'You're on,' said Roy.

We approached the desk and Roy asked for a court in the usual way.

'Name?' enquired the old man.

'Forbes,' said Roy. 'Gordon Forbes, the famous South African.'

'No courts,' said the old man gruffly.

'It's all right,' I intervened quietly. 'He's playing with me. I'm Emerson!'

'Ah, Emerson,' he said. 'Yes, well, court thirteen is about to come off. You can have that one!'

We took the balls and went off to practise, laughing delightedly.

'You see,' I teased Roy, 'the *name* he knows, not you personally!'

For some reason, that incident must have impressed the old fellow's memory, for the next day when Roy went to ask for a practice court, giving his name as Emerson, the old man looked up at him sharply.

'You're not Emerson,' he said, 'You're Forbes.'

'Can't be Forbes,' said Roy. 'Not thin enough to be Forbes.'

'What do you mean?' asked the old man.

'You have to be pretty skinny to be Forbes,' said Roy. He bent his arm sharply and pointed to his bicep. 'See that,' he said, 'that's a muscle. Forbes doesn't have any of those!'

At that moment I arrived on the scene, ready to practise. The old man looked up at me, then at Emerson, then back to me.

'Who are you?' he asked gruffly.

'I am Emerson,' I said.

With a contemptuous glance at Roy, the old man handed me the balls.

'Come on, Forbes,' I said to Roy. 'Let's go and practise!'

Thereafter, nothing would persuade the old bloke that I wasn't Roy Emerson. Emerson, he regarded as a lowly South African of meagre talent.

'Hope the old bastard doesn't have anything to do with the draw,' was Emerson's wry comment. 'It's bad enough being Forbes in practice; wouldn't like to be him in a match!'

The weather cleared, the sun came out, hot and steamy, and play got under way on damp, heavy and not-too-even grass courts. Forest Hills can be desperately humid. By the end of the warm-up one is wet through and physically, there, matches are largely a matter of keeping one's body lubricated. Allen Fox used to spend about half an hour before each match, quietly eating salt tablets and glucose; to 'hydrate himself'.

Rod Laver was by far the best amateur in the world at that time, under any conditions and on any surface. He didn't even need to 'hydrate himself'. No one has ever played tennis more positively than he. He controlled his matches absolutely; quietly, simply, modestly even, but also superbly, with a control so rigid and purposeful that it seemed that every shot he made was part of an unwavering scheme to win.

120

Other players guided their strokes. Rodney fired his at predetermined points. It was *not* simply a matter, as he used to so often claim, of just 'keeping the ball in play and giving the loose ones a bit of a nudge.' More accurately, his game was a grand, deliberate and inevitable road to victory.

When he was young, he was a wild and woolly player. Every ball got well and truly hit, and I remember laughing at some of his early matches, watching his forehand and backhands flying, out of control, into the backstop. Yet, never did Harry Hopman, the great Australian strategist, and Rodney's adviser, suggest that he play more carefully. 'One day,' he said to me, long ago, as we watched him spray balls over a particularly broad front, 'he's going to start hitting all those shots in and then, my boy, what a player he will be!'

That year, at Forest Hills, the shots all went in. Rodney won his grand slam and Hopman's prophecy came true. What a player he was.

VIRGINIA WADE

DAVID GRAY

Nothing much is hidden. On court and immediately afterwards, there is only a thin mask on the public face. At Aix-en-Provence, the French had just beaten Britain in the Federation Cup. The tie had been decided by the doubles in which Rosie Darmon, playing every point as if it were a delicious adventure, and Gail Chanfreau had lobbed and out-manœuvered Virginia Wade and Glynis Coles. They embraced. Virginia and Glynis left the court very separately. If it had been a cartoon there would have been a large black cloud over her head.

British television followed her to the pavilion, collecting shots of dramatic anger. Tosca. Lady Macbeth. Medea. The BBC had sent a crew to Aix to interview her. ('She's in America all the time,' one British correspondent moaned.) Sensibly and discreetly, the other members of the British press kept out of her way.

She was conducting her post-mortem, a soliloquy from the lower depths, when John White, the chairman of the British LTA, appeared. 'Bad luck,' he said tentatively. The tigress looked piercingly, scornfully through the bars of her cage. There was a pause. 'Bad luck?' Virginia replied. 'Bad luck. It was disgraceful. Totally disgraceful.' White retreated. For five more minutes the withering commentary continued.

A man who didn't play tennis (his eyesight was too bad) wrote that line about treating triumph and disaster identically, which makes any competitor with passion and imagination laugh hysterically. Virginia had never believed that. Victory is pleasure; time and carefully acquired discipline haven't made failure easier to accept. She finished third on the Virginia Slims circuit. She knows how to adapt herself to America and living in a group – both of which she once found difficult. She counts the money that she wins but still regards it as currency from Wonderland ('amusing' was the word she used). She played team tennis last year and confounded everyone by making herself the heroine of the New York Sets – a distinction she may have to share this time with Billie Jean King. And there are fewer bad losses because she has improved technically and temperamentally.

She is more relaxed, more confident and more professional. She has stopped being the glorious British amateur who could have a wonderful conquering fortnight at Forest Hills and come home as the first U.S. Open champion, then lose to Winnie Shaw at Stalybridge and Mary Ann Eisel at Perth. Most of the times when she loses now, she has to be beaten. She feels that she is out of her self-destructive phase, that she no longer presents her opponents with unexpected victories. The doubles at Aix was a journey backwards, but she and Glynis only play together twice a year and their matches always look like that.

Every defeat is still etched into her heart. ('Every time I lose I'm miserable. Tennis is the most heartbreaking game of all.') And she has a long memory for grudges: the bottle of orange squash that Chris Evert broke over her new dress when they changed over in the crisis of last year's Eastbourne final ('I lost my break and I can't get the stains out of the dress'); the way the umpire overruled a line judge when she was leading in her Los Angeles semi-final with Navratilova; how the Italians always put her on the noisiest court at the Foro Italico with the worst of their bad umpires. But then that is every other player's grudge about Rome, too.

The anger springs from the same passion, the same streak of artistry, the same fiercely competitive spirit, which makes her produce spectacular shots in dramatic rallies. Applause still intoxicates her but she has a better head for it in her thirtieth year than she had at the Wimbledon when she was so determined to demonstrate her virtuosity to the Centre Court that she almost forgot that she was also playing against Pat Walkden . . . and lost. Most people think that she once said that she would rather play beautiful tennis than win. That is a misquotation, but it has looked like that sometimes. Certainly, she enjoys thinking of herself as an entertainer, but most of all she enjoys winning. Being on top. As long as she 'doesn't have to submerge her personality.'

'Tennis has been such a natural for me. I've always enjoyed playing, but I don't try to do anything competitive without wanting to win.' Would she have found it even more enjoyable if it had mattered less, if she hadn't been such a perfectionist, if she had been less fascinated by what's difficult, if there had been fewer aching joys and dizzy raptures, if she hadn't begun with a devastating service and then had to learn almost everything else about the game, if she had not been such a focus of national interest for the British (players from other countries could have bad days and sling rackets, but if Virginia slung one it always hit a British reporter), if she hadn't labored for five years under

123

the burden of being the only woman player from whom we really expected success?

She arrived from South Africa, luckier than most British juniors in that she had been able to learn the game in the sun, at the end of the best post-war decade in British tennis. Angela Mortimer, a persistent, determined loner, had won Wimbledon in 1961 and Ann Jones, who set her an example by going to America and acquiring a disciplined approach to the game, ended her career by winning it in 1969. Shirley Bloomer, running forever, had run away with the major clay court titles and Christine Truman had been the British Mary Pickford, bombarding the world with a huge forehand, the model for all the middle-class schoolgirls in straw hats, playing the kind of tennis that anyone could understand. She was immaculate and beautifully behaved.

Virginia may have been immaculate, but she certainly wasn't beautifully behaved. When she played for Tunbridge Wells Girls' High School in the Aberdare Cup, none of the school mistresses had ever seen so many flying rackets. At her first Junior Wimbledon, Allison Stroud, who became Mrs. Mark Cox, beat her, quietly returning the ball until Virginia made mistakes which were the result of her ambition outrunning her control. 'Come and look at this girl. She is good,' said Dan Maskell, the LTA's training manager. We watched her blown away in the wind of her own wildness.

She never won a junior title, but she celebrated her 19th birthday by taking Margaret Court, who had been the runner-up at Wimbledon the week before, to three sets at Edgbaston. All the way through her university career – can you really imagine her taking maths and physics? – her promise flared intermittently. She travelled with Ann Jones but lost to her so frequently that in the end their doubles partnership quietly disintegrated. She beat Ann at Bournemouth to win the British Hardcourt title – her first national championship – in 1967 and from then until last year when she finally decided to play regularly on the Virginia Slims tour, her tennis career was full of peaks and valleys. We never knew whether it was going to be 'Brilliant Virginia' or 'Canon's Daughter Explodes on Court.'

Always there were headlines. When she won, she tended to give euphoric press conferences at which she found difficulty in resisting the temptation to give flippant answers to naive questions. She was always surprised when these appeared in cold print. Some of these remarks are still being taken terribly seriously. When she lost, often there were tears, public or private. 'How could you see to hit the ball when you were crying?' someone asked her when she once lost to Christina Sandberg at Wimbledon.

But always she wanted to be left alone to work out her problems. She was bored when tennis tacticians came to her with diagrams pointing out her errors. She liked regular practice partners, but she had no regular coach, no Vic Edwards in the background. She reacted best to criticisms from the other players. Julie Heldman had only to write that Virginia's forehand volley was suspect for Virginia to produce the best forehand volleys of her career in their next match. When Billie Jean commented on the lack of variation in her rallying, Virginia took notice and improved.

She is in a curious position now in women's tennis. Evert and Navratilova, the new generation, are setting the pace. No one knows whether Evonne Goolagong will be on the tour next year. Margaret Court must be coming to the end of a great career. Rosie Casals seems to have lost her appetite for the game and tennis is only a part of Billie Jean's empire. All of which leaves Virginia as the leader of the middle generation with a unique opportunity to climb over them all.

MOMENTS IN TIME

Occasionally a journalist enjoys the luxury of writing what his editor likes to call a 'considered' piece. That usually means he has a couple of hours to sit around and think about it. The following articles are not considered pieces. Mostly, they were written amidst the clatter and chaos of a press room with a deadline of minutes rather than hours. They were written in the mood and the emotion of the moment and, because of the talent of the men who wrote them, are all the better for it.

PATTY EARNS TITLE
Frank Rostron, *July 1950*

Budge Patty is the new name that deservedly goes down in golden letters on the championship roll of the All-England Lawn Tennis Club at Wimbledon.

Yesterday this 26-year-old handsome six feet two inch ex-G.I. proved superior to 22-year-old Frank Sedgman, of Melbourne, whom he beat 6-1, 8-10, 6-2, 6-3.

The match lasted one and three quarter hours – a mere trifle compared with their four hours ten minutes doubles clash the night before.

How much that dramatic eve-of-the-final struggle affected the final match will long be argued.

The result was certainly a triumph for Patty's fitness campaign.

No boaster is the quickly spoken Parisianised American boulevardier. But he told me in Paris last month, just before beating Billy Talbert and Jaroslav Drobny in successive rounds: 'I am a different man this year. I'm fitter, tougher and stronger – so watch me at Wimbledon.'

Yesterday, although the standard of play was uneven and both players had occasional lapses in a match that was not really close enough to carry the usual drama of a final, Patty was the master.

Deadly cool, determined and with a resolute grip of his highly strung temperament, Patty combined the delicate touch of an artist with ruthless smashing and volleying as soon as he had manœuvred the speedy

126

young Australian out of position.

Sedgman confessed to me afterwards that he found Patty's service even more difficult to take than Drobny's.

After Sedgman had dropped the first set at 1-6 Drobny turned to me and said prophetically, 'Sedgman can't get away with a start like this for the third time in succession.'

And so it proved.

Sedgman used his great speed of recovery and a truly astonishing backhand passing shot that saved frequent aces to pull up from 1-3 and later 2-4 to 4-all in the second set.

At 5-all Patty made a fatal mistake. Requiring only a point for a service break he hit a volley gently into the net with the fallen Sedgman on the grass.

Sedgman finally broke through Patty's service in the 18th game, after Patty had saved two set points and took the set at 10-8.

There were faint visions of another famous Sedgman rearguard action.

But he seemed wearier than his opponent and as a result of his big second set effort, which involved panicky running to parry Patty's deep-volleying thrusts, he seemed to have slowed up.

Patty, formerly notorious for his lack of stamina, remained outwardly unruffled and fresh. He clapped on extra pace, making the ball shoot with his wristy 'squash court' action to take the third and fourth sets comfortably.

He bowed in demonstration of exhaustion after he had clambered wearily over the net at the finish – but the champion was still fresher and faster than his opponent.

HOAD BEATS ROSEWALL
IN WIMBLEDON FINAL
Lance Tingay, *July 1956*

Lew Hoad beat Ken Rosewall 6-2, 4-6, 7-5, 6-4, to win the men's singles championship here to-day and to fulfil three-quarters of a major project.

The champion of Australia and France is now champion of Wimbledon, and if, as seems not unlikely, he goes on to gain American laurels he will equal the record of Donald Budge in taking all four major lawn tennis titles in one year.

Princess Margaret and the Duchess of Kent saw a worthy champion gain the most desired distinction in the game. There have been more exciting finals but none since the war where high quality of play has been so well sustained and where both winner and loser played to their best capacity.

In a rich lawn tennis feast, the basic issue between the two contestants was clear. Both were artists, but Hoad, befitting his burlier physique, plied his strokes with heavier touch, like the painter in oils who wields a knife rather than a brush. By comparison Rosewall was a water colourist, his effects more delicate and less permanent.

Hoad joined a not over-long list of Australian predecessors on the championship roll, Frank Sedgman in 1952, Jack Crawford in 1933, Gerald Patterson in 1922 and 1919, Norman Brookes (now Sir Norman) in 1914 and 1907.

It is tempting to question whether he is as great as they, but I hesitate to say. Such comparisons are made in the light of history rather than in the heat of current success.

Among post-war champions, Hoad stands well. Jack Kramer and Frank Sedgman certainly rank above him and possibly also Tony Trabert.

Hoad is an enigmatic champion, inconsistent except in vital issues. If he equals Budge's famous record he will not do so with the same distinction, for Budge was immune from defeat, not only in the big events, but also in lesser ones. Hoad has already suffered many a minor fall.

He is a player without half measures, an all-or-nothing man. This accounts for his rather high proportion of errors which, some would say, marred his play.

Yet the number of mistakes must be balanced against his startling winners. It is significant that the only post-war final that can be compared with to-day's match in quality of performance is that of 1954, the year J. Drobny won.

Rosewall was also the losing finalist that year. His opposition has twice inspired a touch of greatness, a tribute to his splendid qualities.

More than most finals it was curiously lacking in emotion. Whether the crowd was partisan it is hard to say, though possibly Rosewall, ranking as the underdog, had the more supporters. Yet there was not much on which to make a choice between one Australian or another, both of the same age, born and bred in nearby Sydney suburbs.

The players themselves, Hoad, fair hair short-cropped and with a solid, athletic frame, Rosewall, dark, strong-legged, but less robust above the waist, took the contest without strong feeling.

Just now and again, Hoad, bouncing a ball harder than usual, expressed mild annoyance at a stroke ill-executed, while Rosewall occasionally indicated fleeting despair when his shot went awry, but generally they took the ups and downs placidly.

The final lasted one hour and three-quarters. There was probably more wind than Rosewall liked, but apart from that conditions were ideal.

When Hoad finished the first set, as Princess Margaret arrived, I made a note that this was the performance of a master. Such, indeed it was.

He won it rather easily. Rosewall looked more delicate then than, in fact, he proved to be. He was swamped by the weight of his rival's punishing aggression, and his own weakness, lack of service power, stood out glaringly.

The first four games were shared uneventfully, a mere preliminary sparring and test of strength. The disaster for Rosewall came in the fifth game when he won no more than two points on his service.

Hoad did not sustain his advantage without difficulty. In striving to increase his lead to 4-2, which he did in fact achieve, he thrice had game point against him.

His reserve power got him over each crisis magnificently. At this stage Rosewall was a little less nimble than he afterwards became, and the depth and sting of Hoad's volleying, shots executed with contemptuous ease and strength, especially from the forehand, met with inadequate response.

In the next game, in which Rosewall again lost his service, there was one rally, a brief affair, that showed the extraordinary skill he was up against.

As I have written before, Hoad's reactions are abnormally quick. He was standing on the service line when Rosewall smashed at full strength.

Normally it would have been a killing shot. Hoad played the ball from the ground exactly as Fred Perry used to wield his forehand and projected back at twice the speed a scintillating winner.

Probably it was in the nature of a fluke, but the fact that he brought it off indicated the sharpness of his reflexes. Few other players would have got a racket near the ball.

Hoad finished off the set 6-2. He had then won five games in a row and it almost looked as if a disappointingly one-sided combat was to come.

On both sides it was perpetually aggressive lawn tennis, the quick exploitation of a slight opening with a forcing shot. This thrust and counter-thrust was, of course, mainly based on service, but Rosewall, unless he got his first serve in, usually had to delay his net advance until the next stroke.

Hoad often came netwards on his return of service. When he did

Rosewall closed in as well and in the short, sharp exchanges following this manœuvre Rosewall mainly had the best of it.

In the second set Rosewall led as far as 2-1. In the next game Hoad, serving, stood 15-40. He braced himself for a cannon-ball. The ball left his racket with every indication that it would be one, but here Rosewall surpassed himself.

From the forehand he projected it back faster than it came. Hoad was not caught unawares, and there followed a rally of eight superlative shots, every one worthy to finish off the point, that had the crowd in a roar.

How each man contrived to get across to the ball and then to make so fine a return on each occasion surpassed comprehension. I can safely write that no finer rally has been played at Wimbledon this year.

A high forehand passing shot to Hoad's right-hand corner finished off this incredible rally. It made Rosewall 3-1, then 4-2, with an exchange of service games, Hoad balancing, as he had done more than once before, a double fault with an ace.

For a spell Rosewall had seemed a wizard, but his finer inspiration left him. Hoad got back the service break, to be 3-4. Then Rosewall was up and at him again, and ahead 5-3 with yet another service break. These break throughs did not come from service weakness on Hoad's part but from the surety of return.

Rosewall, with new balls this time, served in the ninth game. Once again Hoad pulled him back, only himself to fail to consolidate what in normal sequence should have been his.

Hoad, serving for 5-all, showed lack of confidence for the first and only time. A double fault, his fourth so far in the match, was not compensated by an ace. And when 15-40 down his first delivery was noticeably a wild affair.

He did save one set point, but Rosewall induced a forehand volley error to take the set 6-4 and they stood on level terms.

The issue had now become speculative, but Rosewall led only twice in the match. The first was the minor advantage of being one love ahead in the third set.

He seemed all set to lead 2-1 if 40-love means anything at all. If there were a definite turning-point in the match it came when Rosewall failed to win any one of the three points he had for this game.

In a sense it was Rosewall's failure, for one of the points he lost was a double-fault. Yet it was also Hoad's triumph and not the least striking characteristic of his sterling game was his ability to get out and get his winning shots whatever the score.

Hoad pursued his path to a 4-2 lead. The fifth game had a rally worthy of comment for on the last point, won by Rosewall who held his service, the combatants engaged in the only exchange play entirely from the baseline.

The fluent backhand-to-backhand strokes took one back to a different lawn tennis world, when all was finesse and netplay was not universally employed. One thought of Jack Crawford, but this flashback to the past was fleeting.

Rosewall broke back in the eighth game to square the set and then led 5-4. Hoad's delivery stood between him and a lead of two sets to one.

It proved a formidable barrier for Hoad took a love game to make it five-all. How one sighed then for a really forceful service from Rosewall, for he who should have gone to 6-5 himself lagged 5-6.

With another love game Hoad served himself out for the set at 7-5. He was now completely in the ascendant, though three games earlier the same position was almost Rosewall's.

The excitements were not yet done, but now one had the feeling that only miraculous play by Rosewall could save the day. Rosewall, desperation adding sting, did lead 4-1 in the fourth set, but that was the end of his effort, a far from negligible one.

Hoad's rise from 1-4 down was a tremendous upsurge of all-conquering strength. Two service aces plus two service winners gave him a love game.

He then took Rosewall's service for the loss of only two points and won his own for the loss of only one. That made the score four-all.

Rosewall again lost his service to 30. As he lost it he made a gesture of despair, for he must have known then that the prospect of the Wimbledon title had, for the second time, gone beyond recall. Hoad served to 40-15 and quite simply won his first match point with a backhand volley.

The Wimbledon crown was his. When he went to receive the gold cup from the Duchess of Kent there was much laughter as he had to be steered this way and that like a burly schoolboy fumbling at a prizegiving. What a contrast to his splendid footwork and anticipation throughout the match!

The fourth leg of what would have been Hoad's Grand Slam was denied him in the Forest Hills final by none other than Rosewall. The irony of these two great Australians was that they frequently deprived each other of honours they deserved. Rosewall was certainly good enough to have won Wimbledon and Hoad, at the peak of his majestic power, was good enough to have joined Don Budge and Rod Laver in the exclusive Grand Slam Club.

131

SANTANA: CLASSIC AGAINST OSUNA

Lance Tingay, *June 1963*

There are times when the lawn tennis championships transcend their own high standards and to-day was one of them. I doubt if anything more magnificent will be seen this year than the match by which the Spaniard M. Santana, the second seed, put himself into the last 16 of the men's singles.

I can seek only superlatives in attempting to describe the manner in which Santana beat the Mexican R.H. Osuna in almost 100 spell-binding minutes on the Centre Court.

So fine was the artistry of these two Latins, so superb their touch and control, so rich their imagination, so competent their mastery over the ball, so flexible were they in manœuvre that one realised that much of what takes place in the men's game to-day is expert wood-chopping and little more.

Artistry came back to Wimbledon and, if justice were done, this would have been the final. From first to last the contest was sweet symphony: there was hardly a discord to mar it.

Some lawn tennis matches rise to heights because of the closeness of the issue and others because of the intrinsic quality of the game. On both counts Santana versus Osuna was memorable, and must be recorded as a classic.

Santana, notorious for needing the incentive of a deficit to find his most persuasive strokes, won after yielding the first two sets.

The score was 2-6, 0-6, 6-1, 6-3, 6-4 and, remarkably, not only did the contestants win the same number of games but the same number of points. If it were possible to have a tie in lawn tennis that would have been an entirely just outcome.

All else that occurred to-day was of necessity mundane compared with the beauty – there is no other word for it – of Santana's narrow mastery.

Among the men there are now 16 survivors including the Britons R.K. Wilson and R. Taylor. Wilson won well against the Dane J. Ulrich and for the third time did not lose a set. Taylor ran a harder course.

He threatened a quick win against the Californian J. Frost but in the end implemented his two sets' lead with difficulty – by the margin of 9-7 in the fifth set, when a service break to love enabled him to finish what he had threatened all along.

Looking back at the enchantment of Santana against Osuna, one sees that Osuna roughened his artistic attributes rather more than he could afford in taking the first two sets.

But what else could he do but play all out and stretch every fibre of his lawn tennis talents? Even if the Spaniard, as he usually is, were a little short of his peak of effort, he was still good enough to yield to nothing but the superfine.

Thus it was that in a rapturous half hour of consummate Mexican service returns, of hair's breadth magic shots that clipped the line, of adroit angles and bewitching lobs, Osuna climbed two-thirds of the way to victory.

To lead 6-2, 6-0 looks one sided, but it was really nothing like that at all for then, as to the end, the gap between Spanish skill and Mexican control was minute.

Half the time taken to play the second set was used up by the opening game. Santana lost his opening game. Santana lost his service then after coming eight times within points of holding it and after nine calls of deuce.

It took eight minutes for Santana to yield this game and he lost the next five in the same interval. Those unaware of his recuperative powers might have thought he was resigned to defeat for it almost seemed he was prepared to acknowledge Osuna's flowing expertise with a rueful grin.

Santana, having lost 12 out of the first 14 games of the match, took 16 out of the next 21, and the entire course of his climb back to lead 4-1 in the fifth set was under his command.

It is hard to see why, having lost so much, he should have been able to win so much.

I suppose the most potent factor was an improvement in his service. That against which Osuna had been hitting searing winners became productive of less efficient returns. More and more Santana was able to utilise the wondrous strength of his forehand, a shot certainly no other amateur can equal.

Santana went on winning much but there never was a rally that was not decided on the closest margin. That there were human failings now and then, a double fault here and there, served only to bring the quality of all else that took place in sharper relief.

I do not recall a mundane shot and every superb stroke was liable to be countered by one more brilliant. And with it all there was no delay, no interval while the players towelled themselves, only a smart readiness to resume the conflict.

When, early in the fifth set, Santana fell and slipped underneath the net, the most solicitous among the thousands present was Osuna. Throughout, each artist acknowledged the other's genius with generosity.

133

Osuna held the lead in the match until Santana won, with three service winners, the first game of the deciding set. Then, when the Spaniard had reached his commanding lead of 4-1, the binding spell of the quality of the play was augmented by the excitement of an uncertain issue.

On the telling power of service games Santana progressed to be first 5-2, and then 5-3. He began to serve to take his victory.

The electric Osuna charged his batteries anew as Santana's touch indicated nervous tension. The Mexican won the game to 30, with a stop volley that caused Santana, wrong-footed by its unexpectedness, to slip on the base line and fall flat on his face.

Accordingly Osuna was in the match again. Santana then revealed his genius. When the Mexican served at 30-40, he hit a backhand passing shot that was so fast and so sure that no player alive would have got it back. Not even one as fast as Osuna.

MASTERFUL LAVER EARNS HIS MONEY
Geoffrey Green, *August 1967*

The unique experiment of Wimbledon – the first world championship of the eight outstanding tennis professionals – yesterday reached its climax before a crowded, shirt-sleeved and admiring gallery on the centre court to suggest that the venture holds a successful future that may one day help to open other doors.

First, the left-handed, ginger-headed R. Laver, as expected, beat his Australian compatriot, K.R. Rosewall 6-2, 6-2, 12-10 in two hours to claim the singles crown in the shape of a £3,000 cheque, with £2,000 for the runner-up; next R. Gonzales and A. Gimeno, the Latin partnership, took the doubles against Laver and another Australian F. Stolle by 6-4, 14-12. Since that held a bonus of £800 for the losing pair (£400 less than for the winners) Laver, in three days earned enough for a ship shape second-hand Rolls Royce. Or in less arguable figures a total in all of 75 games of singles alone earned him £40 a game.

It was quite a holiday indeed for him and in terms of skill alone he was worth every penny of it. On a heavy, humid afternoon for summer dresses and fluttering ladies' fans, a 14,000 crowd found itself in a royal presence. For the first two sets of the singles Rosewall was systematically and clinically dissected. Beaten for pace of service and service return, speed of reflex and all-court control, the former champion was left prostrate as a stream of dipping backhand and forehand passes whistled past him.

The ball always seemed to be where he was not. To reduce a player of Rosewall's ability to such pygmy stature is proof enough of Laver's scintillating qualities. Loose limbed and quick as light, he released a phantasy of stroke play which would have destroyed any player. It was virtually 'no contest', a one-sided exhibition of uninhibited power artistry, achieved by ground strokes of every known range and angle, and not by the interminably boring stacatto sound of the serve-and-volley game.

Laver in his world has what Bradman once had in his at the wicket – a quicker eye than the next man, lithe speed, perfect balance, and an early take of the ball on the rise. His wrist is of steel, his sense of timing and accuracy of the masked return quite uncanny.

Rosewall for that opening hour could scarcely live with him. The crowd almost mesmerized, sat lost in admiration, silent as medical students in some operating theatre observing the great surgeon at work. Laver, attacking even from defensive positions, made winners off smashes and lobs. It was wonderfully cruel.

It was only later when the little man, wearying perhaps of perfection and hibernating in lost concentration, trailed 2-5 in the third set, serving double faults – there were seven of these from each man in all – and making unforced errors in experiment, that the skeleton at last became clothed in any flesh and blood.

At the first signs of a real battle the centre court gladly became a wind-tunnel of applause. Laver pulled back to 5-all, broke to 7-6, and then was denied victory as Rosewall levelled at 7-all with a tremendous backhand return of first service and a last forehand pass off the net cord. Rosewall kissed the wind gratefully then, just as later he applauded his own first service ace to go 10-9.

But the end was always predestined. It finally came as Laver, his racket once more singing like a lute, broke to 11-10 to love and finished it off. As in 1954 and 1956 Rosewall again left this same centre court of his amateur days as the bridesmaid, just as Laver raised the echoes of his 1961 and 1962 triumphs. The one difference was that both men in lawn tennis terms now made a mountebank of the social Wimbledon we know each summer.

BUSY CHAMPION ANN
Arthur Hopcraft, *July 1969*

It is the conflict between the flummoxed manner and the exact strokes that makes Ann Jones's tennis so disconcerting to the spectator. It is like watching a woman knitting under stress. Mrs Jones is her own *tricoteuse*.

Now she is the Wimbledon singles champion, a heroine from the very heart of suburban England, with a Birmingham accent, to send our thoughts instantly to the Bull Ring and Mitchell's and Butlers' mild, a fluency with the gentler oaths and the bright bloom of personality that often comes to the successful woman who was a plain girl.

Mrs Jones will be 31 in October. Her husband, Pip, is a retired businessman 30 years older, who films her and deprecates solidly at one side. There is a domesticity about her that contrasts affectingly with the conscious glamour identifying the international tennis circus.

After Friday afternoon's victory over Billie-Jean King, she said she had a busy week ahead: 'I've got Pip's suitcase full of clothes to wash, and mine, and my parents will want to see me, and I expect we'll be going to a few parties at Birmingham.' She might have been a pools winner back from the cruise.

Women's tennis at its best can be sensuously beautiful, as it was with Maria Bueno, and it can have an elastic athleticism, as with Margaret Court. Mrs Jones brings the extreme of concentration to the game. Her central quality is patience, even though it is alarmingly obscured by her manifold expressions of anxiety.

She shuffles frantically on the baseline before a service, as if a milimetre of inaccuracy in the arrangement of her feet would be calamitous. She hurries to and from the umpire's chair, head down and shoulders rocking as if she's got to get home before the Brussels sprouts boil over. Her face is always narrow and taut under the Alan Ladd hairdo.

But after 15 months of contract-professional tennis, by which she is guaranteed 25,000 dollars a year for two years she now shows an unremitting competitiveness. Margaret Court, the favourite for this year's title, said after the English player had beaten her in a brilliant semi-final that it was the best she had ever seen Mrs Jones play. More significantly, perhaps, Mrs King's comment after the final was: 'That's how she plays when we practise. She bombs me off the court sometimes.'

Mrs Jones's career has been marked by the near misses that go with lack of dominating talent. As Ann Haydon she lost in the singles, doubles and mixed doubles finals of the table tennis world championships in Stockholm in 1957; she has lost one Wimbledon final, seven semi-finals. She has had her successes in France and Italy, but in the big events on the speed of sunlit grass she has been disadvantaged by other players' bigger games. This year she has been not only more obstinate but more combative.

Those who have watched her abroad this year agree fully on her increased assurance off the court; the greater sense of security, the more ready responses to interviewers and line judges. Against Mrs Court she interrupted a service game to ask the umpire if he would instruct one of the judges to call the faults earlier. Afterwards she explained cheerily: 'It's a hell of a walk back from the net. And then you've got that big thing peering at you from the other side. . .'

The match against Mrs King, three years in succession the Wimbledon champion, did not have the style and the dangerous ambition of the semi-final. But it made the nerves thrum, as much by its mistakes as by its fitful flash. The Centre Court was at its shrillest, its disappointments mostly relieved by being flung at a vast, contralto line judge, braced at attention as if about to deliver Rule Britannia.

Mrs King, scowling and grunting, gave the distractors a sarcastic curtsey which, she said later, 'I thought was a nice way of saying, "Please be quiet".'

So Mrs Jones arrived at 5-1 in the final set, wiped her feet on the baseline, threw the ball in the air and caught it again as nervily as if she thought she'd thrown her racket up instead, and lost the game. It was appropriate to the brittle character of the whole affair that Mrs King should concede match point with a double fault.

The American girl looked close to crying when she arrived in the interview room afterwards. But she knows the duty of being a champion defeated, and was quickly generous and informative. 'I feel much older now,' she said. She is 25. She gave us explicit indications of the tensions the new champion will be under from now on: 'When you reach the top you realise you've just started. People expect you to win everything: every little tournament, every big one.'

She made some carefully phrased comments about British women players that astonished the packed Pressmen. Ann was the most underrated British player in the game, she said; and that was a just compliment. 'She is better in every way than Virginia Wade,' she said; and that was an elaboration of the strictly non-decorative kind.

Mrs Jones, only the second British champion since the war, told us she had been hampered by a strain in the left thigh. 'I think it's called the riding muscle,' she said, shrugging at the indiscretion of the detail.

She wore no make-up. (Mrs Court in the interviewee's chair on

Wednesday had clearly given her eyes minute attention). She was brisk, collected. If she could begin playing tennis all over again she knew exactly what she would emphasise. 'Three types of service – a kick, a slice and a fast one.'

She was asked if she regretted having got the last point on Mrs King's double fault. 'I couldn't care less how I won,' she said. There could be no thought of retiring now, as there had been earlier in the year: 'I shall defend the title.'

Mrs Jones later took up Mrs King's point about her following in Britain. Billie-Jean had told her often she could not understand why the public had not 'taken me to their hearts like Christine Truman and Virginia Wade.' The answer, surely, is that in the past she has merely scraped our nerves too much. She had to let her own spirit roar before she could lift ours. She did it last week.

SMITH: UNFORGETTABLE FINAL AGAINST NASTASE

Rex Bellamy, *July 1972*

We shall not forget the first time we watched a Wimbledon final on a Sunday afternoon. It was an occasion that so delighted, thrilled and bludgeoned the senses that by the end of it the nerves of players and spectators alike must have been numb. What happened, in plain terms, is that Stan Smith beat Ilie Nastase 4-6, 6-3, 6-3, 4-6, 7-5 in 2hr 41min. In the skill and virtuosity of its content, the shifting patterns of its dramatic crises, the continuous sharp contrast of style and personality, it was one of the great matches of Wimbledon history.

On the one hand was Smith, 6ft 4in tall, and sometimes known as 'The Blond Bomber'. On the other was a superb athlete and a gloriously resourceful stroke player, the lank-haired Nastase, the first Rumanian to reach the final. Here were a craftsman and an artist. Here was a tingling clash of power and finesse. Here was calculated discipline opposed to whiplash flair. Yet at times each borrowed the other's virtues, so that we were often startled by Smith's subtlety or by Nastase's strength as the richly embroidered texture of the match was spread before us.

At the climax each seemed inspired by the heights to which their splendid endeavours had raised them. If they had any nerves left, those nerves were firm. If they had any doubts, those doubts were suppressed. They plundered their reduced resources for a last, desperate exchange of flashing strokes, as if aware that fortune could only favour the brave.

Moments in Time

An incident at the Wimbledon Ball on Saturday evening should have told us what to expect. In the absence of a men's champion, Billie Jean King opened the ball with her husband: but Smith cut in. That was a neatly-timed and popular initiative. In the third rally of yesterday's match Smith was suddenly plunged into another, much wilder dance. A marvellous rally was upon us; as if to put the stamp of class on the match that had just begun.

Immediately Nastase was under pressure, hurtling about the court with demoniac vitality. His retrieving was incredible. Whenever he had a chance to attack, he had to cut his margin of error to nothing because of the span of Smith's leaping, lunging reach. Quickly, too, we noted the cutting effect of Nastase's backhands down the line. If they were not outright winners, they tended to enforce errors from Smith.

Nastase's first volleys were sound but relatively lightweight, so that Smith usually had a chance to get a rally going. Nastase's half-volleys often popped up in an alarming way, inviting Smith to mayhem. But all this was happening partly because of Smith's searching service returns, especially when he advanced menacingly on Nastase's second ball.

Smith had the better second service and his volleys, though sometimes erratic, were mostly punched hard and deep into the corner. His ground strokes have seldom been better. Though swift to use his heavy artillery when there was a chance to do so, Smith was also coolly adept at picking returns from his toes, using the short angles, and nudging the ball softly over the net whenever Nastase seemed to be safely parked at long range.

In short, Smith's tennis was not merely powerful. It was also cutely conceived. If it sometimes seemed that Nastase was being pounded into submission, that the waves of artistry were dashing themselves on the rocks, this was only because of the basic contrast between them. Just as Nastase was rising to the challenge of a big occasion on grass, so was Smith proving himself far more than an expert exponent of the service and volley.

In the first set Smith had two break points, Nastase nine, before the Rumanian achieved the only break. Twice in that set Nastase resolutely quelled his rebellious spirit after disturbing decisions. Clearly, he had no intention of beating himself. He was the first to break service in the second and third sets, but lost both.

He became gloomy and sullen. He muttered fretfully to his lawyer, up in the crowd. His rackets had been restrung and the tension was too tight for his liking. However much this affected his touch, it certainly affected his confidence and inevitably his concentration. But in the fourth set the fires of his ambition were rekindled. Again he broke through in the ninth game. Minutes later, it was two sets all.

The last act of the drama was upon us. For a time it seemed that cracks were appearing in Smith's heavily fortified blend of courage and will. In the fourth game he threw away an easy point with the whole wide court open to him. In the next, probably the crux of the match, 20 points sparkled this way and that – including seven game points to Smith and three break points to Nastase. Yet when every nerve end within him must have been twanging with apprehension, Smith remained cool enough to win that game with a gentle backhand drop shot.

But he was not done with adversity yet. At 4-4 he was 0-30 down, at which point he hit a winning stop volley off the wood. That piece of luck must have encouraged the massive American. In the next game he had two match points, but could not win them. At 5-6 down Nastase roared away to a 40-0 lead, but was then afflicted by some scorching service returns and a double-fault. Smith had two more match points and finished the job with a lob that unexpectedly induced Nastase to cut a high backhand overhead into the net.

Smith flung his racket high and leapt the net. He beamed, stretched his arms to the skies, and blew a kiss to the rapturous crowd, who knew that this Sunday afternoon at Wimbledon would stay green in the memory. With one mighty hand he held aloft the burnished trophy that is the most coveted in tennis.

VANTAGE POINT
Eugene L. Scott, *July 1975*

Indulge the writer one final gasp on why Arthur Ashe beat Jimmy Connors at Wimbledon. Everybody's had their say including Ashe himself in Sports Illustrated. It will save me explaining my version for the zillionth time. I can merely whip out tear sheets of the column.

You see, I was there, which puts me in no more state of grace than those who watched the tube or read Fred Tupper's account in the Times. No one ever really knows why someone wins, though the world will listen to the winner's version glassy-eyed – as if he carved his passage according to diagrams and charted chalk talks. The truth is that many winners could play to identical patterns the next day and lose as convincingly as they had won the day before. Chemistry, destiny, motor control, and energy levels are all elements that may count as much as forehand matchups.

Ashe is more intelligent than his tour brothers and his explanation for winning Wimbledon was sound. I'm not sure he wasn't tongue-in-cheek on occasion. He was right on target in describing himself in Twilight Zone throughout the Connors' final. Arthur did so many things so well for so long, it's difficult to imagine his duplicating the combined feats again.

Arthur was also correct in analyzing a Connors' weakness as a wide serve to the backhand in the deuce court. What Ashe did not say is that he has the best wide serve to the deuce court in the game. And he executed this serve especially well – not wide and deep but wide and short which makes Connors do an impossible stretch. It's a tough serve to perfect, because the net is higher on the side angle and there's not much room for the ball to land safely in court. That Connors rarely returned this serve at all is testimony to the strength and accuracy of Ashe's delivery that day. John Newcombe had tried the wide serve in his challenge match against Jimmy and was crunched because the serve went deep to Connors' forehand not short and wide.

The single most quoted reason for Ashe's victory was his use of 'junk' and 'nothing' balls. While Ashe was racing to a 6-1 lead, the press stared in stoney silence as if they were watching science fiction. No one believed the first set and a ghosty mist clouded centre court. It was very unreal. One writer mumbled, 'He's killing Connors with junk.' A line of heads nodded as if a divine message had explained the inexplainable.

Nothing balls had nothing to do with this match. In the first place, Ashe served half the games and his serve isn't junk. Ashe also volleyed brilliantly. Crazy volleys an inch from the baseline.

Ken Rosewall is considered the game's best volleyer. He smacks the volley – but not deep – there's no margin for error there. Ken drills the ball cross court going for the outright winner but maintaining a safety factor. There was nothing safe in Arthur's volleys which pinned Connors to the baseline.

Another thing. Connors has been schooled by Segura and Gonzalez to play the game from on top of the baseline. Not three feet back of it. This is boldness in extreme and blends perfectly with Connors' ubiquitous aggression. The only difficulty comes when a bloke is 'in zone' and pounds the baseline where you're standing. You have no room to manœuvre.

Ashe jibed that Connors choked. He pointed to Jimmy repeatedly slapping balls into the net as evidence. Here Arthur's scholarship breaks down. The netted balls in question were on approach shots – long a Connors' weakness. The nature of the shot is an underspinned chip – a muted stroke – and not in keeping with Connors' roundhouse swinging style.

141

This weakness was also evident in the Newcombe challenge and has nothing to do with choking.

One final note. Arthur says that Jimmy plays well when in front but 'we don't know much about how he reacts when he's behind.' Here he's calling Jimmy a frontrunner which is absurd. Arthur simply has not reviewed Jimmy's record over the past 18 months which is understandable since the pair have rarely played the same circuit. But Connors' performance when behind has been outstanding in particular against Stan Smith and Mal Anderson in the past two Pacific Southwest Championships when he was down match point and won.

For what it's worth, this writer has his own theory about why Ashe won. It has to do with hybris. If Connors had won another Wimbledon, he would have approached a kingdom of sports' immortals at too early an age. The gods kicked him down from their heavenly territory. And Arthur Ashe, a unique hero, was carefully selected to be the instrument of their pique.

THE CANNONBALL BLASTS CONNORS

Laurie Pignon, *June 1976*
Like many aggressors before him, Jimmy Connors, the 1974 champion and 11-10 favourite this year, lived by the sword and died by it on a stunned Wimbledon Centre Court yesterday.

This greatest of lawn tennis arenas, which has known a thousand different moods, was never more like a parched battlefield than when Connors was humbled in 107 minutes by a barrage of artillery from the fluent racket of Leonard Roscoe Tanner III.

The 6-4, 6-2, 8-6 quarter-final score was almost an exact reversal of their semi-final last year. Tanner's power yesterday was magnificent, even majestic, and laced with cunning. His big serves – 19 aces ricocheted off the browning turf – were almost faster than the eye could follow in the blinding sunlight.

Connors, with the eye of a hawk and lightning reflexes, had to stand 12ft behind the baseline even to have a chance of returning the 140 m.p.h. plus serves.

At times he pointed his finger, shook his head in bewilderment, and slapped his thigh like a jockey whipping a tiring horse. In one moment of almost unbearable frustration he let go an anguished oath.

Considering the punishment – more severe than Arthur Ashe dealt him in last year's final – his behaviour was beyond reproach.

The aggression was there in brilliant flashes, and when they came the heartbeats of the packed stands kept pace with the fluttering fans trying to muster a little artificial breeze.

But for all this, against Tanner, who in this match could do little wrong, Connors's efforts were like those of an angry mouse trying to take on a revenge-hungry cat.

Among the spectators was Leonard Roscoe Tanner Junior, Roscoe's father, from Lookout Mountain, Tennessee. Roscoe's wife, Nancy, was missing. She preferred the calmness of a television screen in her London hotel.

From the brutality of the action, no-one could have guessed these two have been friends and playing against each other since they were 12 year olds.

Afterwards an understandably delighted Tanner, who beat Connors 6-3, 6-4 in the final at Beckenham two weeks ago, told me: 'I decided to vary my serve. Any time you serve two alike he knocks the second one off . . . unless he's already knocked off the first.

'I had him confused quite a bit for sometimes he was looking the wrong way – different to last year when he stepped in to my serves.'

But six-foot Tanner did more than serve hard and intelligently. His return of service, the most important stroke on a fast court, became better and better until he outmatched Connors. His volleying was accurate and full of venom.

Connors began like an actor speaking familiar lines. He broke Tanner's service to 30 in the first game and held his own to love.

Tanner started the third game with his first ace, a warning shot, and his second double fault. He repeated the presciption on his third service but was still 4-2 down.

That was the last time Connors was in front. In the eighth game Tanner broke back at 4-4 and he now had an important psychological edge. Connors conceded the first set with his first double fault.

Tanner twice broke Connors's service in games which went to deuce, to take the second set.

Tanner led 3-1 in the third and had three match points at 5-2, but Connors served an ace, forced Tanner into a forehand error and produced an unreturnable backhand volley to save them.

Connors was fighting for his life. He broke back at 5-5, but Tanner could afford to wait. At 15-40 in the 14th game he played a full-blooded backhander down the line to take the match.

BRITAIN'S DAVIS CUP DOUBLES TRIUMPH
Rex Bellamy; *August 1976*

The brothers David and John Lloyd, who helped Essex win the inter-county championship a fortnight ago, yesterday achieved one of the most glorious and astonishing triumphs in the history of the Davis Cup competition. From two sets down they saved five match points, won 11 successive service games that they had to win in order to keep the tie alive, and finally beat Paolo Bertolucci and Adriano Panatta 6-8, 3-6, 6-3, 18-16, 6-2 in three hours and 50 minutes.

Is it possible, just possible, that Britain could bounce back to win the tie after losing both singles on the first day?* They have done that only once before, against Germany at Queen's Club in 1930. This time, of course, adversity was even deeper because at one time it seemed likely that Italy would achieve a winning margin at the cost of no more than the three sets they lost on Thursday.

After those five match points yesterday, today's tennis is a bonus for Britain, anyway. 'We are lucky to be still in the tie', Paul Hutchins, Britain's captain said last evening. 'David played really well. He held them together. He did so much, so often.' Hutchins also had a good word for Bertolucci, whose service returns, he reckoned, were 'by far the best' on view.

What a pleasant change it is to have a variation on the hackneyed story of gallant British losers in the world of sport. Already this has been Britain's best run in the Davis Cup since 1969. In terms of crowd participation (a prosaic word for the emotional poetry of the occasion) it has also been a revolution and a revelation for genteel old Wimbledon.

Those West Indian cricket crowds seem demure by comparison. Yesterday the Italians were in full voice again, chanting, singing, clapping their hands in unison and waving their flags. But the British made just as much noise and eventually even more: and by way of substitute for a trumpet lead, they had a deep-toned horn that sounded like a cow with bronchial trouble.

What a din they all created and what provocation they had for it! Let us first introduce the characters in this sporting epic. There was David Lloyd, bandy-legged, strutting about in his restless cocky way, a bundle of nervous energy – though there could not have been much of it left after his mighty endeavours yesterday. There was Bertolucci, a

---

*Italy, in fact, denied Britain further miracles and went on to win the Davis Cup that year by beating Chile in Santiago.

beefy, bulging man with short but powerful legs, a sadly bored demeanour, but a sure touch and an artful tennis brain.

There was Panatta, intimidating at the net, imaginative, and resourceful in almost all he did, yet hoping – as John Lloyd doubtless did – that his partner, who had not played singles, would take most of the strain. Finally, there was John Lloyd, half-expecting his brother to go into vertical take-off at any moment, yet determined to keep the ball in play and tie up any loose ends David left lying about.

For two sets and a half the four of them did not have much to offer. They were doing what they could and by Davis Cup standards – always afflicted by nervous tension – it was good enough. But there was nothing much to distress the pulse rate. Not, that is, until Panatta, on the first break point of the match, won the first set by somehow improvising a forehand winner as he was tumbling backwards on the baseline.

Britain lost the second set, too, though they were the first to break service. The 18th game of the match was the first to go to deuce. The third set also progressed quietly, though the Lloyds were now experimenting with a tandem formation. There still seemed to be no spark of hope for Britain. Then the Italians played three loose games. Doubtless, with victory round the corner, they relaxed the intensity of their concentration.

Britain had two break points for 4-2 and broke to 5-3 when a casually half-volleyed forehand by Panatta landed clearly but as it transpired, controversially, out of court. David Lloyd held his service for the set and, after the interval, the full weight of the day's drama hit us like a crumbling wall.

Britain broke through in the first game of the fourth set, which was to last an hour and 54 minutes. Italy broke back. Britain broke again, to 5-4. With David Lloyd serving for the set they had three set points – and Italy five break points – in a thrilling game of seven deuces.

Italy won that argument and from that moment were the odd game up, with the Lloyds serving repeatedly to save the match and the tie. Britain had three break points but, at 9-10, John saved a match point with a drive-volley. At 14-15 there were four more match points for Italy. David Lloyd rose to supreme heights of agility and racket control to save one of them.

Little incidents were crowding upon us. A fierce smash by Bertolucci threatened to dislodge David Lloyd's foot but, instead, hit his racket, and the ball reeled drunkenly in the air and landed in court. Bertolucci smashed the frame of his racket trying to return one of David Lloyd's services. A backhand volley by John Lloyd gave Britain a break to 17-16 and in the ensuing tumult an elderly lady stood up waving a Union

145

Jack in each hand. Once again David Lloyd served for the set. Bertolucci played a startling half-volley, all instinct, to give Italy a break point. Britain survived it. A forehand volley by John Lloyd made it two sets all.

David Lloyd had been playing well. But now he played as if, for 22 minutes that he will remember until he dies, he thought he was the greatest player who ever lived. The man had been working himself into the ground for three hours and a half. But now he actually accelerated. He broke a racket. He was running, leaping, lunging, hurtling about like a racing car that had gone out of control.

But David Lloyd had not gone out of control. He knew what he was doing – and of those four tired men it was David Lloyd, restored to the team last month for the first time since 1974, who had the reserves – of energy and inspiration to blast Britain through the breach that fourth set had created. With that, the Italians were cooked, physically and mentally. Today, they will remember yesterday.

VIRGINIA FIT FOR THE QUEEN
John Barrett, *July 1977*

It was, in the end, an occasion fit to set before the Queen as Virginia Wade overcame early problems to defeat Holland's Betty Stove 4-6, 6-3, 6-1 and win the centenary Wimbledon for Britain.

The Centre Court was awash with emotion as the 31-year-old Miss Wade, competing in her 16th Wimbledon, triumphantly held aloft the gold salver for the women's singles victor after the Queen had presented it to her.

Hundreds of Union Jacks were waved, the crowd broke into a chorus of 'For she's a jolly good fellow' and the Duchess of Kent saluted the British victory by raising her arms over her head in the style of a winning boxer.

Miss Wade, who spent some time before the match sitting out on the Centre Court ('It is absolutely necessary in order to absorb the atmosphere,' she explained), said afterwards: 'The whole thing was like a fairy tale, so wonderful. It means everything to me to win. Everybody thought I was past it, but I feel I am so much better now and I worked incredibly hard for this tournament.'

She was also made to work hard in yesterday's one hour 37 minute final by the 6 feet 1 inch 32-year-old Dutch girl who reduced the Centre Court to virtual silence by capturing the first set in 38 minutes.

The first game lasted five minutes and went to four deuces, with Miss

Stove having a point for a break, before the British girl held service.

Miss Wade herself had three break points in the next game, but Miss Stove, whose style was very much hit or miss – hitting some stunning winners, especially volleys, but perpetrating some awful misses, including nine double-faults – held on with the aid of an ace and a smash.

She also profited from four Wade errors to break in the fifth game, but was immediately broken in turn. Still Miss Wade was treading a dangerous path, holding the seventh game after surviving three break points. But her next service game was Miss Wade's undoing. She was broken to love, and Miss Stove volleyed her way to the first set.

If she was unnerved by this setback, Miss Wade showed no sign as she set about repairing the damage. She led 3-0 in the second set and had a point for 4-0 when Miss Stove double-faulted, only to be pulled back to 3-3.

Once again her response in this see-saw match, which was occasionally short on top-class tennis, but never lacking in excitement, was hearteningly positive. She served out to love, broke Stove to 15, and won on her second set point with a fierce smash to which the Dutch girl could get only the faintest of touches.

Roared on by an ecstatic audience, Miss Wade was in full flow. In the first game of the decider, she broke to 30 when Miss Stove netted a backhand volley. In the second she gratefully accepted four Dutch backhand errors. In the third she survived two break points, and it was no wonder Miss Stove buried her head in her towel at the change of ends.

The fourth game, too, went to Britain despite Miss Wade's first, and only double-fault of the match. The next game was the best of the match as Miss Stove fought back bravely from love-40 to hold service.

But there was no halting Miss Wade now. She served her way to a 5-1 lead without conceding a point, and when Miss Stove served to stay in the match she was immediately in trouble. Miss Wade conjured a winner off the wood, sighed with relief as a Dutch forehand volley fell narrowly out and another one rattled into net.

On her first match-point it was Miss Wade's turn to net a forehand, but on the second her return of Miss Stove's serve was so good that the Dutch girl could only push the ball into the bottom of the net.

So Miss Wade finally won the championship she has promised to take for so long, adding it to the major titles she won of the United States (1968), Italy (1971) and Australia (1972).

So at the end of an emotional afternoon, Miss Wade had finally scaled her Everest at the 16th attempt. It was in 1953 that the Queen was given a Coronation present when Sir John Hunt's party conquered the mountain. How appropriate in this Jubilee year that Miss Wade should add this illusive title to her first previous successes at the first U.S. Open (1968), in Italy (1971) and in Australia (1972)!

It was never a great match, but, nevertheless, was a great personal triumph for someone who had promised us that her days of nervous inhibitions were behind.

Elated, she said: 'I have felt this week that I was by far the strongest person in the dressing-room, and I thought that was what was going to hold me through. The thing that excited me about to-day was standing out there holding the trophy, and the thought of opening the women's matches on the Centre Court next year.'

HARRY CARPENTER'S WMBLDN
Clive James, *July 1977*
In what Harry Carpenter calls Wmbldn, but other people refer to as Wimbledon (BBC1 and 2), the gifted nutter, Nastase once again blew his ego all over the court. Bits of his personality were left hanging from the grandstands, the net posts, the umpire's nose. It was a spectacle more to be rued than scorned. Nastase would be a man of genius if he had command of himself, but as things are he seems doomed to remain merely talented.

'Nastase, will you come here a minute, please?' called the umpire after the petulant star had tried to drill a tennis-ball-sized hole through Borg. 'What I do to heem?' whined the rebarbative Romanian, coyly dragging a toe. 'I'm reporting you to the referee for calling me Nastase.' Doubtless mentally rehearsing some of the other things Nastase might usefully be called, the umpire stayed cool. Borg stayed even cooler, profiting from the hiatus to regain some of the strength expended in the top-spin duels and frantic chasing after lobs and drop-shots that any opponent of Nastase is bound to find himself involved in. Nastase is a winner everywhere except inside his fat head.

Borg went on to meet Gerulaitis – the man with the looks of Apollo and the name of a skin-disease – in a five-set thriller that had your reporter rolling off his lilo in excitement. Dan Maskell was more excited still. He has seen every great tennis match in history. He was ball-boy for Henry VIII and Cardinal Wolsey at Hampton Court. But he had never seen anything like this. Unfortunately his range of encomiastic outbursts is somewhat limited, rarely extending beyond a polite cry of 'Well played! Well played *indeed!*' In the end this did not matter, since even the Borg–Gerulaitis nailbiter could only be regarded as marginal compared to the uproar aroused by Virginia Wade reaching the final.

As you would have had to be dead not to notice, the media experienced a collective sexual climax at the thought of Ginny the Loser finally getting a crack at the big prize. The Press, in particular, went insane. Even before the final, the newspapers were already in a state of total hysteria. After it, they went berserk. In view of these patriotic caperings, it is hard to see how anybody could think the British Press deficient in positive spirit.

NOAH TAKES WILANDER'S CROWN
John Parsons, *June 1983*
Yannick Noah presented an ecstatic French crowd with the honour they have been demanding for 37 years yesterday – a champion of their own at Roland Garros.

With a masterly exhibition of physical power and athletic control, Noah, 23, had the courage and the skill to attack defending champion Mats Wilander, the most stubbornly difficult European clay court player there is to beat, until even he had to submit.

As the Swede, who had never lost here before even in a junior match, overhit the backhand service return which signalled Noah's 6-2, 7-5, 7-6 victory after two hours 30 minutes, the crowd rose almost as one to salute this commanding young man for whom this surely will not be his last grand slam tournament triumph.

Even when he broke back for 5-5 in the second set, Wilander allowed the Frenchman straight back in at the one moment he might have faltered, with three errors and then a winning Noah lob.

The pattern of the third set was in much the same vein as the first two except that now tension played an increasing part, but in the end Noah even won this battle as well.

Wilander was deep with a lob on the first point of the tie-break and Noah served into a 6-2 lead. Another Wilander lob saved the first match point, but the power of Noah's serve was too much for the Wilander backhand on the second.

The only pity is that Noah, who might be suspended later this week for missing a match in the Nations Cup in Dusseldorf last month, is not playing Wimbledon because he does not believe he can play on grass.

The positive, exciting tennis he played to become the first Frenchman since Marcel Bernard in 1946 to win the French championship was proof enough that he could be a champion on any surface.

There were astonishing scenes. Noah's father, Zacharie, literally stumbled from his seat at one end of the court to jump down and embrace his son who then ran to the other end to Patrice Hagelauer.

It is Hagelauer who, for most of the time since Arthur Ashe spotted this rich hidden talent on a visit to the French Cameroons 11 years ago and arranged for him to move to Paris, who has groomed Noah to his present success.

Noah sensed that his best, possibly only chance, was to impose his aggressive game as quickly as possible and sustain it in such a way that there would be no possibility for Wilander, with his eroding accuracy, to escape and then wrest the initiative for himself.

Apart from a tentative spell at the start of the third set and then another flutter of nerves when he served for the match at 6-5 and was broken to 15, that was precisely how it happened.

Bounding about the court, using his pace and reach to carry him to volleys and overheads which were then ferociously put away, stepping in and hitting tremendous forehands off anything short and pulling out big serves just when they were most needed, Noah's game at times was almost arrogant.

Such was the pressure on Wilander that, apart from the lob, even some of his normally most reliable shots such as the ground strokes, approaches and passes broke down. Indeed, I do not recall his being forced into so many errors on such an important occasion.

OFF-COURT CRISES

Off court, two great upheavals have helped shape the world of professional tennis during the past two decades.

The first was the advent of Open Tennis in 1968, pioneered to a large extent by All England Club chairman, Herman David, and supported with surprising fervour and courage by the British LTA, as Laurie Pignon, then with the Daily Sketch, *describes here.*

BRITAIN DEFIES WORLD OVER OPEN TENNIS
Laurie Pignon, *December 1967*

British tennis defied the world and decided yesterday with overwhelming unity and commendable courage to go it alone on open tournaments from April 22. At the annual meeting of the Lawn Tennis Association in London only five of the 210 members present voted against an amendment to hold a springtime pistol at the heads of the International Lawn Tennis Federation.

Under threat of suspension from the Federation – world rulers of tennis–representatives from clubs and counties all over Britain supported a motion that the LTA should only legislate for players – thus losing the amateur and professional definitions and clearing the way for open tennis, including Wimbledon, and honest payment.

The original proposal was to start on January 1, but yesterday's discussions had barely got under way when it became obvious it was not a matter of what but when. Two amendments were tabled.

The first, by John Archer, of Hurlingham, was to delay action until January 1969. The second, by Cecil Betts, of Middlesex, was to make the date April 22, two days after the International Federation management committee have their next meeting.

Betts was seconded by Derek Hardwick, of Dorset, the new LTA chairman.

Those who argued for a year's grace said it would give the world body

151

time to find a peaceful solution. Those who wanted April claimed the Federation had had a decade to clean up the game and had closed their eyes to exorbitant payments to amateurs.

Hardwick won over many waverers when he said: 'Never will Britain have another opportunity like this to lead the world.'

The effect of the vote is drastic. It means that from April 22 all British players will be OUTLAWED from international competitions and tournaments and all overseas players will be FORBIDDEN by their national associations from playing here.

But I know two top Frenchmen are prepared to defy their officials and play at Wimbledon.

The first tournament affected will be the LTA's own national hard court championships at Bournemouth. These start on the fateful day of April 22.

Herman David, chairman of the All England Club, who has been fighting for an open Wimbledon but did not speak yesterday, could not conceal a massive grin when he saw the forest of hands shoot up in favour of the motion.

Later he told me: 'I am delighted. We started this in 1956. It's a great and courageous step by this democratic body.'

Eaton Griffith, Britain's representative on the Federation, was just as happy. He told me: 'Those in the world who strive for honesty in the game will be delighted that Britain has not ratted on them.'

Among speakers against the proposal was Ben Barnett, Australian representative on the Federation. He said Australia did not support Britain, but this claim was challenged when it was pointed out that his country had not had their annual meeting.

Proposing the original motion Derek Penman, chairman of the LTA rules committee, said: 'It's wrong to get the impression the LTA are doing this to get an open Wimbledon. The idea is to rid the game of a shame. We believe players should be able to earn honestly, according to their ability.

'How can the United States LTA be against such a plan when they pay their Davis Cup team £3,000 a year each? Behind the Iron Curtain the stars are all civil servants – tennis playing civil servants.

'We have kindled a fire, but if we let it die now it will never be relit.'

Fears were expressed that if Wimbledon gates suffered next summer lack of finance would embarrass the LTA. But honorary treasurer Sir Robert Fraser quickly killed these by pointing out:

'After the war we only had £32,000 to keep the game going. Now we have reserves of £120,000. That should be enough to keep us going for one or two years.'

I think the LTA took the only possible course. Everybody knows top stars are being paid.

Delaying tactics would have been a sign of weakness, considered overseas as an almighty British climb-down.

There was no devaluation yesterday.

ILTF CAPITULATE
Lance Tingay, *Paris, April 1968*

Concessions had to be made, but in the balance the British lawn tennis revolution, brought about last December when the authority of the International Lawn Tennis Federation was flouted, was successful.

The historic emergency session of the Federation here yesterday capitulated to the British *fait accompli*. It created new amateur rules which, while allowing for amateurs and 'registered players' for those who want them, permits self-determination by nations on such matters.

With this freedom Britain's abolition of the amateur–professional status was legalised. Great Britain, despite her rebellion, emerged from the meeting still a solid member of the international game.

This was undoubted victory. At the same time, Britain yielded ground and accepted a limitation on the number of tournaments open to all classes of players and such events must, in fact, now be sanctioned by the management committee of the ILTF.

Britain was today granted four open tournaments, Wimbledon, the hard court championships at Bournemouth, the Kent championships at Beckenham and the London championships at Queen's Club.

There will be hard feeling elsewhere – Bristol, Newport, Hoylake and the like – at a more meagre ration than hoped, but short of falling outside the international game, the British delegation had no choice but to accept.

The ILTF yesterday defined the status of a professional for the first time. He is one who gets money either from teaching the game or who plays in events not controlled by the amateur associations.

But from a British viewpoint a professional is one who does not accept the disciplinary control of the British LTA. On this score Roger Taylor, for instance, is barred from all British tournaments save those designated as 'open' while at the same time British teaching professionals, who acknowledge the LTA's control, are free to compete in any British tournament.

'Registered players,' a category France will certainly adopt, will in effect be non-teaching professionals who acknowledge their association's authority. No one will pretend they are amateurs.

All these sweeping changes were accomplished surprisingly peacefully. Even Iron Curtain diehards did not cast a vote against reforms, doubtless because they feared a worse evil to them of the disintegration of the Federation. Their feelings were assuaged by keeping the word 'amateur' among the rules and by promising the inauguration of specifically amateur tournaments, notably one for the championship of Europe.

As for the Davis Cup, the Federation had no authority to rule on that. However, they urged that organisation to regard as amateurs all who were technically of that status on March 29 and it is almost certain that the competition will go on as usual, complete with Great Britain.

Five years later, the ATP boycotted Wimbledon. It was an inevitable clash between the old world and the new and amidst the ensuing hysteria, only occasionally were the real issues presented to the British public. Reams were written but the three pieces that follow make more sense than most. In his lucid style, Rex Bellamy lays out the nuts and bolts of the extraordinary crisis as it developed on the eve of Wimbledon 1973 and a Daily Telegraph *editorial echoes sentiments that were being hurled at the public in less rational tones by the popular press. John Crosby, the American columnist who was once Art Buchwald's stablemate on the back page of the* International Herald Tribune, *took a viewpoint in the* Observer *that closely mirrored my own. So, with all the license at an editor's disposal, I am happy to resurrect it!*

THIRTY-FIVE WITHDRAW FROM WIMBLEDON
Rex Bellamy, *June 1973*

Thirty-five men, including eight of the singles seeds, yesterday signed the forms withdrawing their entries from the Wimbledon championships, which will begin next Monday. The seeds concerned were Arthur Ashe, Tom Gorman, John Newcombe, Tom Okker, Cliff Richey, Martin Riessen, Ken Rosewall (who arrived from Australia on Sunday), and Stan Smith, the champion. That list will expand when other members of the Association of Tennis Professionals, including those competing at Eastbourne, have had the opportunity to sign.

The only men's singles seeds so far certain to compete are Ilie Nastase and Jan Kodes. But there are other 'acceptors' whose presence should ensure an interesting if sub-standard tournament. These include James Connors, Owen Davidson, Jurgen Fassbender, Zeljko

Franulovic, Neale Fraser (the 1960 champion), Karl Meiler and Alexander Metreveli.

The defections have occurred because one of the ATP directors, Nikola Pilic, has not been allowed to compete. He has been suspended by the International Lawn Tennis Federation after refusing to play for Yugoslavia in the Davis Cup competition. The only thing that could save the men's events from mediocrity is an ILTF decision to lift Pilic's suspension. But Allan Heyman, president of the ILTF, told me yesterday that there was no possibility of an emergency meeting. 'There's nothing to meet about. There is no room for compromise. The players say: "Pilic plays – or else." There is no in-between solution.'

The draw, which should have been held yesterday, has been deferred until 11 o'clock tomorrow. A new men's seeding list will be announced an hour earlier. Meantime, there are rumours of discontent among some of the women. There is no question of a similar boycott, because they could not achieve any kind of solidarity at such short notice. But the women reckon (vainly) that the prize money should be adjusted because of the reduced quality of the men's field. The men are to receive £32,000 compared with the women's £20,200. The women are to meet this evening to discuss the formation of an association of their own.

It is bitterly regretted, by the players as well as their critics, that the tournament to suffer from this dispute with the ILTF should be Wimbledon, which was largely responsible for making the reputations and the fortunes of many of the men now deserting it.

It was Wimbledon, too, that insisted on the introduction of open competition in 1968, an innovation that led to an astonishing advance in the player's earning capacity and the game's development as a sector of the entertainment industry. At the same time, the boycott is a rebuff to all those who thought tennis players would be too selfish to miss the tournament that means (or meant) most to them. Because of what many leading players regard as its relatively low prize money, Wimbledon has lost some of its old allure.

Such comfort as can be drawn from the mess concerns the distant rather than the immediate future. Mr Heyman and the ATP president, Cliff Drysdale, think on similar lines in proposing the 'liaison committee' which Mr Heyman has long advocated and the 'tennis council' to which Drysdale referred in the small hours of yesterday morning after that historic boycott decision at the Westbury Hotel.

Mr Heyman's idea, which he has yet to sell to his ILTF colleagues, is for a committee of six or seven consisting of the present and two vice-presidents of the ILTF (from different continents), representatives of men and women players and a representative of the tournament directors or sponsors (or both). Drysdale's scheme covers a similar spectrum of opinion and the two proposals are so close that there is obviously room for compromise.

The ATP board meeting lasted two hours and a half and was held in a room next to swing doors marked 'Emergency Exit'. But the board needed no escape route. However we may differ about their decision, they provided firm leadership at a time when it was needed. They voted seven to one in favour of a boycott, with two abstentions. Later in the morning an assembly of 47 members unanimously supported the board's decision.

Drysdale, who had no previous experience of what was basically an industrial dispute, has emerged with his personal reputation enhanced. At a time when others on both sides were making inflammatory statements, his own were always considered, cooperative and constructive.

The men in the middle of the dispute have taken up such entrenched positions that it was refreshing and instructive to listen to two distinguished overseas tennis writers who are impartial and well informed. 'I'm disturbed', said Bud Collins (*Boston Globe*), 'by the utter failure of the British (the LTA, the All England Club, and the Press – and I'm very fond of all of them) to try to understand the players' viewpoint and what this means to them. Not necessarily to approve.

'It is a movement and its time has come. It is being called an insult to Wimbledon, but it isn't. And I don't think it has anything to do with Pilic. The players want freedom of choice and movement. They are going forward with what the All England Club courageously began in 1967. But once that is in motion, we see a reversion to attitudes they had prior to 1967. It's like freeing the slaves and then suddenly saying: "Hey! We didn't mean you to be *that* free." '

Judith Elian (*L'Equipe*, Paris) said: 'I'm terribly sorry it was Wimbledon. But at some time something had to happen. Because during the past four or five years everything that has occurred in tennis has been so peculiar. This can be the start of a completely new era. Everything is changing so much. The whole structure (it's almost anachronistic) is blowing up. Wimbledon is only part of a much broader picture. And the players have to stick together.'

The last such challenge to the authority of the ILTF was made in 1967 by one of their constituent national associations, that of Britain, who threatened that if need be they would 'go it alone' in introducing open tennis. That internal dispute was settled without recourse to the law courts. The danger now is that the players' disaffection with the ILTF and many national associations may induce several leading players to sign contracts with the new team tennis league in the United

States. In 1967, a similar disaffection encouraged a flight of professionalism, involving contracts that took the players outside the authority of the ILTF.

The basic issue is a determined and concerted effort by the ATP to establish the freedom of professional tennis players to pursue their living as and when they wish, as long as they honour their commitments (a hotly debated reservation in the Pilic case).

The ILTF would be wise to note that the ATP forces ranged against them are not a small group of ill-advised malcontents and agitators. The significant thing is that, though tennis is regarded as a selfish sport, so many players from a wide variety of national, social, and political backgrounds have so swiftly found common cause (the ATP was formed only nine months ago). We may question the wisdom of the ATP's decision. But they have made it clear that they are going to be pushed around no longer.

The ILTF committee of management could not begin to challenge the ATP board's collective knowledge of the modern professional game. This does not mean that the ATP should govern tennis. It does mean that within their own sphere they command more respect than the ILTF, and that, as Mr Heyman and Drysdale agree, they should have a bigger say in the conduct of their own affairs. But the professional game is only the tip of the iceberg, the bit that sparkles in the sunshine of public acclaim.

The ILTF, for all their imperfections, have much wider responsibilities and must maintain their status as the governing body. But they have been in so much trouble in recent years (in the Pilic case they did not have the unreserved support of their constituent national associations) that it is no good pretending they are like those motorists who keep having accidents but are never to blame. As presently constituted the ILTF cannot adequately govern professional tennis. They need help. It is available. They would be wise to accept it.

DOUBLE FAULT: ATP BOYCOTT
Daily Telegraph Editorial, *June 1973*

Most tennis fans will find it hard to understand why a quarrel between Mr Nikki Pilic and the Yugoslav Lawn Tennis Association should effectively ruin the Wimbledon championships. Since all the players, professional and amateur, really want to take part, and the public certainly wish to see them play, it speaks little for the maturity and common sense of those involved in the conflict that no solution, apparently, can be found. The tournament of course, will go on. Yet without the participation of most of the professionals, who include in their ranks nearly all the best players, it will be a pale shadow of what it has usually been in the past: the premier tennis tournament in the world.

Why should this happen? The root of the matter is the desire of the Association of Tennis Professionals for some say in the running of the game. At present they have no place in the International Lawn Tennis Federation. Yet, since they are the 'stars' of the game, the men who pull in the crowds and the revenue, they think that their importance should be given constitutional recognition. Their case may be a good one. But their decision to take a stand on the case of Mr Pilic shows poor judgment, since he voluntarily accepted the jurisdiction of his national LTA, and then broke faith with it. What is more, the Federation is willing to negotiate with the professionals on the substantial issue. So there seems little justification for this boycott. Tennis fans will probably conclude that the professionals are getting too big for their tennis shoes.

ON THE SIDE OF THE PLAYERS
John Crosby, *June 1973*

The papers have now agreed with great huzzahs that Wimbledon has won a mighty victory over those great bullies, 70 of the world's best tennis players, conceivably the greatest exercise in self-justification since the United States decided it wasn't going to be pushed around by little Cuba any longer and organised the Bay of Pigs.

Am I alone in thinking the players were dead right in this affray and the International Lawn Tennis Federation dead wrong? I feel strongly that if Nikki Pilic didn't want to play Davis Cup tennis for Yugoslavia, he shouldn't have to. It would be a different matter if he had been contractually obligated to play, but he wasn't, and there seems to be no evidence that he even said he would. I was fairly stupefied by that British judge who said he'd heard no reason why Pilic didn't play. The same reasons I didn't play in the Davis Cup this year, Judge. I just didn't *feel* like it.

In any disagreement between tennis officials – we have had some lulus in the US – and the players, I am always on the side of the players. It is one of Crosby's Laws, based on long observation, that all tennis officials are boneheads.

We used to argue in Bleeck's saloon about how they elected amateur athletics officials (having rejected the superstition that they spring full-grown from exploding footballs). We decided they presented the candidate with a choice of 10 decisions of varying degrees of dumbness and if he didn't automatically choose the dumbest, he was ruled out of contention.

The supreme example, of course, is Avery Brundage, until recently chieftain of the Olympic Games, a very important position indeed, who has set all kinds of Olympic records for making the most idiotic decisions, over the longest period of time. When I was a mere stripling, Brundage – in one of the great sports brouhahas of the 1930s – ousted our best and prettiest backstroke swimmer, Eleanor Holm, from the US Olympic team for sitting up late drinking champagne with the boys on the boat on the way to the Berlin Olympics. Well, she was a fun-loving girl. At a stroke Brundage succeeded in making an unholy ass of himself, depriving the US of its best and most personable swimmer and achieving nothing at all. A very good score for a sports official.

The fact is that these people and tennis associations themselves are becoming increasingly irrelevant. The tennis players are showing a distressing ability to run their own affairs very skilfully, although this is being fought every foot of the way. Some papers seem scandalised by the fact that tennis players even have their own lawyers. My goodness, next thing you know they'll be demanding civil rights.

Athletics officials have always felt They Know Best. Just like nanny. Stand in the corner, they like to tell the players, play when and where we tell you to and shut up. And get to bed by 10, mind you. Well, I feel that now they have lowered the voting age to 18, athletes might be permitted to make up their own minds about whom and where to play, and whether they want to go out with girls or to booze it up – if they choose.

We had a fellow at baseball long ago named Babe Ruth (his fame must have crossed the Atlantic) who used to stay up all night, drinking incredible quantities of beer and laying an extraordinary number of girls – and he still managed to hit the ball farther and oftener than any other member of the team. This behaviour outraged the purists who felt it set a bad example to the young for Ruth to be so good at baseball while flouting all the training rules. I felt a sneaking admiration for your George Best, who looked marvellous on the field even after he had been up all night. (That is, when he showed up at all.)

In spite of all these strictures, I was right there in front of the set when Wimbledon came on the screen and I'll stay glued there until it's over. Dan Maskell and Billy Knight, the commentators, assured each other happily that Wimbledon had survived. (The monarchy has survived, too, but is this relevant, I ask myself?) Several spectators said to the cameras that anyhow we'd be able to see the talented youngsters now. We will indeed. And talented oldsters, too. But what will happen to the boast that Wimbledon is the place and the *only* place where all the best players in the world may be seen?

The opening Monday was the second-best Monday in the history of the championships, confirming the suspicions of some cynics that the populace is really there for the strawberries and to show off their bonnets. The tennis is incidental.

My own feelings were best summed up long ago by Wilson Mizner, who was found playing roulette in a Western mining town. A friend whispered to him that it was a crooked wheel. Mizner shrugged and said: 'It's the only wheel in town.' Wimbledon's the only wheel in town too.

PANCHO GONZALES

GIANNI CLERICI

The feeble light that filtered through the dusty windowpanes bright-ened one corner of the room, casting the rest of it into dark and somber hues. Lost in a deep sleep under a coat, a naked man lay breathing. His long hand, with its slender and tapered fingers, had swept clean a tiny spot on the dusty floor as the sleeper unconsciously moved his arm. His long, dark hair was streaked with silver, and his thick, sensual lips signaled fatigue. They were the only visible features of the face, half hidden by a strong forearm. Standing out in the subdued mauve light, a scar on the right cheek grew ruddy as the blood coursed beneath it. The heartbeat rhythmically lifted the coat above the chest.

Richard Alonzo (Pancho) Gonzales was asleep. After the match against the Englishman Mark Cox, the first one lost by a professional to an amateur in history's first open tournament, the reporters had left Gonzales alone and were swarming around his blond rival in the packed clubhouse. It was April 1968 at Bournemouth. Pancho had collapsed on the soft cot and slept deeply as only the poor can or those for whom sleep is the only release from an immense grief. The walls of the old club, which protected the sleeper from the rainy gusts of wind, were no more worn than those of Arzy Kunz's store in Los Angeles. Pancho had once loved to call Arzy's place the 'pad', and as a small Chicano boy he treasured that refuge where he could engage in the luxury of admiring the brand-new rackets. At the pad Pancho had learned to re-pair his first enormous, fourteen-ounce racket, worn and scraped by visits to the courts near the Los Angeles Coliseum. His mother, Car-men, would often come looking for him there, complaining loudly that this son of hers was always out in the street, always running around in bad company and managing to play tennis all day long, and that he would forget his supper when he got absorbed by the same Western film for hours on end.

In the Gonzalez household, meals were served with regularity to please the head of the family, Manuel, a decent man who had immig-

rated to Arizona from Chihuahua, the town famous for its lap-dog and for its poverty. In Arizona, Manuel Gonzalez had married Carmen, and their arduous journey had come to an end in Los Angeles. Near Wrigley Field, the sports stadium, Richard came into this world on May 9, 1928, as the depression was gathering strength in the United States. Richard, and then Bertha, Margaret, Terry, Manuel and Ralph had grown up in two rooms in that neighborhood, and in two others elsewhere when the family was pushed out by new waves of immigration and saddled with debts. The children were raised on spoonfuls of beans, omelettes with stewed tomatoes, and oatmeal patties. Not even the most optimistic prophet would have predicted that such a slow and awkward youngster as Pancho would one day be transformed into a prince on the tennis courts, a splendid warrior, 1.8 meters (5 feet 11 inches) in height, well armed with both serve and backhand, hard on the referees, the fans, and himself, but just and occasionally generous toward his enemies in the lists.

Even today the yellow ribbon still rests in a position of honor in his collection, next to a copy of the Davis Cup of 1949 and the rusty medal won for an oratory decathlon, together with other awards for paddle tennis, dice, chess, pool, basketball free throws, croquet, coin pitching, horseshoe pitching, and table tennis. Filled with pride, Pancho had run all the way home to give his mother the yellow ribbon, pinned to his torn sweater and awarded him for first place in the tennis tournament at Slauson Park. Carmen gave him a kiss and told him he was a fine boy, the best in the whole family. Encouraged by her praise, he quickly won two other events, and the *Los Angeles Times* devoted a few lines to him in the paper.

Pancho's dedication to the sport helped Frank Poulain to come to a decision. Like Arzy, Frank was interested in the boy's welfare. They would go to see Perry Jones, the tennis czar. Pancho immediately wanted to know if Jones was a great champion. Poulain said he was not. Pancho wondered why he was called a czar then. Poulain answered that Jones was an egotistical man. Not knowing what that meant, Pancho gingerly nodded in assent. Beyond a network of courts, meeting rooms, and dressing rooms swarming with attendants, Pancho found himself in the czar's office. Smiling but also showing misgivings, Jones looked at the boy from behind the metal frames of his glasses which ringed his weak eyes and seemed connected to them. Poulain noticed his suspicions and attacked at once. 'Here is the future champion of the United States,' he said proudly.

Perry looked Pancho over with the eyes of a horse trader. 'Perhaps,' he murmured skeptically. Then with sudden enthusiasm, 'That's a long road, a very long road.'

'He'll make it,' Poulain insisted.

'I've seen hundreds of them,' Perry growled, angered at such a show of faith. 'Almost none of them passed my easiest tests.'

'Try him out.'

Perry took off his glasses and began to clean them with a handkerchief embroidered with his initials and the emblem of a tennis racket. 'The only positive proof,' he muttered, 'would be to take a dozen or so of them up on the roof and throw them off. A couple would survive and the one with the best reflexes *might* become a champion.'

Perry laughed wickedly, and while Poulain was doing his best to do likewise, Pancho jumped to his feet. 'Let's go up on the roof, Mr. Czar!' he said determinedly.

'I'm not as bad as all that. Let's go out on the court,' Jones answered. After ten minutes of volleys he turned angrily to Poulain: 'Can't you see he's a cream puff? He doesn't have any drive. His metabolism must be off.'

'His metabolism is better than mine,' Poulain answered heatedly. 'Richard is a fighter who shows his stuff when the chips are down. Send him East with your boys; you'll see what he can do.' Jones shook his head. Gonzalez's high-school transcripts, he said, showed too poor a scholastic record. An educated man himself, Jones was not in the habit of aiding and abetting illiteracy. He was sorry, but he had already wasted enough time.

Glumly silent, Poulain and Richard drove home in the old Ford. Finally Frank broke the silence and asked Pancho about school. 'I'm through with school.' Pancho's eyes were cold and unrelenting. 'All I want to do,' he sighed, 'is to play tennis. From morning to night. My whole life long.'

After a bad year, Pancho finally felt at his ease in the Forest Hills locker room, in the process of performing the same rituals and gestures that had preceded his victory over Sturgess twelve months earlier, a victory marking the conquest of the American title. It had been a surprise for everyone, but not for Pancho's young bride, whom he married secretly and who was already expecting a child. Henrietta had seen him rise from one success to another, and she was certain that there wasn't a man in the world who was stronger and braver than he. Pancho had been suspended for two years for his stubborn decision to quit school. Then they had reinstated him, and he quickly vindicated himself by beating Herbie Flam, their favorite son. Jones had then been clever enough to admit his own mistake, and he courted Pancho by providing him with equipment and a little money.

Faced with conclusive proof that such a foolish game was a moneymaking proposition, Pancho's father Manuel finally relented. By working overtime, he managed to scrape together the funds to buy his son a Dodge, a veteran of eleven years on the street. Pancho had dismantled and souped up the motor in order to compete with the sports cars owned by his rich adversaries. That noisy piece of junk ran like a top, and beating it was a risky business. Pancho drove it like a parking-lot jockey with no consideration for others. In that car he had rambled from tourney to tourney, winning matches and charming audiences. His name, corrupted into Gonzales, began to appear in the newspapers with greater frequency. By the end of the season, he was ranked seventeenth in the nation.

By 1948 Kramer was already with the pros, and Schroeder, too busy with his work, did not sign up for Forest Hills. By dint of extremely hard-placed serves, Pancho finally beat Drobny, who had led for thirty-seven games before letting himself be broken. In the finals Pancho also took the elegant Eric Sturgess to pieces. His victory was greeted with enormous enthusiasm by a public that was still smarting at the resignation of Kramer. But at his first errors, at his first defeats by the hand of Schroeder, directors and reporters turned against Pancho and left him to argue with Henrietta, who was by this time the mother of a little Richard junior and expecting once again.

Pancho finished lacing his shoes as he thought over all these problems. He scowled at his reflection in the mirror: these little tournaments, played in the South in order to be close to his wife, had slowed him down and were making him put on weight. There were newspapers on the floor where they had been thrown about in a gesture of anger. They reminded him that this new finals match at Forest Hills would be decisive for his brief career; only *The New York Times* was nonconformist enough to list him favored. Beyond the wall, in a room like his, waited Schroeder, a middle-class type with his house in order, a German name, bravery in the war, a degree, a good job in the packing plant, and an irresistible drive that had brought him the Wimbledon title. Pancho would have to anticipate that damned serve, keep the ball down near his feet and attack him with no errors, while holding firm to his own serve, always alert for changes in the direction of Schroeder's passing shots.

'Mister Gonzales, it's time.' The pink-faced gentleman, wearing the tie of the club and a ribbon in his buttonhole, smiled paternally. The thought suddenly flashed across Pancho's mind that behind this man disaster might await him, *el diablo de los pachucos*. The huge horseshoe frame of the stadium resounded with voices and the September grass was turning yellow like the threshing floor of a barn. Pancho found himself standing beside Schroeder, who already looked like the winner as he confronted the barrage of the photographers' cameras with a confident smile on his face. Pancho saw Henrietta in the stands. She was leaning on the arm of Frank Shields, his only friend. Pancho smiled and then realized with a sudden shiver that she would soon begin to cry. His hand grazed his heart, forehead, and hair, an automatic gesture related to his Catholic upbringing.

Pancho made the sign of the cross and then tried, together with Henrietta, to erase from his mind all negative impressions from the past year. But his hatred for the rich and beautiful white society of the tennis world could not help but cross the net and engulf Ted, who had beaten him seven times to his one victory. Ted Schroeder stood there smiling like always and rallying with insulting indifference. He sent the balls back lightly or else suddenly with tremendous speed, keeping his opponent cold and unable to center his shots. Pancho answered with his serve and hit thirteen balls with increasing violence, while Schroeder stood his ground, keeping his legs wide apart as he eyed his opponent with irony. The umpire thought it opportune to end the warmup. 'Play,' he ordered simply.

Gonzales had not yet recovered from the shock of the first two sets having been lost and of the third set received almost as a gift from an absentminded Schroeder. He lifted his face toward the needles of the shower, and then Shields came to him, breaking the silence of the dressing room with his deep voice. 'When Ted is a point ahead,' the old champion repeated, 'he always plays a slice instead of a cannonball.' How could Pancho not have noticed that? Shields, however, did not give him time to reply before continuing: 'You're staying too far back, and as a result you don't pick up that short ball of his. If you don't see what I mean, if you can't get it by yourself, pay attention to my hands. When he serves you a slice, I'll grip the railing.'

When the game was resumed, Pancho cast a glance toward Shields, ready for his signal. He moved up two paces and suddenly there was the ball on his racket, ready to smash to bits. Before Schroeder could regain mid-court, the projectile had whizzed past him. Pancho continued to blindly follow his friend's signals, and, as if by magic, he got the break. From the fans a voice blurted out: 'Put him on ice!' Schroeder lost his cool and requested silence. With a bellow, the crowd turned against him. Pancho ran off with the fourth set, 6-2. Schroeder was proud of his record as a winning player in fifth sets. Only Jack Kramer had managed to clobber him in a final set. He threw himself grimly into the game.

The game followed the serves up to four all. Pancho risked two anticipated shots and two forehand passing shots and made the break. A double fault and a net volley showed how nervous he was and cost him a 15-30 score. A volley on a ball possibly out put him in trouble, 30-40! Schroeder's lips rounded in a sneering grin. Pancho really drove the serve home twice and then closed with a volley. Match point. He kissed his racket and then served. Ted rushed the return with his forehand, and Pancho saved himself with a half-volley, while his opponent advanced to finish him with a drive. The ball flew out of reach near the line. The umpire raised his hand. 'Out!' Pancho was the winner. Thirteen thousand fans got to their feet to applaud. Henrietta had begun to cry again, her head cradled on Shields's shoulder.

After his victory in the finals at Forest Hills, Pancho Gonzales joined Jack Kramer in the professional ranks. Bobby Riggs signed them up for a tour that was a financial success. After 96 matches lost in the long string of 123 challenge matches played against Kramer, Gonzales put $75,000 in the bank. But at the same time Pancho ruined his reputation as a tennis player. Listening to his wife's advice, he bought two small houses, gave one to his parents, and then bought himself a pair of red morocco leather slippers. His unfulfilled desire for competition and for danger soon drove him into playing poker and gambling for high stakes at an illegal establishment. After a couple of months he had lost everything and knocked on Riggs's door. The old champion was frank if cruel with him: 'You're a drag on the market, Pancho, and your name isn't worth a red cent. Get in shape, start practising, and bide your time. You've got to be patient.' The insult was lost in the sound of the door being closed. After a long walk, as rambling and disjointed as his thoughts, Pancho found himself once again in front of Arzy Kunz's sporting goods store. 'Don't you think you have worked here long enough?' he asked his friend. 'Why don't you sell the store to me?' Kunz agreed.

After a few days Henrietta could see, tearfully, that it was impossible to transform Pancho into a small businessman. He would leave notes written on the windowpane, and off he would go to compete with the boys on the drag strip. In bowling he often scored 250, and in two week's training he played a round of golf in 75. Against his better judgment, he tried coaching in Hollywood, making Henrietta wrongfully jealous. When a starlet propositioned him, he threw her into a bed of tulips in her yard and shouted, 'My tennis is not for sale!'

The few dollars Pancho was able to raise came from playing semipro basketball. He tried giving tennis lessons but had no success whatsoever. It was not his thing, and after a few attempts, he managed to alienate all the rich clients and found himself reduced to one student, Oscar Johnson, who would later climb to prominence as an Afro-American star. Angered by Riggs's indifference, Pancho finally rebelled and signed a contract with Jack Harris, which turned out to be a mistake. Within two years, Pancho was to win a pro championship of the United States which was boycotted by Riggs. At the end of 1953, Pancho was invited to visit Kramer in his new office.

Dressed in a dark suit with a twenty-dollar tie around his suntanned neck, Jack encouraged him to sit down, then slumped into a comfortable revolving armchair. 'Aren't you weary of being retired by now, Pancho?' he smiled. He had replaced Riggs, he explained quickly. It was a euphemism for what really had transpired, which was lost in Pancho's amazement. With his eyes glued to the contract that Jack was waving around like a fan to punctuate his elegant sales pitch, Pancho gritted his teeth, unable to hear a word of it.

At last, when he had finished his discourse, Kramer himself lost his customary calm just for a moment. 'There is only one thing that keeps me from signing, Jack,' Gonzales had observed. 'I never carry a pen with me.'

The tourney with Sedgman, McGregor, and Segura was not very profitable in the United States, but in Australia the crowds were staggering in proportion. In 1954 the Aussies were mildly intoxicated by the success of their own champions and identified themselves with their domination. The arrival of Pancho and his sixteen victories against nine for Sedgman, his fifteen triumphs that shut out McGregor showed to those with eyes that professional tennis was something more than a badly controlled amateur status. The strongest player in the world was a professional without a penny in the till.

In 1955 Gonzales became the victim of a curious phenomenon which had afflicted some other highly gifted professionals of the sporting world, like Joe Louis, Bobby Jones, or Willie Hoppe. Pancho was out of work because he was too strong for the competition. At the age of twenty-six, he played such an excellent game that Gardini and Merlo, Eleanor Tennant's guests, were able to take from him only one game in two successive singles matches of two sets each! Another tour in Australia ended with forty-five victories for him against seven for his opponent Pails. Little by little the crowds began to dwindle. At the end of the tour Kramer invited him into his office, and, with a little more elegance, repeated Riggs's old argument. 'I can't put you out on the court until I get Trabert, or Rosewall and Hoad.'

Kramer tried in vain the get the Wimbledon and Forest Hills champion and the two young holders of the Davis Cup into professional tennis at the same time. His attempt to keep Pancho on the sidelines also failed, and he was forced to organize a challenge between the amateur champions and the professional stars. The large sum that he advanced to Trabert was a mistake: Gonzales would earn only $15,000 as opposed to $80,000 for his rival, whatever the outcome. Pancho certainly had no need of special provocation to dislike poor Tony Trabert. He grew so bitter that he refused a practice set before the tour began. 'We will meet on the court one hundred and two times. Don't you think that's enough?'

Every evening, after his long and solitary car trip, Pancho would meet Tony and Jack in a new town. Under feeble lightbulbs, on treacherous canvas that covered a playing surface of wood or ice, in dancehall or circus tent, he unleashed himself against his adversary, pitting himself against his boss at the same time. At the end of the tour, with 75 victories to 27, Gonzales felt repaid for all the humiliations of the first tour and at the same time free of the hatred he had felt for the tall, good-looking, rosy Trabert. He was ready to discuss a seven-year contract with Kramer.

Up until 1960 Pancho would continue to match wits with the strongest opponents that the impresario could muster, the great Rosewall and Hoad. The ascent of Rosewall did not throw him out of the running, especially in the individual matches and in the tournaments: regular as clockwork, Pancho would combine the best tennis with the highest prizes. In 1966, at the age of thirty-eight, Gonzales would take Wembley, beating Rosewall in the semifinals 13-11 in the third, and Rod Laver in the fifth set of the final 10-8. His career was not yet over.

DIARY NOTES

ARTHUR ASHE

Friday, November 16, 1973 – London
We fly out tonight on BOAC, a through-flight to Johannesburg, with a stopover in Nairobi, but even as late as this afternoon, in my room at the Westbury Hotel, members of SANROC – the South African Non-Racial Olympic Committee – tried to convince me not to go. We argued for several hours, going round and round the same points, but I remain convinced that my way is the one that can best serve the purpose of eventual equality. Economic sanctions have been tried against South Africa, legal appeals to domestic courts and world courts, political pressure and the force of international public opinion, and all of them have proved unsuccessful at breaking apartheid. On the other hand, the country bends a little for sports. South Africa seems more upset when people won't play with it, than when they won't trade with it.

The country is, after all, ideally situated and structured for playing games. It has a subtropical climate which encourages year-round outdoor activity, and it has a year-round subservient population to do the dirty work and allow whites leisure time. Not surprisingly, South Africa also has among the very highest indices of divorce, suicide and alcoholism in the world. You see, idle hands are the devil's workshop.

Spectator sports have no competition with television either, since South Africa holds back the tide of human communications from its blacks by denying television to everyone. Thus, the whole land focuses heavily on major sporting events. Bob Foster, the American black who is light heavyweight champion of the world, arrived in Johannesburg earlier this week to start training for a title fight on December 1 with a white South African challenger. This is the first interracial fight in history in South Africa, but once the appetite for the best boxing is whetted how can it be the last? Same with tennis, or any sport.

Diary Notes

Saturday, November 17 – Nairobi/Johannesburg

The flight was crowded, and I was jammed into an inside seat, next to Nailbags. He slept better than I did. Our travelling party included Donald, who has the flu, and his wife, Carole; Richard Evans, a British journalist who is also the press officer for ATP; Frank Deford, who is covering for *Sports Illustrated*; and Bud Collins of the Boston *Globe*, who is to join us in Johannesburg from Australia. I wish *Jet* or *Ebony* had sent a black reporter along too.

At quarter to four, London time, when the morning sky was just beginning to color over Africa, Donald and Richard took me upstairs to the first-class lounge to try and prep me for the press conference I would have to face when I arrived. One of the more curious inconsistencies of South Africa is that it still has a relatively free press. There is a certain oblique censorship and a greater implied censorship (if you go too far), but the papers do enjoy a surprisingly large degree of freedom. The Afrikaans-language dailies seldom exercise the right. The government of South Africa has long been run by the Afrikaners, the Boers, descendants of the Dutch, who were the first Europeans to settle southern Africa. The British came later and now dominate the cities and the business of the country, although they are a white minority. The English-speaking dailies, notably the *Star* and the Rand *Daily Mail*, can be quite outspoken, even altogether critical of the Afrikaner government. As long as the government has the Afrikaners in the bag though, it seems content to let the English-language newspapers lurch and snap to no real avail; all the while making the country appear freer than it really is. So I could face some tough questions from the English-speaking press.

I had agreed as part of the deal that I would keep my counsel and hold any substantive opinions for my departure. This would also serve to keep the press from hounding me, so that I would be able to concentrate on playing tennis. I decided to start my statement this way: 'I'm here in a spirit of cooperation. I've come as a man, nothing more, nothing less, and I look forward to a fascinating twelve days . . .' Pretty pat stuff – but, as it turned out at the conference, everybody was being so polite to me that my remarks were accepted with ponderous courtesy.

It was, all things considered, a mellow welcome to the land. Shortly before the plane landed, a little man came up to me, and said: 'Mr. Ashe, I'm one of those horrible South Africans'.– and he paused – 'and I just want to wish you the best of success. I promise you we're not all as bad as we're supposed to be, and you mark my words: three fourths of the people will be pulling for you.' When we landed, this gentleman

171

came down the ramp right after me, and another white South African who had also wished me luck came up on the other side, and together they sort of convoyed me into the terminal.

There were a few black people waving and snapping photographs from the balcony, but it was a quiet reception, and of course deceptive, too, because the international building, where we came in, offers a sort of diplomatic immunity to blacks. There are no separate facilities there, no physical evidence of apartheid. It was just like landing in Sydney or Rio or Brussels or any damn place. It was very disconcerting that way.

And, like a lot of places, the customs line was long. When my turn came, the official took my passport without offering me any special recognition and flipped through it till he came to the visa stamp. He glanced at it for a moment and then abruptly turned and took it back to a uniformed officer, who seemed to be in charge. This guy looked like he just came in from the Boer War: starched short-pants, long-socks uniform; swagger stick; bushy mustache. He exchanged a word or two with the customs man, who turned, walked back to his cubicle and stamped the passport with no more to-do. As I passed, the officer with the swagger stick said, 'Welcome to our country, Mr. Ashe.'

I had flown for more than half a day and missed most of a night's sleep, but I felt fine physically. Emotionally, however, I was shot. But I put on my mask, the one I must keep on for the next couple of weeks. I have this ability to take it all in and never to let on how I am feeling. Nobody can tell the difference.

Owen Williams and his wife, Jennifer, drove us from the airport through the city to the house where we were going to stay, in Sandton, the best section of town. My first impression was that apartheid was a much more subtle proposition than I had anticipated. If you were white, I doubt if you would even have seen anything out of the ordinary. It is what you *don't* see. During the entire trip from the airport, nearly an hour's drive, I saw only two blacks driving cars. All you see are the Africans walking – and walking slowly, as if they really have no place to go.

We are staying in the house of a wealthy insurance/real estate man named Brian Young. He is Jewish, recently divorced, and lives alone in this huge, opulent place – alone with the usual complement of servants, of course. He is away this weekend, on a trip to Swaziland. One wing of the house is turned over to four of us: Frank Deford and I each in a private room, Donald and Carole in a suite. Richard Evans and Bud Collins (when he arrives) are staying in private houses nearby. While

Brian is away, our host is Gordon Forbes, a contemporary of Owen's and once a world-class player himself, whose sister, Jean, is married to Cliff Drysdale. Forbesy is divorced too, so he has moved into another of Brian's guest quarters to look after us.

The place is very Spanish, sprawling, with the obligatory trappings of the neighborhood: a Mercedes or two in every garage, a swimming pool, tennis court, gardens, the majestic purple jacaranda trees and a burglar alarm system. There is a cook, a maid, a gardener. Forbesy orders steaks all around for our luncheon as soon as we arrive. Steaks, apparently, are the everyday staple of the cuisine and are served like hot dogs. And when I ask for a cold drink, the maid, Anna, drops her eyes and says: 'Yes, master.' *For God's sake.*

So here is little Artie Ashe, the skinny black kid from the capital of the old Confederacy, all set up in a mansion, carrying on jes' like the white folks, and gettin' hisself called Master. I knew in advance that a lot of people would call me a hypocrite for living in a white man's house – and the matter was discussed, very carefully, at length. But the only other alternative would have been to stay in a first-class hotel, such as Bob Foster and several of the white tennis players did. When we were invited to use Brian Young's house, we were assured that our host genuinely wanted our company, and it provided me with a privacy and a convenience that was bound to help my tennis. Staying in Soweto, that grim black 'city' that serves Johannesburg, was really impossible. I did not come to South Africa in a sackcloth and ashes to serve penance. I know damn well how badly the Africans in this country live, but I cannot see how it would serve any useful purpose for me to live like one myself. I know I'll catch a lot of heat for this, but I think it's best this way.

This night we went to a cocktail party that was given by the various South African breweries which had joined together to sponsor the Open. It was the very essence of brotherhood: whites, blacks, Coloreds, Asians all eating and drinking together. Of course, it was all illegal too, because whites are not permitted to provide drinks for persons of any other race. (And what do I call these persons? You can't just say blacks, because there are also categories of Coloreds and Asians too. And you can't say minorities because the minorities are the majority here. I hate to say 'non-white,' which is the accepted term, because that means that a race is defined foremost by the absence of what it is. To be devilish, I'd like to call the whites 'nonblacks.' Anyway, I use nonwhites under protest.) After the breweries' illegal party, Owen called ahead to a little restaurant, and we all went out to dinner. Everybody was just lovely to me. If I had been a native nonwhite, I would

173

not have been permitted in the place. Hell, if I had been a native non-white, I wouldn't even have been permitted to be up that late in Johannesburg. There's a curfew for all nonwhites at 10 p.m.

Somebody told me today that the only way to understand South Africa is to assume that it is either run by madmen or evil men. I'm catching on.

Sunday, November 18 – Johannesburg

Went out to Ellis Park today for a hit, and saw my first WHITES ONLY signs. You know, since every visitor who takes a picture in South Africa finds it easiest to portray the fact of apartheid with restroom signs, most people who have never been here think, I'm sure, that the whole country is nothing but a land of public toilets. I was almost relieved at last to see some segregated restrooms; otherwise, it would be like going to Paris the first time and not seeing the Eiffel Tower or visiting Egypt and missing the pyramids. And right away, somebody wanted to take my picture in front of the HERE BLANKES or DAMAS BLANKES Afrikaans signs. It does freak you out to see those things though. It wakes you up.

I had a hit with some of the country's best black players. I'm afraid that none of them is very good, though, which, considering the tennis facilities and coaching, is not very surprising. You can't just bring a handful of them into the Open, beat them love and love in the first round and then send them back to nowhere till the next year's Open. We've got to obtain the right for the best players to compete on the Sugar Circuit – a series of top domestic tournaments – and at all levels of competition.

Luckily, I don't have to play my own first-round match until Tuesday, which should give me enough time to get acclimated to the altitude here. Jo'burg (everybody calls it Jo'burg) is 500 feet higher than Denver. This is surely the reason that almost all South African players have the same, limited style: short, blocky swings. The ball moves fast in the light air, but inversely, the Dunlops they use here fluff all up and get very heavy on your arm. The South Africans could always handle everybody else's case when they got them down here in their own air. They even won the women's Federation Cup when that was played down here a couple years ago – and there isn't a single outstanding South African woman player.

I'm going to get an oxygen tank tomorrow for courtside. You've got to limit yourself. Forget about angles. Just try to hit the ball in the middle of the racket. If you hit it off centre, it's liable to soar on you. I

174

mean, balls you hit out won't just go a little long – they'll hit the back-stop.

Luckily for me, as badly as I'm playing, I've drawn a first-round opponent who's coming in from New Zealand tomorrow, so he's bound to be less acclimated to the altitude than me. It's Sherwood Stewart, ranked thirty-sixth in the U.S., from Goose Creek, Texas. I go halfway around the world, and finally get into South Africa, and how do I make history: I play a guy from Goose Creek, Texas.

Monday, November 19 – Johannesburg
I saw my first reference book today, the odious pass that all nonwhites must carry, signed by their employer. The blacks call it, I learned, 'my stinker.'

Still, apartheid is handled with such sophistication that it is sometimes easy to forget that South Africa is nothing less than a police state. The injustices here go far beyond the seminal matter of racial inequality. Informers of all races are everywhere. The secret police – Bureau of State Security, or BOSS (isn't that magnificent? – straight out of Ian Fleming) are ubiquitous. Arrest is arbitrary, incarceration capricious, and there is an execution, on the average, every nine or ten days. Without any trial, you can be imprisoned for three months at a clip – and they can repeat that each and every three months, ad infinitum. There is something especially unsettling about hearing the expression 'go inside' being tossed about in any conversation, in the most respectable company. Jail is an everyday fact of life here.

House arrest, or something known as 'banning,' is virtually as effective though. Banning is an insidious device which permits you to exist but not really to live. If the government bans you, you cannot publish, attend a university, visit a library, travel or even meet with more than one person at a time. You could not, for example, even play a game of doubles. Seventy persons have already been banned this year. They just banned a swimming administrator who was too outspoken on the subject of multiracial swimming competition.

There is, in fact, increased repression in South Africa, belying the well-publicized 'liberal' breakthroughs which have permitted me to play here and Foster to fight. The universities and churches are being pressured by the government to conform, and, for the first time, the newspapers are genuinely concerned about the full threat of censorship. Today, out of the blue, the government declared that blacks and Coloreds could not compete against each other in amateur sports. It is as if they have unscrewed the top off one bottle of apartheid and given the rest of the world a good heady whiff of that but then screwed the lid even tighter on all the other bottles – and tightest of all on those that are concerned with men's minds: the schools, the press, the churches.

I had met some black journalists at Ellis Park and was chatting with them near the courts, when, suddenly, one of them said: 'Please, Arthur, we cannot talk here, this is a public place.' So some of us moved on to the privacy of the players' lounge (presumably it's not bugged), and they emphasized to me what I already knew – that many blacks do not want me here, that they feel my being here legitimizes the government and lends it some credence. As Cliff Drysdale explains it: 'If you accept the hypothesis that all this must end in violence, then any visit from an outsider – Arthur's, Foster's, anyone's – any dealings with the government only prolongs that agony.'

After the other writers had left, a reporter named Don Mattera, of the Johannesburg *Star*, stayed and we talked by ourselves for a while.

'Do you think I should have come?' I asked.

'Oh, I'm glad you're here,' he said, ' We need some contact, we need to be periodically assured that people in the rest of the world still understand and care. Commited black Americans should visit South Africa.' He paused; he spoke softly, evenly. 'But someone like Foster only hurts us. That kind of person should stay away.' Foster had already spent a week in Jo'burg without making any contact with the black community. Moreover, he had declared that he 'loved' South Africa and might like to build a vacation home here.

'Will you write that about Foster?' I asked.

'No,' Don said. 'I wouldn't criticize another brother. There'll come a day when we'll have the luxury to criticize, to disagree with each other in public, but right now we need solidarity above all.'

Mattera, who is classified as a Colored, is a poet as well as a journalist, and Nikki Giovanni saw his work when she visited South Africa and was much impressed with it. Don has his first collection of poems at the printer right now. That stuns me: how anyone could perform any serious creative effort in this atmosphere. Everyone must be so careful politically not to offend the government that I would think that this fear would inhibit the spontaneity of life that results in the creation of any art.

Not long after Don left, I met the President of South Africa, Jim Fouche. He is an old man, the ceremonial head of the nation, the best equivalent for royalty in a land without royalty. 'How do you like South Africa?' he asked me.

'How are you enjoying the tennis?' I answered.

Tuesday, November 20 – Johannesburg

Bud Collins, the Boston writer, arrived last night and came over to Brian's for breakfast with us this morning. 'I flew in with Sherwood Stewart,' Bud said. 'You know why he's here? He thought he would come because he wanted to see something historic. He thought it would be interesting to be here to see you break through in South Africa. Now he flies ten thousand miles and finds out he's the poor sonuvabitch you've got to break through.'

Sherwood and I came out to play just after noon. There was no wind to speak of, and in the warm stillness, a few small clouds spotted about a high blue sky. The courts at Ellis are cement, and the center court is surrounded on all sides by a dandy little covered grandstand, which seats several thousand. The roof is aluminium, topped by several light towers and embroidered with a few billboards, one of which, for Scotch, actually says: 'Time to serve Black & White.' The stands were not quite filled, but for a weekday the crowd was quite large, and I could see blacks scattered all about the place, including one whole boxful at courtside. I learned later that an usher had run up to Owen about this time, and distraught, cried: 'Are you Mr. Williams? You must do something. The blacks and the Coloreds are sitting in all the white seats.'

Owen said: 'I'll take care of it.'

For the record, I won the first point that a black who had been persona non grata ever played on the center court at Ellis Park, in Johannesburg, Republic of South Africa. It was a forehand, down the line. I won that game, a service break, and the set, and the match: 6-1, 7-6, 6-4.

Afterward, I decided to go out to Soweto. I had an informal agreement with Owen that I would keep him posted at all times as to my whereabouts. He wasn't going to stop me from going anywhere, he just was concerned. On his part, it was superfluous, because by now I was convinced that I was being tailed wherever I went anyway. I'm not paranoid to think that anybody was out to get me; I imagine it was just to make sure that nobody killed me or kidnapped me and brought South Africa a lot of bad publicity.

But it was eerie, anyway. I've never been tailed before – and for cops and robbers writers, I have some friendly little advice: if the gasoline crisis remains with us, tailing is going to be an increasingly difficult operation. The Arabs are pretty tough on South Africa because of its Israeli sympathies, and already there are tough gasoline restrictions here. Among other things, there is no gas sold anywhere on Sunday, so there are virtually no cars on the road on Sunday. And Sunday was when I became positive I was being tailed, because the only car around was the one always back of me. Believe me, it is going to be very difficult turning a good dollar in the tailing business from here on.

Owen's car is at my disposal, along with his driver, Solomon. He is a perceptive black man from Mozambique, friendly, shrewd, indispensable to Owen, with such a broad knowledge of the events and the people of Jo'burg that I thought initially that Sol must be an informer. But he is not, I am sure. For one thing, aside from his Man Fridaying for Owen, he runs a large dance troupe, which performs the indigenous tribal dances of southern Africa. The ensemble has received several offers to perform in the U.S., but the government has forbidden them passports. Presumably, informers get better treatment.

Soweto sounds like some quaint old African name, while actually it is just a bureaucratic abbreviation for Southwest Township. And I always visualized it in terms of the usual suburb, hard by the city. But suddenly Solomon and I were buzzing along an open road, passing nothing but gold mines. 'Hey, where's Soweto?' I asked.

It was seventeen miles from Jo'burg. And not only do the blacks have to train and bus in and back every day for work, but they must buy most of their goods from the white man. Soweto has a population upward of a million, but it is not a city so much as it is an urban reservation. The government owns all the houses. No public transportation within the city. One fire brigade, one hospital, one switchboard for 500 phones. Plumbing is rare, and perhaps a tenth of Soweto has electricity. Unlike the whites, who have free education, the blacks, who can least afford it, must pay tuition, so that thousands of kids never go to school, and roam the streets, idly passing all the formative hours of their lives.

All of it sprawls. The best of it is endless rows of tiny little cottages; the worst, shacks of paper, of wood, of tin. The last tableau remains the most vivid, and the most heartless somehow. It was late in the afternoon now, and the thousands of workers were coming home from the long day in Jo'burg. Many had risen before dawn, and many were burdened with food and other items they had to buy in the city. There was the train station, and before it, a great field, maybe half a mile wide, which they had to cross before they even got to the houses of Soweto. We watched as they came, hundreds, thousands of them, filing toward us as the sun fell across their backs. Suddenly it occurred to me that I had seen something very much like this once before, and then I remembered that that scene was in Africa too, a time in Kenya when I saw hordes of wildebeest crossing a broad savanna.

'Let's go back, Sol,' I said. The servants cooked a steak for me as soon as I came into the house.

178

Diary Notes

Wednesday, November 21 – Johannesburg
The paper was waiting for me with breakfast, and the story on the front page: they had banned Don Mattera. The banning order must have been in process, even as I sat talking with him Monday.

I beat Barry Phillips-Moore in straight sets this afternoon, four/four and one, and then this evening several of us went down-town to the headquarters of the United States Information Service to attend a reception for black journalists. Foster had also been invited, but declined.

It was dusk when we arrived, and the lobby of the building was dark, but there, standing at the bottom of the stairs, was Mattera. He was alone, except for an agent from BOSS. Don greeted me warmly, so calmly, and seemed mostly only apologetic that he could not attend the meeting upstairs – the one he had personally organized. 'I don't want to do anything to jeopardize your visit, Arthur,' he said. I shook his hand and commiserated with his fate. He only shrugged, 'They have banned me, but they cannot stop me,' he said. 'If they put me in jail, they put me in jail. But they cannot stop me.' He shrugged again.

He is thirty-seven years old. His livelihood is journalism, or was, till this morning. That is denied him now. He has six children and lives surrounded by squalor and violence. He has no electricity, just as he has no plumbing, so he writes his poetry by candle, or gaslight. I did not know it then, but he was writing a poem about me at this time. It reads:

I listened deeply when you spoke
About the step-by-step evolution
Of a gradual harvest,
Tendered by the rains of tolerance
And patience.

Your youthful face,
A mask,
Hiding a pining, anguished spirit, and
I loved you brother –
Not for your quiet philosophy
But for the rage in your soul,
Trained to be rebuked or summoned.

179

As for me,
When I asked them for bread,
They gave the wheatfield,
And I thought they loved me.
When I asked for water,
They gave the well,
And I thought they cared.

When I asked for freedom
They took back the wheatfield
And the well,
Tightened the chains,
And told me I asked too much
Now, I no longer wait for
The wheat and water, but fight
For freedom. . .

Mattera is a unique person, which, of course, is why they banned him. When he was a teenager, he was recognized as the toughest kid in a community that features the casual violence of a doomed people. Don headed a gang called 'The Vultures,' and he even killed, but they only put him in jail, because he merely killed other Coloreds or blacks, and the government is really not to be bothered with that kind of intramural mayhem. But inexplicably Mattera was somehow mystically transformed in jail, he came out for the last time at eighteen, went back to school, educated himself, married and began to write his poetry by candlelight. Even now, they say he is something of a legend where he lives. It is said that he, the gentle poet, is permitted to walk the dark streets unmolested. The thugs, penniless and hopeless, understand that they must not attack Don Mattera.

And so, as he watched us go, we climbed the stairs to attend his meeting. I agreed to speak in the auditorium, so long as I could ask questions as well as answer them. There were about seventy-five of us jammed into this small, windowless room – counting the man from BOSS and a predictable number of informers. The atmosphere was charged with fear and passion, and the place was as hot from the tension as from the crush of people. I did not really understand how scared the people were, though, until I looked over at one of the group's officers and saw that his hands were trembling – and that he could not stop them.

. He stood first, and talked of Don Mattera: 'He has spoken out for the common brotherhood. So our time must be short too, for so do we. We may be called on very soon to say no more.'

'Power, power!' some of the people said, and others: 'Shame, shame!'

But they did not spare me. I heard one man mutter 'Uncle Tom' at me, and others were no less opposed to my being there. 'You come here, our people play in a tournament once, and the situation remains unchanged. The black man still has his place – cleaning toilets. You stay away, all of you. All right, Arthur?'

'You mean you want me to stand on the outside and just watch you suffer?' I said. 'That makes me very sad.'

'If we isolate them, they're forced to change,' another said. 'Cut off South Africa, boycott it. Don't you see: we blacks wouldn't suffer any more than we already do. We are used to suffering. Only the whites would suffer more.'

'Power, power!'

'Your presence delays our struggle. You go back to New York. Stay away, stay away. You come here and save their tennis. Soccer is dying here because of the sanctions placed on it.'

'Sanctions won't work,' I said. 'When there's a choice, money over morality, it's always money that wins out. There's ten southern African nations trading with this country today. If the blacks cannot keep up a boycott, what makes you think the whites will?'

'We don't just want equality, as you do,' a young woman said. 'We were dispossessed. We want our land back.'

'Look, I'm not saying that the United States is a proper analogy here,' I said. 'I'm not telling you how to live your lives. But I am saying that history shows that progress does not come in huge chunks. It comes bit by bit. There was the lady named Rosa Parks on the bus in Montgomery, and she was tired, and she said, *No, I'm not moving*, and the whole thing for us started from there.'

'She would have been banned here,' a man shouted, 'and Martin Luther King would have been put on Robben Island.'

'Please, I know these things,' I went on. 'Of course I know it's infinitely harder here than it was in the States. But I still see my being here as a start. You've got integrated seating out at Ellis Park. It was never there before. And we're trying to get black players on the Sugar Circuit. There will be something left when I'm gone. I'm always thinking of the guy behind me, so I tell my head to hold my tongue.

'Maybe I'm naive, but I think, when you're mapping out a plan for progress, emotion cannot be allowed to play a large role, except for drumming up support. I had a very wise man who taught me to play tennis, to play against whites, and in places no black man had ever been before. His name was Dr. Walter Johnson, and he used to say: "Those

181

whom the gods wish to destroy, they first make mad." '

I don't know if I convinced anyone. It was a time for declaring one-self, not for swaying others. I gave them an excuse to air all the things bottled up inside, even though they realized that everything they said would probably be in a report at BOSS the next morning. And there were many who supported my views. I don't know, maybe the crowd was split fifty-fifty. 'You know,' a funny little guy named Patsy said, 'they tell me I can't sleep on the white man's sheets because I'm black, but they let you come and they find you the best beds, and if you're black and good enough to sleep on sheets, well so am I. Everytime they do something like this, they kick their own policies in the backside.'

'Somebody like you comes,' another man said, 'it shows us an inspi-ration, not just to excel at something, but not to be intimidated by the bully. Enough of you come and show us, then pretty soon, we don't have no bully no more.'

'You're not an inspiration to me,' a large man said. 'But you're a chal-lenge. I see you and other free blacks who come here, and it is a chal-lenge to me to be like you, free, and if not me, my sons.'

'Power, power!'

Downstairs, Don was waiting patiently, just to say goodbye. 'Go well, brothers,' he said to us, clasping our hands, 'go well, go well.'

Shame, shame.

DAVIS CUP AND DRACULA IN BUCHAREST

RICHARD EVANS

One dark Romanian night I went driving with Ilie Nastase to a monastery by a lake where Count Dracula is supposed to be buried. It was, I admit, a little eerie, but I only got really scared when I read an article by the brilliant *Los Angeles Times* columnist, Jim Murray, a couple of months later. It is one of Murray's more imaginative pieces and well-worth quoting at length:

'The first look you get at Ilie Nastase . . . you close your eyes and picture a lightning storm playing around this lonely castle and your car mysteriously breaks down and you knock to get in out of the rain and this big door opens and there he stands grinning in his evening cape and top hat and his eyes glow in the dark and he has this ghoulish pallor, and he says, "Goot evenink, von't you come in?" and he keeps staring at your wife's neck and his teeth start to drip. Off in the distance you hear a wolf howling and the pillow in the coffin in the corner looks slept on.

'You resist the temptation to ask him what time he turns into a bat or how his pet lycanthrope is doing.

'I mean, it's a great part for Bela Lugosi. Bram Stoker should cover his matches. "Count Dracula goes to Wimbledon." . . . Crowds shout, "Hey Ilie, your casket is ready!" Or, "Hey, Ilie how do you want your blood – straight up or over the rocks?"

'You're sure he lives in a place where the eyes in the portraits move and everyone is afraid to go down to the cellar. And the shutters bang all night and you don't want to know what it is that's howling in the basement or moaning under your window. You try not to look at the tombstones in the backyard.

'This is the image Ilie Nastase projects on a tennis court. Linesmen

183

are afraid to look into his eyes for fear they'll find themselves roaming across the countryside on moonless nights wearing a shroud and blank eyes.

'It is an image which is worth, perhaps, half a million a year to him and half a game a set. People love to come and shudder when he approaches the baseline, brandishes a racket at an umpire or goes after a heckler.

'His opponents buy the psyche and, nine chances out of ten, they come on court tight-lipped, tense, jumpy and angry and ready to take desperate chances to teach this terrible Transylvanian a lesson. In other words, just the way Ilie wants them.

'Now, will the real Ilie Nastase please stand up?'

On closer acquaintance Murray, like everyone else, found Ilie a little different.

'The real Ilie Nastase would make as lousy a Dracula as Jimmy Stewart. Vincent Price would turn the part down cold. If he lived in a castle, the only howling would come from Elvis Presley records. He drinks 7-Up not Type O . . . Take the racket away from Ilie Nastase and you go from Count Dracula to the Count of Monte Cristo, a suave, hand-kissing type, a lover not a lug.'

Perhaps it was a good thing I knew all that when on our first night back in Bucharest, Ilie and I set off to find a dinner party which was being held for Horst Dassler, the youthful boss of the vast Adidas organization. Dassler had landed at Bucharest Airport just a few minutes after us to begin a three-day business trip to Romania. For both professional and personal reasons he also wanted to spend as much time as possible with one of the biggest names his star-studded company has under contract. So when a dinner was arranged for Horst at a country lodge about twenty miles from the city, Ilie was asked to join the party as soon as he had finished practising at the Progresul.

'They say it's just ten kilometres past the airport,' said Ilie optimistically as we set out. 'I've never been there but we should find it OK.'

It soon became quite evident that we were not going to find it very quickly. Ilie may drive around the wide boulevards of Bucharest like James Hunt in pursuit of Nikki Lauda, but as soon as we hit the smaller roads on the other side of the airport, he dropped his speed to little more than 25-35 mph. It was easy to understand why. The road had become a paved but narrow strip running between rows of self-built cottages. Apart from slits of dim light peeping from behind half-drawn curtains, the only other illumination came from the head lamps of the Lancia. It was a good thing they were powerful because practically none of the bicycles we encountered had rear lights and every few hundred yards an enormous black mass on the side of the road would finally materialize into a parked lorry. If we came upon one of these at the same moment as Ilie had to dip his headlights for on-coming traffic, some rapid braking was required, even at 25 mph.

'If a foreigner drives out here for the first time at night, he will kill many people,' said Ilie. 'It happens sometimes.'

It was easy to believe. After a while we stopped to ask for directions, and Ilie was distressed to be told that the place was still twelve miles away. 'Shit, we're going to be late,' said Ilie, pushing the little car forward in short bursts of high-powered acceleration whenever he was absolutely sure there was a clear stretch of road in front of him. But that did not happen often and it was tiring work.

'Silly sons-of-bitches,' Ilie would exclaim as cyclists wobbled along the middle of the road. Eventually he fell silent – or at least verbally silent. For soon his strong, finely drawn right hand, resting on his knee when he was not changing gear, became his voice. One quickly got to understand the language. When we circumvented a truck or cyclist without too much trouble, the hand would flutter briefly like the wings of a bird, denoting mild annoyance. But if danger loomed too close, it would take off in a full sweep of anger and then settle, twitching, as we continued to dodge the shadowy figures thrown up by the dark Romanian night.

Finally we reached a junction with a sign for a place called Snagdov. 'We're supposed to turn here and then turn left after the monastery,' said Ilie. 'You know the Wallachian prince they based the legend of Count Dracula on? Vlad the Impaler they called him. He's buried near that monastery. Down by the lake somewhere.'

Terrific. I thought that was probably all we needed: Dracula's ghost leering through the car window offering directions. In fact when we did make another stop to ask the way, the two characters who helped us were more likely to have been invented by Peter Cook and Dudley Moore than Bram Stoker, author of the nineteenth-century novel *The Passion of Dracula*. They were a couple of peasants meandering their way home, their wide-brimmed hats pulled down low on the forehead, baskets over their shoulders; too drunk to risk riding the bicycles they were wheeling beside them.

'We're looking for the lodge where the big party is,' said Ilie.

The tall one, 'Pete,' stuck his head through the window, mixing the clear country air with the light alcoholic breath of wine and vodka. Grubby fingers stroked a long, stubbly chin and then the eyes flickered with comprehension as Ilie's question sunk in. Withdrawing himself from the car, he announced, 'Yes, sure I know where the party is. You

185

must turn round.' He swayed convincingly to demonstrate the required movement.

'You sure you know the party I mean,' asked Ilie suspiciously. It was obvious that 'Dud' and 'Pete' had found a very good party of their own. In the background I caught sight of the little one, 'Dud,' making faces and grinning inanely.

'Sure, sure I know,' replied 'Pete' with as much conviction as he could muster. 'Big party, lots of cars. You go back down this road and take the first left after the monastery when you have passed two signs.'

We left them standing in the middle of the road, going through sweeping movements with their arms like a couple of inebriated traffic wardens, chuckling happily.

They had given us tremendous directions. There weren't any signs and there was no first left after the monastery. After making another about turn just to make sure we hadn't missed it, Ilie pulled up in front of the huge wooden archway leading to the monastery. We both gazed up at it for a minute, a dark silhouette against the night sky. I knew what Ilie was thinking before he said it.

'You think we ought to take a look up there?' he asked. At that point Jim Murray might have run off screaming down the road, but as Ilie looked just about as scared as I felt, I thought we might as well venture on together.

It really was a bit eerie. The long, winding pathway up to the monastery was overgrown and hemmed in by trees and shrubbery and when the Lancia's headlights finally hit the outer wall, the whole area was suddenly flooded by a ghostly glow. Nothing stirred. It was about 9.30 p.m. by this time and the monks were either asleep or praying silently for Count Dracula's soul. 'Somehow I don't think there's a party round here,' said Ilie and our laughter broke the tension.

We made it back to the main road before anything fanged and frightening sprung from the bushes, and reverted to our original course, this time ignoring the turn off for Snagdov. 'Bloody people gave me the wrong directions,' said Ilie banging the steering wheel in exasperation. 'Turn left the guy told me and so did those couple of idiots back there. Somewhere there's got to be a road to the left.'

But there didn't seem to be. We drove on for about a mile until a car a few hundred yards in front suddenly pulled off the road – to the left! When we reached the spot where the car had disappeared, there was no signpost, not even a road. All we could see was a barely discernible track leading across an unkempt field.

'We might as well try it,' I suggested. 'There don't seem to be too many alternatives.'

After a few hundred yards, the rear lights of the car in front disappeared around a bend and when we made the turn, we found that the driver had pulled over to the side under the cover of some trees. Leaning across me, Ilie rolled down the window and called out. 'Is there a lodge further on? We're trying to find a dinner party.' The young man in the driver's seat stared at us blankly for a couple of seconds and then his face took on an expression of suspicion and disbelief. Ilie Nastase, possibly the most famous Romanian alive, was obviously not the person he had most expected to find in the middle of a field in the dead of night. 'Yea, I think so,' he replied cautiously. 'There's a house or something a few meters further on just by the lake.'

Just as we drove off I caught sight of a pretty blonde in the passenger seat. She had been leaning back to avoid what little light was filtering into the car.

'It's a good thing those two were looking for a place to make love, otherwise we would never have found the place,' I said.

'You mean there was a girl in the car?' Ilie asked. 'I never saw her. Jesus, that's great. I hope they have a good time!'

The young man had been more than just a determined lover. He also knew what he was talking about, which made a refreshing change. The lodge was there all right, and we were led straight through it out into an untidy garden back where some twenty people were seated at a long table. The grass was ankle high, and the cluster of trees stretched down to the lakeside where the throaty chortling of frogs could be heard competing with the babble of human conversation. And directly across the lake, huge, dark and forbidding in the moonless night, stood the monastery. Before anyone noticed his arrival, Ilie bounced up to the top of the table and greeted the guest of honor. 'Horst! So sorry we are late, but we would never have found it at all if we hadn't followed a couple looking for a place to screw!'

From then on, it became a pretty good party.

This was more than could be said of the Davis Cup against Britain. The odds on a Davis Cup tie passing without incident in Bucharest are never very good. But they verge on the ridiculous if you have two personalities like Ilie Nastase and David Lloyd in opposite teams. They simply become lightning rods for disaster.

With three brothers, David, John and Tony, all playing at international level, the Lloyds have become the first family of British tennis, rivalled on the world scene only by the Amritrajs from India who also have three brothers on the pro circuit. The Lloyds have been great for the game in Britain, giving our national teams a competitive backbone

187

they have often lacked in the past. As that is such a vital ingredient of any successful campaign at international level, it might seem counter productive to complain that, on occasions, the Lloyds as a family and David in particular suffer from a surfeit of nationalistic feeling. Their laudable competitive spirit is too often fired by an innate and somewhat old-fashioned belief that anything foreign is suspicious, probably devious and possibly not to be trusted at all. As David fights like a bulldog as soon as the action starts, this can often lead him into situations of unnecessary ill-feeling. And so it was in Bucharest.

But there was, as usual, a calm before the storm. On Friday, June 10, Britain battled through a hot and humid afternoon at the Progresul Club and ended up two rubbers down. That came as a disappointment to the young British captain, Paul Hutchins, who had expected that his No.1 singles player, John Lloyd, would defeat the inexperienced Romanian No.2, Dmitru Haradau. When Lloyd won the first set 6-2, there seemed every chance that he would. But Haradau proved himself a powerful and determined competitor and when Lloyd started to get cramp in his racket hand, the match slid away from him.

In the opening singles, John Feaver had performed creditably against Nastase in his first ever Davis Cup rubber. Like all players who suffer from periodic neurosis about various aspects of their game – which is 98 percent of pros on the tour – Feaver had, at that time, lost confidence in his serve. As the big West Countryman has one of the deadliest first serves in tennis, it was a considerable handicap to go into a match against Nastase in Bucharest with one's best shot on crutches. But when John started slicing his first serve instead of hitting it hard and flat, there was no doubt that it was in need of mental, if not physical, repair. Yet even without that potent weapon, Feaver showed a surprising aptitude for sticking to it on slow clay and, after winning the third set, he led 4-2 in the fourth before Ilie capitalized on a few English errors and ran it out 6-4.

The day's play had presented few problems for the experienced Spanish referee, Jaime Bartroli. The line calling had been above average and, to the occasional surprise of the large crowd, what few dubious calls there were tended to be called in favor of Britain. And from the point of view of clashing personalities, there was no problem between Nastase and Feaver. They had played doubles together once on the U.S. Indoor Circuit and had always gotten along.

But the next day the players on court produced very different vibes. Ilie Nastase and David Lloyd should never be separated by anything as frail and inadequate as a tennis net. A concrete wall, perhaps, or, if they insisted on being able to see each other, bulletproof glass might

188

suffice. But nothing which allows their high voltage nerve ends to rub themselves raw. With two people who basically find each other irritating, it is only a question of time before the sparks create an almighty explosion.

On this occasion it took a little over an hour. Nastase and Tiriac had won the first set 9-7 and the Lloyds were leading 2-0 in the second when, in play reminiscent of Dibbs in Dallas, David Lloyd chased a wide ball at such speed that he ended up on the Romanians' side of the net. As fate would have it, David and Ilie were in the net positions as John Lloyd prepared to serve the next point, so verbal contact became all too easy.

Nastase began making some funny and relatively harmless remark about David trespassing on Romanian territory. Whether David heard what Nastase said correctly or not is a moot point. What is clear is that he had been waiting for Nastase to make a wrong move. And at the first suggestion of it, Lloyd, bristling visibly, pounced.

'What was that you said?' David snapped back, cocking his head in Nastase's direction. Even from the stands, his whole stance, expression and attitude seemed provocative, and from a distance of five feet across the net there was no way that Ilie was going to have enough self-control or sense to resist what seemed to him to be a challenge.

So he replied with a phrase that threatened to give oral sex a bad name. David heard that clearly enough and still not satisfied that he had hooked his fish, said, 'What was that? I didn't hear.'

Nastase was probably quite well aware of what he was letting himself in for, but there is something in his character which will not allow him to back away, even if the bait is clearly marked 'DANGER – DON'T TOUCH.' So once again he repeated the insult and Lloyd had got him.

'That's it, that's it,' David shouted in a fit of moral indignation. 'I'm not taking any more of that.' And he strode off court. The crowd, who had heard nothing of the conversation at the net, were momentarily stunned, but quickly added their own cacophony of boos and whistles to a state of total confusion which had erupted on court.

At first David said he was going to quit in protest. Then in quick succession, David and Ilie started to walk toward each other gesticulating; Tiriac and Bartroli got between them; Nastase tried to tap Lloyd over the head (David later maintained that Ilie hit him with his racket); Paul Hutchins tried to talk to Bartroli; the British coach, Roger Becker, raced down out of the players' enclosure to have a soothing word with David who had been frog-marched backwards off court by Bartroli and Constantin Nastase, the Romanian captain, and up in his chair the umpire made vain attempts to attract somebody's attention. Only John

Lloyd stayed on his side of the net, aloof from the chaos.

After a full ten-minute hiatus, Bartroli got everyone back on court and publicly warned Nastase for insulting behavior. The line calling continued to be generally good and even the British players acknowledged later that Tiriac had been excellent throughout, never disputing a call and once even signalling a dubious decision in Britain's favor. Tiriac seemed to be enjoying his role as the elder statesman in this tie. With much shaking of his curly head and shrugging of the shoulders, he adopted a gently superior air to any dispute that arose, as if admonishing little kiddies for getting up to such childish games. The American Davis Cup team that had battled with Tiriac on the same court five years before would not have recognized him.

But even Tiriac in this benign mood could not prevent further arguments from flaring up as the match progressed. The score had reached 8-7 to Romania in the fourth set when Bartroli changed a call in Britain's favor, thus making John Lloyd 15-30 down on his serve instead of facing three match points. Then it started to rain in earnest. Obviously the Romanians wanted to continue and just as obviously Hutchins wanted to get his team off court. Anything to break a spell when it is going against you. Once again David Lloyd was the most visible advocate for stopping and when Bartroli finally decided to call the players off, David, swathed in a huge towel that made him look like a senator in Ancient Rome, gave the hissing crowd a deep, facetious bow and marched out of the arena.

In the corridor leading to the locker room, Nastase confronted Hutchins. 'You running this match, Mr. Hutchins?' Ilie asked coldly. 'Or perhaps David Lloyd is?' 'It's the referee's decision,' Hutchins replied.

When the match resumed, David netted a forehand volley; John hit a smash out of court; and Romania had gained an unassailable 3-0 lead in the tie. But the drama was not over.

That evening an extraordinary dinner took place in the large restaurant of the Inter-Continental Hotel. The hotel was evidently not very busy that weekend for the British team virtually had the place to themselves. A group of Africans occupied one nearby table and over in a far corner, John Parsons of the *Daily Mail* – the only British tennis writer farsighted enough to have made the trip – entertained Christopher Bullock, the chairman of the LTA to dinner.

Hutchins' team were seated at a large circular table in the middle of the room. Apart from the Lloyds and John Feaver, the party included Roger Becker, a Davis Cup player himself back in the early sixties, and Richard Lewis, a big, blond left-hander who was the fourth man on the squad.

Evidently Hutchins had been at a series of meetings since the end of the match, both with members of his team and with Jaime Bartroli; but none seemed to have helped to alleviate the feeling of acute disappointment and nervous tension that still pervaded the group. And one major and quite startling suggestion remained unresolved: A move was afoot for the British team to pack their bags and leave without completing the remaining two rubbers, as both Davis Cup rules and sporting etiquette demanded. Needless to say, it was David Lloyd who was advocating this drastic action, and he was supported by Roger Becker.

'Even if there's a small chance of it doing some good, it would be worth it,' said David. 'Sometime, somewhere, someone's just got to take a stand against Nastase's type of behavior and we have a golden opportunity to do it right now. How is anyone ever going to be able to persuade kids that Nastase's antics are not the proper way to behave on a tennis court if we go on condoning it?'

'But we've lost,' Feaver interjected. 'It would look like sour grapes.'

'Quite apart from that, we've got a problem with Bartroli,' Hutchins added. 'He says he never heard Ilie make those remarks to David and never saw David being hit over the head with a racket. He feels that in the circumstances, he cannot put those incidents in his report to the ITF. So without evidence from the referee to back our action, I think we'd just risk having ourselves banned from the Davis Cup next year.'

'Then it's not worth it,' said John Lloyd. 'British tennis would lose and the Romanians would get off free. What would be the point in that?'

Becker shook his head. 'I tend to agree with David. No matter what the consequences, I just think it is time someone took a stand.'

'That's right,' said David vehemently. 'You guys can do what you want, but I'm on that early flight in the morning no matter what.'

'How can you leave the team now?' Lewis shot back heatedly. 'We've worked as a team, trained as a team, played as a team and we should stick it out as a team. How can you bugger off now just because you're upset?'

'Well, I'm sorry but I'm going and that's that,' David replied. 'If you're gutless enough not to come to a decision either way, I can't help it.'

'Well, I wish you'd fuck off right now,' Lewis retorted, his blond features suddenly turning crimson with rage. 'And if you're going to call me gutless, you can step outside and we'll discover who's gutless. No one's ever called me that before.'

If honor and moral behavior are close relations then one could argue, somewhat ironically, that it was David's complaint about the lowering of the standard of behavior which had created the row in the first place.

Even so, the elder Lloyd had to keep a very firm grip on himself to avoid getting dragged into a brawl. For Lewis suddenly slammed down his soup spoon, jumped up and grabbed David by the collar, twisting it in a large fist and in an effort to yank him to his feet. Refusing to react, David stared down at his plate and said nothing. Everyone round the table froze in a mixture of shock and embarrassment. The French-speaking Africans at the next table were the first to react.

'*Eh, doucement, mon ami,*' one of them said.

'Oh, shut up,' snarled Lewis, who eventually responded to the more recognizable tones of his captain and his coach by resuming his seat.

'Bloody idiots,' someone muttered as the Africans cracked jokes about what to them must have seemed an amusing scene.

'I think,' said Feaver, 'they would have more right to call us idiots.'

'Look, try and calm down,' Hutchins interjected. 'We're all uptight and it's getting to us.'

'You mean, *he's* got to us,' replied Lewis who was slowly returning to his normal color. 'Bloody Nastase's the one who got through us.'

And of course Richard Lewis was right. With one obscene and insulting phrase repeated twice across a net, Nastase had set friend against friend and temporarily disrupted the excellent team spirit – so eloquently voiced by Lewis in his moment of anger – that Hutchins had carefully nurtured. That was much more than Ilie had intended, if, indeed, he had intended anything. Having had the red rag waved in his face, he had simply unsheathed his horns and gored. The wounds, as usual, had run deep.

If any player but David Lloyd had been on the other side of that net, it would probably never have happened. (But Kipling did not write 'If' with Nastase in mind. 'If you can keep your head when all about you/ Are losing theirs and blaming it on you. . .' No, no – Ilie can never be counted on to handle stuff like that.) Occasionally, Ilie can surprise everyone with his reaction to adverse circumstances, as he was to demonstrate at Wimbledon just a few days later, but generally it is no use lingering over 'ifs' with Nastase. (A lot of things could have turned out differently for him if. . . .)

But there weren't many question marks left when this particular situation had run its course. After a long, heart-searching talk with Hutchins after dinner, David Lloyd reluctantly agreed to stay with the team. But when the ITF pronounced judgment several months later after reading Bartroli's report, David was partially vindicated even though he did not escape mild censure himself. For the International Federation decided to get tough with Ilie and banned him from all Davis Cup play in 1978 – Bartroli having finally decided to back up Hutchins' sweeping condemnation of Nastase's behavior in his own report. The Spanish referee did, however, point out that Lloyd himself had acted in a provocative manner. It was a fair judgment.

JIMMY CONNORS
FRANK DEFORD

A man who has been the indisputable favorite of his mother keeps for life the feeling of conqueror, the confidence of success which often induces real success. SIGMUND FREUD

Jimmy Connors was the indisputable favorite of his grandmother as well, and so, he is most abundantly infused with this magic milk. It surges through his veins, suppressing every doubt and every defeat. And why not? The two women had promised him the world, and, just so, he grasped it in 1974: only 21, but already champion of all he surveyed, Alexander astride Bucephalus astride the globe. He won the Wimbledon final with the loss of but six games, Forest Hills with the loss of but two. Wise men in tennis sat about and seriously contemplated whether he would win every major title for, say, the next decade.

Conqueror was what he was, too, because Connors did not merely win. He assaulted the opposition, laid waste to it, often mocked it, as well, simply by the force of his presence. The other players feared to go against him, because the most awesome legend that can surround any athlete sprang up about Connors: the better any mortal played against him, the better Connors became. So, he became invincible upon the court, just because no man could beat him, and he was inviolate off the court, because his mother had told him so.

Two months ago, on July 8, Connors lost the 1978 Wimbledon final, winning only seven games against an ascendant Bjorn Borg. Since 1974 Connors has played in seven major finals and lost six.

What has happened is disillusioning for Connors and his mother. They speak of the latest rack and ruin by Borg in hallucinatory terms, and Jimmy fitfully retreats to the glorious conquests of yore. 'They'll be talking about '74 when I'm dead. . . . Don't forget what I did in '74 . . . Nobody can ever take '74 from me.' On and on like that. And the greatest irony is that '74 will be devalued if he does not triumph over Borg in '78, because this year Borg can win the Grand Slam and the Davis Cup – and as extraordinary as '74 was, Connors did not achieve that. For history, then, what would '74 become but a real good year a kid had just before Borg became great?

And that was so long ago – 1974. Since then Connors' father has died, and his surrogate father – his manager, Bill Riordan – has become estranged from him. His only male instructor, Pancho Segura, has been discharged. His engagement to Chris Evert, the one sweet love of his life, was called off, nearly at the altar. Looking back, it all began to unravel then, the loss of dear ones and tournaments alike. A kind of incompleteness has come to plague Connors. In the big tournaments, the ones he shoots for, he virtually never loses until the finals. What is it there? What seizes him at the last step? There is a flaw somewhere, something that denies him consummation in his life.

'It happened so fast,' Chris Evert says. Oddly, she and Jimmy have matured more in the difficult ways of their love than they have as players in a simple game. 'There was no emotional foundation, nothing to fall back on.' Evert says. 'You must never forget that he made No.1 when he was 21, and now he's not No.1. That makes him so defensive. You see, he's still a champion. He isn't No.1, but he hasn't lost the qualities of a champion.'

It is suddenly fashionable to blithely dismiss Connors as a mere cipher again. Borg – as easy as it once was to consider Connors unbeatable. But no, there is too much of the sublime in Connors' game to suggest that anyone ever could own him. The technique is still all there, but the passion has been muted. So now, starting this week at the U.S. Open, we shall find out if the man is capable of what once the boy and mother accomplished. For that matter, we shall find out soon enough if there is a man to surmount the boy.

In retrospect, Arthur Ashe may have dismantled the invincible Jimbo by upsetting him in the 1975 Wimbledon final. Although he won Forest Hills in 1976, Connors has never really been the same since. In the months before the Ashe match, in the period after Jimmy and Chrissie broke up, Connors had already begun to self-destruct – ballooning in weight, running imperiously over good people and firm obligations. But by Wimbledon time he was primed, and all the more forbidding for the callousness he had displayed.

Now rampant upon the court, he did not lose a set in the early matches at Wimbledon. In the semifinals, he came up against Roscoe Tanner, who has the best service in the game. That day Tanner was serving at his very best – yet Connors obliterated him 6-4, 6-1, 6-4. *The New York Times* correspondent, Fred Tupper, an able – and restrained

– tennis authority for several decades, wrote in awe, 'Did anybody ever see a ball hit so hard? . . . Connors' performance today staggers the imagination and confuses the memory.'

Incredibly, Connors rose to this majesty despite a secret leg injury – something called an interior compartment syndrome – which he had suffered in his opening match. After beating Tanner, Connors went to Chelsea Hospital, and as he lay on the examination table the doctors called Riordan aside and told him that the damage to the leg was growing dangerous, and the final could only be played at the risk of crippling Connors, perhaps of ending his career. Riordan broke the news to Connors, who replied that it was the final of Wimbledon and he had to play. Riordan then turned to leave, and Connors called plaintively to him.

'Bill,' he said, 'don't tell Mom.'

Connors and his mother shared a hotel room (they are as frugal as they are close). She knew he was going for treatments, but not that he was putting his playing life – the one she had created for him – on the line.

Ashe beat him badly. There was no evidence that Connors was at a physical disadvantage, but he played as if in a daze. Ashe changed his style for the match, as Borg would come up with new tricks for him years later – but Connors could not, or would not, adjust. There were no alibis afterward. There never are. Although often crude and ill-mannered upon the court, Connors is almost always a gracious sportsman once the game is done. But Ashe had belled the cat. The conqueror that the mother and the grandmother had carefully fashioned was exposed. Riordan, who did not tell Mom, was banished by the end of the summer; Chrissie and Segura were already gone. And also departing soon enough was that unshakable confidence, the mystical armor his mother had spent a childhood dressing him in.

Two months after the Ashe defeat, Connors lost another final, to Manolo Orantes at Forest Hills. By now he was indulging himself with groupies and food, taking both to excess. Under tension, Connors gorges himself. At tournaments, *in training*, he will devour four or five large meals a day. At that time, in '75, lost and depressed, he gained 30 pounds. One day in Acapulco he saw himself in the mirror – 'a spare tire, fat face; I only had slits for eyes.' He reached for the phone, 'After I called my mom, I lost 18 pounds in the next two weeks,' he says.

And so he started back; but something was never recovered from that night at Chelsea Hospital and the next afternoon on Centre Court. By this summer of 1978, even before he fell to Borg, other players had begun to see in Connors a pathetic parody of his old self. 'Jimmy's always exuded such confidence,' Ashe says, 'and real or not, it seemed

196

all the more intimidating because it was cocooned in that aura of bravado and brashness. But now even that seems specious. He's scared about something. I don't know what's happened, but he's not the same.'

'The kid is psyched,' says Riordan. At Wimbledon, Riordan took Borg at 7 to 1 to win in straight sets and cashed in big against his Jimbo.

Gloria Thompson Connors proudly points out that she and her mother are the only women ever to have developed a men's champion. Whatever more Jimmy achieves, theirs was an amazing accomplishment, and no one should be surprised at the obvious – at how much the mother lives for the son and how much he depends on her. Naturally, if this were not so, it never could have worked.

Of the other major influences upon Jimbo, Segura was merely brought in as a retainer, a male totem, to help Connors 'think like a man' on the court, while Riordan was tapped as something of a necessary evil in the shattered times after the grandmother, Bertha Thompson, died in 1972. Bertha was known as Two Mom, a name bestowed on her by Johnny, the older of the two Connors children. Johnny had originally been cast as the future champion, but, as Gloria has noted many times, he lacked the requisite 'guts.' The second boy, the lefthander, did not. Eerily, it was Jimmy whom Gloria was carrying when she personally cut and cleared the land behind their house to build the tennis court that would give meaning to her life.

This sporting monument at 632 North 68th Street, East St. Louis, Ill. is now grown over, in disrepair. But then, so is the whole town run down, forgotten by the whites who abandoned it. But while East St. Louis was never fashionable, while it was always the other side, when Gloria Thompson was growing up there it was a well-kept blue-collar borough, the municipal manor of Mayor John T. Connors.

That was Jimmy's grandfather. Mayor Connors had one son, Big Jim, a good-looking, well-liked fellow of no particular abilities. He was sent off to Notre Dame and, back home, was provided with the sinecure of running the toll bridge that spanned the Mississippi into St. Louis at the other end of 68th Street.

Gloria's father, Al Thompson, was chief of the city parks police. Hers was a disciplined, rock-ribbed upbringing. As the Connorses were open and genial, so were the Thompsons tight and skeptical, even suspicious. Jimmy Connors got his athletic genes from the maternal side. Al Thompson had been a middleweight boxer and a lifeguard, and when he and Two Mom were courting, they shared their love this way: he taught her to swim, she taught him to play tennis. They had one child, and the happiest times of Gloria's life were spent at Jones Park, which she recalls as a nearly idyllic place where she would swim in a sand-bottomed pool and then skip past a beautiful lagoon to the tennis courts. 'Believe me,' she declares earnestly, 'I never went to a country club as nice as Jones Park.' The remark is not offhand. Tennis was a country-club activity, and the Thompsons, the cop's family, insular by nature, grew even more defensive as tennis brought them into contact with the swells across the river.

Says a St. Louisan who has known the family for many years, 'Gloria was taught, "They're all out to get us," and that's what she taught Jimmy. His mother is the only person he trusts. They're really not comfortable with anybody else. They have such overpowering loyalty to each other that they're incapable of any lasting outside relationships. Their own relationship is spooky. I swear, it's always been like there was a tube going from her veins into his.' One of the first things mother and son bring up (independently) is that she can correct his game over the telephone merely by sensing what has gone awry.

Gloria was a fine athlete in her youth but there was no evidence then of the drive and single-mindedness that would consume her on behalf of her son. Pauline Betz Addie, a world tennis champion in the mid '40s, says, 'It's impossible for me to believe these accounts of Gloria today – hard and mean. Never. She was the sweetest, most ingenuous lovely person.' She was pretty, too, a good catch. Surely no one in the world photographs worse than Gloria Connors. In fact, she is a lovely woman, gossamer feminine, all grace and poise. The good-timing mayor's boy, who had had his eye on Gloria since childhood, wooed her, married her, and they settled in the trim little red brick house on 68th Street.

This marriage of opposites never worked. Big Jim died of cancer last year and both Gloria and Jimmy stoutly uphold his memory, but from all objective accounts, theirs was a house divided by tennis. Big Jim learned of his son's engagement to Chrissie over the radio. When Jimmy won Wimbledon in '74, he couldn't be bothered to take his father's congratulatory phone call. Gloria explains it this way, 'My husband enjoyed being around people in the evenings, and, of course, he had to take care of Johnny. We all had to sacrifice. You see, we more or less had to part ways if Jimmy was to play the tournaments he had to. Two Mom and I had a job to do.'

Unlike Johnny, now a teaching pro in Atlanta, Jimmy's interest in competitive tennis never flagged. 'I've been known as a pushy stage-door [sic] mother, but my biggest problem was to stop him from playing tennis,' Gloria says. 'He's always been the same. Why, he couldn't wait to kick the slats out of his playpen and get started in life. *But al-*

198

ways a homebody. Johnny would like to spend the night at other boys' houses. Not Jimmy. He was so happy just being in his own home. You know, he was so much like his grandmother especially. Why, we were a team. We were three peas in a pod.'

Soon everything was devoted to Jimmy's tennis potential. It was Gloria's pleasure to become, as she describes it, 'a human backboard.' No detail was overlooked. On the boys' circuit, free tournament housing would be declined, and the team would spend money it really couldn't afford to spend to stay in a motel, so that Jimbo would not get chummy with the children he had to beat. In St. Louis, Gloria would transport him about to clubs, soliciting good adult players to hit with the child. Those who lacked the zeal for this pastime were dismissed as snobs. At the same time, those pros who took an interest in the boy and sought to help his game were suspected of trying to 'steal' him from his mother.

Two Mom told Gloria. 'Don't bring anybody else into the picture. You made him, Glo. Don't ever hand him over to anybody.' If there is one thread that weaves most prominently through the whole fabric of the relationship, it is this one. And yet, contrary to what is generally assumed, Mrs. Connors does not appear to be motivated by selfishness. No, she is simply and utterly devoted to this son, and she is convinced that no one else can serve him so well as she.

'Yes, sir, we fought it,' Gloria says. 'But if no one would play with Jimmy, *he had me.* I played him every day – every good day – of the year, every year. And we played hard. We taught him to be a tiger. "Get those tiger juices flowing!" I would call out, and I told him to try and knock the ball down my throat, and he learned to do this because he found out that if I had the chance I would knock it down his. Yes sir. And then I would say, "You see, Jimbo, you see what even your own mother will do to you on a tennis court?"

Ah, but off the court he was pampered; bikes and go-carts, a pony. More important, he was spoiled emotionally, always shielded from life's little adversities. This arrangement remains in force to this day. Connors is about as difficult to reach as any public figure in the country; he has been protected for so long that he will go to almost any lengths to avoid personal confrontation off the court; by his own admission he finds it constitutionally impossible to say no. He avoids contention in real life as he seems to seek it on the court.

It is all bizarre and contradictory. Once Connors has been freed, he is not only wonderfully genial, but he also seems to enjoy himself. In paid personal appearances, he is charming, considerate of strangers and supplicants to a fault. He will never refuse an autograph. Children adore him, and he seems happiest of all in the haven of their innocent affection.

But now it seems the price of a lifetime of the Connors insularity must be paid upon the court. Connors seems incapable of making hard decisions – even to honestly assess, much less change, his game or strategy. Out there, on the concrete garden, only the tiger was formed – and his only response is to salivate more tiger juices. That very quality of his mother's that protected him, that let him gain the world championship, now appears to be vitiating him. 'Wouldn't you be different with your mother around all the time?' Ilie Nastase says. 'I don't mean better or worse, I just mean very different.'

Nastase was once very close with Connors. Then, at their TV challenge match in 1976, Nastase was wounded by some tiger-juice insults that Connors hurled at him, and last year, in a match at Caesars Palace – where Connors had never been beaten in a dozen outings – Nastase was prepared. When Connors began abusing him, Nastase stopped him dead by saying, 'You don't want to fight. Go get your mother.' Connors, shaking, was beaten for the first time on that court.

Acknowledging the incident, Nastase adds beseechingly, 'Hey, don't get Gloria mad at me.' For, notwithstanding Pauline Addie's tender memories, Mrs. Connors is feared. She is feared as a zealot, for being an implacable advocate for her son. When, after months of negotiations, Riordan obtained the unheard-of guarantee of $500,000 for a single match – a figure so large even CBS considered it obscene and refused to divulge it – Gloria's first response was that it should be a million. Last year a three-man round-robin among Borg, Vilas and Connors was set up for television. Michelob was bankrolling it for $1 million: $500,000 for the winner, $300,000 for the runner-up, $200,000 for show. At worst, 200 grand for losing two exhibitions over a weekend. 'Isn't there something else?' Mrs. Connors said to the promoter, Gene Scott. 'There has to be an extra $250,000 for Jimbo.' Michelob, aghast at this hubris, walked.

Such examples are legion. The possibility that somebody somewhere might 'use' Jimbo haunts the Connors entourage. What makes this all the more fascinating is that neither Gloria nor Jimmy gives a tinker's damn about money. In all their lives, they have been extravagant only with their love and loyalty for one another.

In her devotion to him, Gloria makes sure that everyone pays in some way to use Jimbo – the press in the currency of delay and exasperation, which it can least afford. She is herself, frankly 'scared' of the press, and she has a right to be, for she is never treated sympathetically, and often savagely. Jimmy's image may be as negative, but the press is hardly to blame; his cockiness and vulgarity, the strut and bluster, are visible enough that they do not need to be filtered through newspaper columns in order to produce a bad public taste.

But poor Gloria: the existing impression of her derives more from deep-seated biases. People who don't know Mrs. Connors from Mrs. Calabash just plain don't like the idea of her. She is, first of all, dead correct in what she has perceived: that she is viewed as a stage mother, and that Americans do not approve of that species. It is dandy for Mickey Mantle's father to instruct his son to switch-hit, but only a pushy dame like Judy Garland's mother would shove that poor kid onto the stage. Moreover, in our affluent society, parents who lavish stereos and Toyotas upon their children are approved of, while those who only devote their time and talent are eyed suspiciously; they make other parents feel guilty. This is all the more so with Gloria, because as a coach she comes in the wrong sex. She and Jimmy are also victims of sexism.

To be sure, it is an unusual relationship. To be sure, Gloria is on guard in private, and Jimmy is obnoxious in public. Guaranteed, they will find a way to louse up public relations. And yet, for all the negative consequences that this unusual relationship might encompass, nobody ever pauses to acknowledge the greater truths: that this relationship contains an extraordinary amount of love, and that this relationship made Jimmy Connors champion of the world.

By now they expect no quarter. Having been cross-examined on their relationship for so long, they are both defensive – as Nastase proved consummately – and they both have pat answers. They maintain that all final decisions are Jimbo's, and both will intimate archly that people who are offended by their relationship probably have very unhappy family histories themselves. Says Jimmy, 'The people who talk meanly about my mom and me are just a lot of people who are jealous. Wouldn't most people like to love their mom or dad the way I do?' He always adds the 'or dad' when making this point.

As important as Gloria has been to her son, she has never really been isolated with him until now. Two Mom was a constant presence for the first two decades. 'Our right arm,' as Gloria always refers to her, Stonewall Jackson to her Lee. Jimmy is just as emphatic. 'Both my mom and my grandma gave me my blood.' So much was Two Mom on the road with Gloria and Jimmy that the family took to calling Al 'Lonesome Pop,' and, after Two Mom died (while in Los Angeles, with Gloria), Lonesome Pop suggested it might be more appropriate for Gloria to take his cemetery plot next to Two Mom's.

One of the reasons why Riordan, the outsider, could come to exert such authority for a time was that he was, in effect, Two Mom's legacy. She had admired him, and suggested to Gloria that if they ever did need a male specialist off the court, he might fill the bill. Riordan, who is in bitter litigation against the family now, is a non-person in their eyes who tried to take over tennis by 'using' Jimmy as the wedge, but the fact cannot be avoided that he was a major male influence in Jimmy's life at precisely that time when he was leaving adolescence and becoming a public figure. With legal suits that became a crusade approaching paranoia, Riordan probably brought a surfeit of contentiousness into the life of a boy already brimming with antagonisms.

But Riordan did provide Connors with a close, influential adult male figure for the only time in his life – and it showed. Away from the tennis Establishment, Connors exhibited an ease and good humor that he has never again shown. Granted, some of his comic material came with lines written, inflection indicated, by Riordan, but the public image was of a dead-end kid who could stop and laugh at the world and himself. Since Riordan's leavening influence has disappeared, this breezy Cagney figure has hardened into a surly and sour wiseguy – the bluster and forced antics culminating in the mortifying episode at Forest Hills last year when Connors ran around the net onto the other side of the court and erased a ball mark that his opponent, Corrado Barazzutti, was citing as evidence of a bad call. (Connors says now he blacked out on his feet and doesn't recall the incident.)

Jimmy was so at home with Riordan because he obviously could see much of his father in him. Like Big Jim, hanging around the Stop Light Restaurant back home, telling stories, having some Scotches, laughing with the gang – '*My husband enjoyed being around people in the evenings,*' says Gloria – Riordan is a social animal, in search of any crowd to which he can distribute his blarney and sly jests out of the corner of his mouth. He really fits in: a conservative Catholic, devoted to tennis, with a strong wife and tight family ties. 'Bill was a father image for Jimmy,' Chris Evert says. 'He put a lot on the line for this guy. I don't mean just his reputation. Jimmy put his emotions up for Riordan.'

Playing, competing, with a racket in his left hand, Jimbo is more a Thompson than a Connors – in a sense, he is Jimmy Thompson. Has any player ever been more natural? But then, in an instant, he wiggles his tail, waves a finger, tries to joke or be smart, tries too hard – for he is not facile in this way and his routines are forced and embarrassing, and that is why the crowds dislike him. He is Jimmy Thompson no more. He is trying so hard to be Jimmy Connors, raised by women to conquer men, but unable to be a man, to be Big Jim or Bill Riordan. He is unable to be one of the boys.

Connors says he 'holds no grudges' against Riordan, but there is no question but that the older man took something valuable of Jimmy's when he was sent packing. 'So much of it goes back to Jimmy's growing up, to the way people back home treated him,' Evert says. ' This was all inside him, and then he confided in Riordan, put his emotions on the line for him, and now he feels betrayed. So now his attitude is: You see, it is true. It is. I can't trust anybody.'

Then, Riordan gone, body and soul, Connors' real father died of cancer on Jan. 30, 1977. Jimmy was holding Big Jim's hand at the end. At the time, Connors' traveling companion was Marjie Wallace, a former Miss World, but she faded from Jimmy's life shortly after his father died, and there has been no serious new romantic interest since then.

Last year Connors was sometimes convoyed about by a hard-nosed phalanx of Gilbert and Sullivan bodyguards, but they have been super-seded, mercifully, by Lornie Kuhle, an affable 34-year-old Las Vegas teaching pro. Kuhle is a favorite practice partner and a devoted friend ('You know what Jimmy is? He's just a good American kid'), but obvi-ously he cannot harvest the emotional ground that lovers and fathers have turned and planted.

So Gloria's universe expands. Now she is everything to Jimmy: mother (he calls her 'Mom' in that capacity), coach ('Coach'), best friend and business manager ('Glo'). So totally involved are Gloria and Jimmy with one another that, since it was knocked down to a two-person operation, the mother and son have engaged in some dreadful arguments; shouting matches in hotel rooms, Jimmy using some four-letter names that tennis people have been embarrassed to overhear. Both mother and son dismiss these episodes as healthy outbursts. 'Look, I can cut it for you,' Connors says. 'First, she's my mom – you know, the one who creates you. She's my mom first and always will be. But she's my coach and my friend too, and if we scream at each other sometimes, that just clears the air. That's good among friends.'

Only Evert appears to be in a position to exert a major influence on Connors. She fills all the necessary criteria. She is female, which he pre-fers – 'I'd rather be friends with a woman than a man any day' – and she is enduring. All of the Connors family intimates must stand the test of time. Besides, it is obvious by now that Chrissie and Jimmy can't get each other out of their systems. That doesn't necessarily mean that they will marry someday. It just means they can't get each other out of their systems.

In fact, what has emerged from a teenage infatuation is a tender, un-derstanding adult affection. 'We fell in love when we were so young,' says Chris, 'before we were friends. Jimmy has always worked harder on the court than anyone, but he's always been completely pampered off. His mom thinks he deserved it that way. So you must be very attentive to Jimmy. And I don't want to sound harsh, please, because much of this also applies to me, to athletes in general. So when we were together, each of us was thinking about ourselves. It's very tough for Jimmy to give on those occasions, because he gives so much on the court, and you come to expect it off. And then, of course, most of the time you *do* get it off the court. Imagine us, two kids so young, in love for the first time, each expecting the other to give.' She shakes her head.

With Chris, with any woman, Connors feels more relaxed 'because I'm never in competition with them.' Besides, as he was schooled to be a tiger on the court, so was he taught to be a gentleman off, and nowhere is this more evident than in his relationships with women. He believes in ladies, old-fashioned manners and modesty. The well-publicized itinerant liaison with Marjie Wallace was really something of a baffling interlude, because the family background, as Mrs. Connors volunteers, was very puritanical. She herself had a 'girls academy' upbringing. Jimmy spent several years in parochial schools, and, indeed, the ostensible reason for Two Mom being drafted as an extra escort was that the family considered it scandalous that a married woman would journey about alone, with only a child. In private conversation, Jimmy can go literally for hours without so much as a 'damn' escaping his lips, and in the men's locker room he is known for his obsessive modesty, never appearing without a towel held primly about his waist.

So here, perhaps, is the greatest contradiction of all between the public figure and the private man: a genuine personal prudery contrasted with the grotesque machismo and vulgarity he flaunts upon his stage. Connors' court pantomimes are invariably sexual, his imprecations obscene, his attempts at comedy and his belligerent statements sexual or scatological. For a time he and Nastase used to drift into a mincing 'queer' act. Jimbo was going to show the world that he is not some sissy or mama's boy, but that he can be as coarse and crude as any father's son.

Not even Riordan could fathom these upside-down transformations. 'Jimbo was so thoughtful,' he says. 'He always called his mom. Whenever he saw me, he'd ask about Terry, my wife. When I first sent him to Europe, he clung to me at the airport. "Bill, please don't leave me," he said. He was such a child. And we had such fun. I could make Jimmy laugh.

204

'But then all of a sudden, out of the blue, he'd be obscene, and I'd just get lost then, because it was so distasteful to me. And I never understood any of that in him, because it doesn't fit. Which is strange, because that's how he is on the court, that's what people see the most. But it's not his dominant side – not at all. And I could forget it and go on being fond of him because we had so many good things, so many good times, and there should have been so much more of that ahead.'

One day, when Jimbo was 11 or 12, Gloria and Two Mom took him out to the backyard court and told him it was time to abandon his childish two-handed backhand and start learning to hit backhands with one hand. This had always been their intention. The two women watched the child hit one-handed for a couple of days, and then Two Mom said 'Let's put it back, Glo. By the time he's 19 or 20 he should be able to tear tennis apart with the two-handed backhand.' Two Mom, as usual, was right as rain.

Still, as great as Connors' backhand is – one of the three or four best shots in tennis history – what always set the kid apart was his ability to be offensively unorthodox; he scores best from defensive situations, especially with the return of serve. No one ever used an opponent better against himself. No wonder players hated to face him.

For power, Connors learned to literally throw himself at the ball. His main source of strength comes from his thighs; it is his secret, a perfect, fluid weight transfer. And then, finally, he grew adept at what is known in tennis as hitting the ball on the rise – meeting the ball as it comes off the court, before it bounces at its apex. That is the ultimate attack taking it on the rise, a man spitting back bullets. It speeds up the game infinitesimally in time, exponentially in fact, by putting constant pressure upon the other man. To hit on the rise requires three essentials: excellent vision (Connors is 20-15), superb coordination (he even slugs with a trampoline-like steel racket) and utter confidence.

And so the Connors' all-court game grew as a whole, each part advancing with all the others, and one day, when he was 16, only five years before he was to win Wimbledon, he beat his mother. He came to the net apologetic, and said, 'Gee, Mom, that hurt. I didn't mean to do that.'

Gloria almost cried. 'No, no, Jimmy,' she said. 'Don't you know? This is one of the happiest days of my life.'

But now it seems that everything thereafter has been anticlimatic. Even winning just came naturally, in the wake. Nothing ever changes. To even acknowledge that changes might be considered would, it seems, repudiate all that Gloria and Two Mom did with a child many years ago. For example, Connors' serve had always been relatively weak, and Borg exposed it at Wimbledon as an outright liability. But when Jimmy and his mother worked out for a week after that defeat no special attention was paid to his serve, to his forehand approach or to any other of the weaker elements of his game. 'His serve is good enough for me,' Gloria says emphatically, peeved. 'We just worked on the overall game. Borg just had one of those days, like Jimmy did in '74 against Rosewall.'

Unfortunately, Borg and Connors only meet in the finals, on Saturdays and Sundays, and those appear to be the two particular days Borg has. Besides, even if Borg did just happen to get hot at Wimbledon, the real crux of the matter is that even just a year ago, under no circumstances could Borg have ever routed Connors in straight sets. But Borg has worked on his game and it has matured. Borg, the machine, the robot – 'The Clone,' his colleagues call him – he, not the exciting, bombastic Connors, has put variety and spice into his game.

Connors is so locked into the past he cannot bear to change even his practice routines. Practices are rugged and spirited physically, but they only amount to 'hits' against lesser players. In Los Angeles, Connors' regular sparring partner is Stan Cantor, a middle-aged movie producer; on the road, he hits against Kuhle. Dick Stockton, who has known Jimmy since childhood, says, 'To improve, you must practise against players of your own ability and you must work on the individual parts of your game. If Jimmy really wanted Kuhle to help him, he'd have him hit 300 balls in a row to his forehand approach. But Jimmy can't change. He only knows one way.'

And that is precisely what Connors himself says, again and again, as a point of pride. 'It isn't me if I don't play the way my mom taught me. . ... My mom gave me my game, and she taught me one way, that lines were made to be hit. . ... My mom and my grandma were the *only* ones who ever touched my game, and they taught me to play one way. There's no other way.'

And as with style, so with intensity. Connors boasts, accurately, admirably, 'I peak every time I play.' He loved to hear Riordan, an old racetrack buff, tell stirring tales of Bill Hartack, the cantankerous jockey who was famous for two things: fighting the Establishment and riding every race as though it were the Kentucky Derby. 'My mom taught me she'd rather have me play correctly for 30 minutes, her way, than play messing around for two hours,' Jimmy says. 'Play 30 minutes right, then I could go ride my pony or minibike.' Thus, even practice games against Cantor or Kuhle are conducted as vendettas, with growling and curses. Every shot is for real. As ever, there is Gloria across the net. *You see, Jimmy, you see what even your own mother will do to you on the court?*

Just as Connors must give his all in every match, so does he exhibit uncommon physical courage. In 1977 he played all of Wimbledon with a broken left thumb. When an X-ray technician brought the news, he said, 'Well, Mr. Connors, I guess you won't be playing tennis for a few weeks.' Connors sneered, 'You want to bet, sucker?' They put on a splint that dug in so hard the blood was gushing down his arm. The Connorses came back for another splint; they never told a soul, there would be no excuses, and he went to 6-4 in the fifth set of the finals, to that very last step, when, as ever, it was not his thumb that kept him from winning.

And yet, in contrast, since 1974 Connors has defaulted from almost 20 tournaments, often with the most transparent excuses of ill health at the 11th hour. ' Why should I let someone make a name off of me, beating me when I'm not right?' Connors snaps. Nobody uses Jimbo. What he does not say is what is apparent, that whereas he needs a physical excuse to get him off the hook, he is 'not right' for psychological reasons. If there is not enough animosity on tap, not enough tiger juices flowing, then Connors does not dare to even venture into competition.

We should remember that 1974, his year, was swollen with vitriol and tension – and he was near unbeatable. And what of 1978? At the time Borg laid waste to him, it was hard to find a player who did not mention how Connors had mellowed, become friendlier. Bill Norris, a tennis trainer and an old friend, says, 'Jimmy's found an inner peace. He's much more aware of other people's feelings.'

'Jimmy was brought up to win on hate,' says a top player, a contemporary. 'How long could anyone keep winning on hate?' If Connors' game is locked into the past, if it remains exactly the same, it may, nonetheless, have diminished in one almost imperceptible way: hitting the ball on the rise. To the keenest eyes, Jimbo does not appear to be taking the ball quite so soon. He has either lost the confidence to perform this feat, or somewhere deep inside a little bit of the killer instinct has paled, and he is giving the poor guy on the other side a chance, an instant more of breathing room. And the balls are coming back.

Borg, though, so bland, so unflappable, is a special problem. Connors tries to dislike him. He tries to hate him. Give Jimbo that. For years he would snarl that Borg had 'no guts', and he always goes chasing after him. After Wimbledon, Jimbo vowed, 'I'll chase the son of a bitch to the ends of the earth.' And in the weeks that have followed, that charge has been embellished: 'I'll be waiting for him. . ... I'll dog him everywhere. . .. Every time Borg looks around he'll see my shadow.'

But the problem is that it is not Bjorn Borg who is the target. It is his own man that the boy is chasing. Jimbo will be 26 next week, and the boy and his mother can only go so far. There must be the man to accept the harsh truths, so that once again he can win finals, win other people. If ever Jimmy Connors would stop trying to be something else, if only Jimmy Connors would again take the ball on the rise, the way he once did, crushing it, crashing forward, taking no prisoners, what a dreadnought he would be. Why, that would make 'em forgot '74 – and serve 'em right!

But no one knows if he is capable of the necessary changes. What we do know is that only one mother has made a men's champion, but that no mother has ever kept a man champion.

'As well as I know Jimmy,' Chris Evert says, 'a lot of times I don't know what goes on in his head. But if he still has me baffled, I know that he's still got himself baffled, too. Jimmy might know himself better if he would ever spend some time soul-searching. But he won't.

'He's always had to hate the men players to be at his best. But they don't hate him anymore. A lot of them have even come to like him. So he's got to find a new motivation, and that's going to be very hard for Jimmy.'

It is strange that as powerful as the love is that consumes the Connorses, Jimbo has always depended on hate in order to win. And all along that must have been the hard way. There is no telling how far a man could go who could learn to take love on the rise.

VILLAINS? HEROES? OR A BIT OF BOTH?

LANCE TINGAY

Whatever one's views about John Patrick McEnroe and his court behaviour in 1981 it is certain that the Wimbledon Championships will stand as a landmark in the story of the game. A tradition was broken. Despite his manifest brilliance as a player, this New Yorker was not made an honorary member of the All England Club after winning the singles.

I know not when that gracious convention started. It seems to have gone on as long as living memory, that the winners of the men's and women's singles should be offered the honour of membership of a fairly exclusive club.

In 1981 the committee felt that because of the disciplinary penalties imposed on McEnroe during the course of the meeting it would be invidious to carry out their normal practice. Of course no rule was involved in withholding membership but nonetheless a sanction was invoked by not maintaining a tradition.

All that is as may be. McEnroe, who is, after all, a lawn tennis genius, perhaps deserves to be judged by the standards of genius. He demands much of himself and he demands much of other people. There are many, mindful that graciousness and good manners have probably become scarcer commodities in recent years, who would cast McEnroe to perdition and ban him for ever.

He will have his defenders, too. There are plenty who take pleasure in watching the sparkling genius of McEnroe and mind not a bit that he often does not combine it with courtesy to those helping him show his skill. And there are many, too, who delight in a good row. One must not forget that there are two sides to the box office appeal of McEnroe, his playing talent and his propensity for provoking scenes.

Even his staunchest defenders would not claim that William de Wykeham would hail him as a man of like mind. And I doubt if the various umpire's associations round the world would, if such were their custom, rush to give him honorary membership.

If McEnroe plumbed new depths in the well of noisome court behaviour, bringing aspects to the relationship between players and umpires not seen before, he was pursuing a custom as old as the game itself.

Let me quote from C.G. Heathcote, one of the founding fathers of the Wimbledon Championships. He was writing in about 1889.

> A well-known player has publicly declared of umpires, that though they are a much-abused body his experience is that they fully deserve all they get.

At the same time he pontificated:

> It should always be remembered that an umpire intends to do his best . . . it will be well, in the plentitude of Christian charity . . . to recollect . . . that he is still a fellow-creature, entitled to so much consideration as is due to the fact that, after all, he is there for your pleasure and not for his own.

That Heathcote could write like that hardly indicates that in the gentle 1880's, in the cradle years of the game, all players were shining white knights, *sans reproche*, so far as their court behaviour was concerned.

Those who love the game of lawn tennis must live with the fact that it has not in its more than one hundred years of history built a tradition of impeccable behaviour; rather the reverse.

Now we have penalty points and the code of discipline in an attempt to give the game a better image in the face of its critics. But it is all a matter of attitudes and such are difficult, if not impossible, to control.

There are, I daresay, two categories of 'bad' behaviour. There is the player who misbehaves as such in a hundred different ways because of frustration. There is the cheat. The players themselves will be forgiving and understanding of the frustrated offenders. But players will not forgive the cheat.

That is where McEnroe will have his sympathisers. For all the convolutions of his behaviour no-one suspects that his motive has ever been to upset his opponent. He may well have done so but it has not been the object of his exercise.

There are cheats and cheats. Beyond the pale are those who would deliberately mis-call a ball in their own favour. But what of those who indulge in what would be called 'gamesmanship'? Surely in competitive lawn tennis the dictum 'caveat opponentem' must prevail.

Let me ask, who was the most popular and sporting player at Wimbledon in the late 1920's and early 1930's? To youngsters, of course, the question may be meaningless but there must be many older hands around who will answer, why, of course, Jean Borotra.

Borotra, the 'Bounding Basque' and one of the 'Four Musketeers' who took the French game to unparalleled heights of glory. He was the 'Bounding Basque' because of his acrobatic volleying.

His game was spectacular, his personality magnetic. Not so much in France but in England, and nowhere more than at Wimbledon, he was an absolute idol. On the Centre Court he held the crowd in sway like Henry Irving in command of an audience at the Lyceum. When pressed his signal for an acceleration of effort was to don his beret while changing ends. It could bring a standing ovation.

The story I tell of Borotra is this. He had something of a rivalry with the British Bunny Austin in the Covered Court Championships at Queen's Club. Usually, but not always, he had the better of their clashes on the very fast East Court.

They met in the final of 1933 and Austin, a player of superb touch but small power overhead, flourished mightily. He led 3-6, 7-5, 4-6, 6-1, 4-1 and was within a point of 5-1.

Borotra made a superhuman effort and projected a winning volley. But as he did so he suffered what seemed a catastrophic fall. He knocked the singles posts flying with his head – the ball was dead so he had already won the point – and lay, apparently unconscious. There was inevitably a shindy. Everyone gathered round his prostrate body, including Austin, who was probably the most disturbed person present. At last Borotra moved. At last he staggered to his feet. Could he stand? Could he play? Yes, play he would. By no means would he deny his old rival a full victory. So things got under way again.

Austin never knew what hit him. There never was such a rapid sequence of games. In hardly any time a bemused Austin realised that Borotra had taken the set 6-4, for the half dead man had come to life with vengeance.

As Borotra strode smartly from the court, clutching his towel and rackets, Phyllis Austin, Bunny's wife, ran across and accosted him at about the service line. She beat him on the chest with her fists, crying, 'You cheated Bunny out of it. You cheated him!'

Is that a cautionary tale? Caveat opponentem! It is entirely true. I make no judgment.

A player who would have appreciated Borotra was the American Gardnar Mulloy. He was men's doubles champion in 1957 with Budge Patty and, at the age of 43 years 7 months, the oldest male to win a Wimbledon championship.

Mulloy had a wonderful gift of talking to his opponents while changing ends. The Church in Convocation could not have taken exception to anything he said. He was pleasant and helpful and encouraging. But somehow opponents were liable to find themselves getting more and more nervous and doubtful of their own ability.

His fame grew to such dimensions that a Sunday newspaper columnist was provoked to suggest he hurl his racket over Beachy Head – and not let go! Mulloy, who was a lawyer, made a start to a libel action but did not persist.

That had followed an incident at Queen's Club, just prior to Wimbledon, when Mulloy had indicated dissent about a line decision by throwing his racket at a linesman. The snag was that the offence was compounded by it being a lineswoman!

Striking a ball may now involve the code of discipline if the direction be unorthodox. In 1962 in Paris, when Rod Laver was in the process of going on to win his first Grand Slam, he survived a match point when he played against Martin Mulligan, the Australian who later played Davis Cup for Italy. Mulligan, naturally fraught when the match began to slide, marked his dissent about a point by hurtling the ball at speed towards the offending judge on the baseline.

There was no question of a warning or penalty point then. But so menacingly did the linesman, who was about six feet six inches tall, face up towards Mulligan that I doubt if he ever dissented in that manner again!

It was in the French Championships, and it might have been the same year, when Willy Alvarez of Colombia ran into trouble. McEnroe was Little Lord Fauntelroy compared with Alvarez in full cry.

Alvarez was indulging in one of his most unpleasant disputations when one of the Committee happened by the court. He was Robert Abdesselam, a French lawyer – and, incidentally, schoolboy champion of Great Britain in his day – and he was so outraged that he disqualified Alvarez there and then.

It is, of course, almost impossible to define bad court behaviour for the purpose of legislation and the simplest thing to recognise it when you see it. Ilie Nastase, over the years, has been involved in so many incidents, been involved in so many fines, that it is impossible to quantify his transgressions.

I thought that nadir had been reached in the last rubber of the Davis

Cup tie, Romania against Great Britain when, in very trying conditions, Nastase and John Feaver completed their postponed singles. Nastase eventually won 6-4 in the fifth set and being twice the player, that was no more than lawn tennis values demanded. Nastase's behaviour was that of a maniac, and I do not exaggerate. The only real excuse the referee had for not disqualifying him on the spot was that he was, in fact, temporarily demented! Or so it seemed at the time.

Eccentricity of behaviour may be said to have been a Rumanian speciality. Between the wars a Rumanian well known at Wimbledon and elsewhere was Nicholas Mishu. No man was more amateur – he was a diplomat – and no-one more obviously played for the fun of it.

He played shots as the fancy took him. He had developed a shot not even Nastase thought of a service projected with his back to the net. Should a bird fly within range he could not resist taking a shot at it! Gamesmanship?

Many must remember Freddie Huber, who came from a nation not all that far away, Austria. I suppose Huber was as talented a games player that ever was. His eye and physical co-ordination was super normal. He had far too good a touch, far too sharp responses to get down to the basics of being a top class player. But he was a very good one, nonetheless, and his acrobatic exploits would not have been out of place at a circus.

Huber was terribly distracting to his opponents. The problem would seem to be as old as the game. For instance Wilfred Baddeley, Wimbledon champion in the 1890's, was constrained to write at about the turn of the century:

> It seems to be the object of some players to cause the spectators as much amusement and to make them laugh as much as they possibly can. To compass their ends, these players resort to the most ridiculous devices, which, perhaps, do excite the risibility of the gallery but which are most annoying to their opponents.

Bad language is hardly a modern phenomena. No-one would condone it. I doubt if it has any relationship with gamesmanship, sportsmanship or anything but a personality which must release frustration in that way.

The Austral-South African Bob Hewitt, I well remember, got into hot water at the Midland Counties Championships at the old Edgbaston Club when he provoked a parson into complaint. Prior to the war there was the New Zealander, Cam Malfroy, one of the best mixed doubles players there ever was, who was always shocking nearby spectators.

Those were the days when simple barrack room phrases were enough to be offensive in lawn tennis circles. But the language which might have surprised, if not shocked, a barrack room came within the last two decades from otherwise charming teenage lasses of impeccable lineage and upbringing. There were two, one from Devon and another from Northern Ireland, and since both have long since given up their curious ways I do not name them.

The dividing line between court behaviour that is reprehensible and that which is fair in a competitive field can be hard to draw. There was a notorious case at Wimbledon in 1936. The British Dorothy Round, the champion of 1934 (and afterwards in 1937), played the German Hilda Sperling in the quarter final on Court One.

In the course of it Miss Round broke the strap of her bra. Seriously incommoded she asked the umpire if she could have a short break while she retreated to the dressing room. He was willing enough but, as a matter of courtesy, asked Fru Sperling (she was Fru, not Frau, because she had married a Dane) if she had any objection. 'Yes,' said Fru Sperling, 'I have. I shall get cold.'

So Miss Round had to struggle awkwardly on and she lost the match. In legal terms those who maintained that she had had a raw deal had no case. The rule was 'Play shall be continuous'. The incident did, in fact, provoke a change allowing for a discretionary interruption of that kind.

In terms of sportsmanship how far do you support Fru Sperling? Do you try to win at *all* costs? Of course, it depends what you mean by *all*. But there were no bad manners about Fru Sperling.

There is a well known English phrase which all foreigners studying our language have to learn: 'It's not cricket.' It may well be that the metaphor has got out of step with the reality but no native English speaker need have its meaning explained.

I think, perhaps, cynically, that in our game we are lucky that an antonym to that phrase has not grown up, 'That's lawn tennis'. Those who offend are very much a minority and always have been but they necessarily make their presence felt, generally by vocal means.

There was a player, an American, who was suspended for life for bad behaviour and it must have been about 25 years ago. He was Earl Cochell. It was not ill manners on court that provoked such drastic punishment by the U.S.T.A. All he did was to punch the referee of the U.S. Championships on the nose! They had penalty points and a half in those days!

BJORN BORG

A MARRIAGE MADE IN GLITZVILLE
Curry Kirkpatrick

Hey, Manny, I got it. The So-Long-Swede Tour. Here's the deal. We run the kid down through the baskets markets – you know, the ACC, the SEC and the Sunbelt and all those other tanktown paradises where they don't know forehands from net-cord judges. We do trade-outs with hotels, limos, the media. Stick ads in all the Baskin-Robbins. Hold press conferences in airports. Get the mayors to read proclamations, order plaques and trophies and humongous multicolored cakes and – get this – ice sculptures. Is this dynamite stuff or what? Then we dress Borg all in white, dim the house lights, turn on some anthem music and round up all the chicks to storm the locker room door. We're talkin' monster time here, pal. Am I right or am I right? Tag it? We tag it Bjorny Does the Bushes, what else? Hey, it worked for Barry Manilow.

And it worked out for Bjorn Borg, or at least for his promoters. So what if the tour turned out to be extremely hoked up, a lot tacky, a bit of a ripoff and inundated with sleaze. This was Borg's swan song in the U.S. Last week it consisted of five one-night stands in five cities. In Charlotte, N.C.; Chattanooga, Tenn. and Norfolk, Va. he played Rosco Tanner; in Baton Rouge, La. and Providence, R.I. he faced Jimmy Connors. This week Borg was scheduled to play an eight-man event in Toronto, and on Monday he's slated to appear in Kansas City for yet another match with the omnipresent Tanner. That could well be the last time anyone this side of the Atlantic sees the best player of the age strike a tennis ball.

It should be acknowledged that the last roundup was planned long before Borg decided – last November or last month or last week or in the last few minutes or whenever it may have been – to retire. These exhibitions, or 'exos' in player lingo, were originally intended to serve

as preparation for Borg's return to the regular tournament circuit. But when news bulletins of his quitting emerged three weeks ago from all corners of the globe and most notably the mountains of Nepal, where Borg, his wife, Mariana, his parents, Rune and Margarethe, and his coach, Lennart Bergelin, were riding elephants, this particular series of appearances loomed as Borg's final fling on North American courts. So there. You didn't really think Borg had retired and then wantonly squeezed out a few more paydays, did you? Perish the thought. The elephant boy would never forget his commitments.

Moreover, who's to say this leave-taking was any less dignified than Joe Namath hanging on for dear life to his Los Angeles Ram earphones or Ray Leonard preening before the celebrity guests at his famous last bash. Still, as Borg wandered zombielike from airplane to limo to hotel to exo and back against last week, it was difficult to forgive him for double-fistedly backhanding himself into such a vulnerable position: a head-banded cartoon character tap-dancing at age 26 through the carny atmosphere of horridly commercial one-nighters. The announcement at the end of Presley concerts used to be so agonizingly final: 'Elvis has left the building.' Why, oh why, couldn't Bjorn Borg, the one and only Bjorn Borg, go out like Ted Williams, hitting the home run, instead of like Presley, wallowing in self-caricature?

On Wednesday, just before Charlotte's Winter Challenge, which is how the Borg-Tanner match was billed on some of the sponsoring beer's posters, the villain of the saga mused on Borg's predicament. 'Tennis is so year-round these days, so involving,' said Tanner, 'that you never get away from it unless you go to the wilderness. You never feel relaxed about *not* playing. Bjorn's decision must have been a relief to him. He's so loose, so on high.'

Indeed, upon arriving from Katmandu by way of Bangkok and his home in Sands Point, N.Y., Borg looked refreshed, healthy, younger than he has since the day in 1976 that he won the first of his five Wimbledon championships. Clean-shaven, his hair clipped, Borg began the tour without either Mariana or Bergelin, whose sharp differences are now public record, at his side. Not that they had disagreed over or influenced Borg's retirement decision. That was his and his alone, and both wife and coach were stunned. According to Borg, after he told Mariana in late November in Stockholm that he planned to retire, 'She thought I was crazy. Lennart was a player. He knows about the day that comes when you have nothing more to give.'

Before the match in the Charlotte Coliseum, the Charlotte Choir Boys sang the Swedish national anthem. The Charlotte Pops Ensemble played the theme from Sylvester Stallone. Borg and Tanner entered the court under raised rackets held by the ball boys. 'I felt like we were getting married,' said Tanner. Borg won in three straight sets before better than 9,000 fans. Later he was asked if he'd had fun. 'Well, uh,' Borg replied, bewildered. 'I had to play the match. I'm pretty pleased.'

In the confusion and crush of teen darlings enveloping Borg's car outside the coliseum, one of his police bodyguards was left behind. 'I was surprised they mobbed Born [*sic*],' said the abandoned patrolman, John Horton, 'but securitywise, this wasn't much, about 15 police. Now, we'll have about 45 to 50 for Ozzie Osbourne.'

On Thursday, black and white limousines rolled out on the tarmac at Lovell Field in Chattanooga. The quarry was whisked away from the crowds to an isolated terminal, where he met the press and was presented the key to the city by Mayor Pat Rose. Then the limos roared downtown, a police escort screaming sirens and running red lights and forcing mere civilian riffraff onto the shoulders. Who was this, Cap Weinberger?

The who was a wide-eyed, gape-mouthed and shell-shocked Borg. The why and wherefore was W.E. Stamps & Associates, promoter of the Chattanooga and Norfolk matches. 'You've got to understand Bjorn is a very, very close friend of mine,' said Bill Stamps. 'We brought him out of retirement at Industry Hills last summer in L.A. [where Borg played back-to-back exhibitions with Connors and Vitas Gerulaitis]. We thought it apropos we put him back to bed, so to speak.' Stamps is a former celebrity agent from L.A. He said he wears his trademark Panama 'so my people can spot me on court fast.' He said he would throw Borg his 'only retirement party' the next night in Norfolk. He said he would fly in some 'stars.' What stars? 'Oh, you know, stars?' What stars? 'Oh, you know, *future* stars.' What stars? 'Look,' Stamps said. 'I'm a celebrity broker. I'll pick up the phone and get some stars. Maybe Donna Mills or Lionel Ritchie. Maybe Rogers will be in the area.'

Rogers? Kenny Rogers? Ginger? Roy? Rogers Hornsby? Before the mystery could be solved, Stamps was introducing his retinue: Mrs. Barbara Stamps, who favors swirling Fawcettian waves and lollipop sunglasses; son Jesse, five, who was packing a plastic machine gun; and housekeeper Antonita from south of the border. 'Hey, don't tell the Feds,' said Stamps. 'Hey Toni, you got a last name?' But that's not all. Stamps then wheels on his producer, Doug Bleeck, 'formerly in late-night TV – *In Concert* and *The Midnight Special*' – and his photographer, Kim Mizuno. He presents them to any and all bystanders with a burst of similarly unhilarious racial-ethnic intros.

That night Borg lost 6-2, 4-6, 7-5, 6-4 to Tanner, who was playing in his hometown. The highlight of the match came in the third set, when the Supreme Court in the Roundhouse arena at the University of Tennessee at Chattanooga split open as Borg took a spectacular dive, landing on his keister. Borg came up laughing, but James Rose, a Supreme Court company employee who had braved possible sniper fire to truck the court up from Cartersville, Ga., wasn't pleased. 'Makes a man prideful to see Be-yon, or however you say his name, goin' out on my stuff,' said Rose. 'But somebody took a damn mop to my court. No tape's gonna stay stuck with a damn mop wipin' the court. My overalls are still soaked.'

Stamps seemed especially upset about Be-yon's behind, not to mention preoccupied with the news value of his spill. 'Terrific,' he said. 'This'll be second paragraph, right?'

Later Borg was asked about Stamps. 'Bill's a pretty funny guy,' he said. 'Actually, I don't know him really well. I think he's from, ah, L.A.'

Friday, Norfolk. Bjorn Borg Goes Navy. The retirement party. Stars. Uh, oh. But first the players' limo couldn't leave the hotel in Chattanooga because Stamps wasn't ready. An elderly woman climbed into Borg's car. 'I'm from the gree-ell [that's grill in English],' she squealed at Borg. 'I want you to write "To Lamarr" on this, Bjorn boy. That's two r's, and make it quick.'

Borg signed, but Bill Ryan, his personal representative for this tour from the International Management Group, was getting itchy. Ryan is believed to be the first male ever to wear a turquoise shell necklace with a button-down Oxford shirt. He has been at odds with Stamps. 'Let's go. We're out of here,' barked Ryan at the driver.

'I don't want to be rude, sir,' said the chauffeur, 'but I don't work for you. I work for Mr. Stamps.' Whoops.

Finally on the road, Ryan plotted revenge. Poring over tickets, bills and receipts, he said jokingly to Borg and Tanner and the warmup singles act of John Fitzgerald and Jimmy Brown, 'Wouldn't it be great if we all just went on to Boston instead of Norfolk? Stamps would have heart failure.'

Thing is, the tour nearly didn't go anywhere. Airport security in Chattanooga nabbed Jesse for brazenly carrying his machine gun past the X-ray machine, and by the time the entourage arrived at the gate, the flight was oversold. Borg wasn't asked if this ever happened when he was in the care of Bergelin.

When Borg finally arrived in Atlanta to change planes, who was boarding the same flight to Norfolk but Martina Navratilova. She carried a fox terrier puppy in a box. 'Her name is K.D.,' said Navratilova.

'Killer Dog. But she's having a false pregnancy. It's sad.'

On the next plane, Ryan to Stamps: ' Can we get Martina into the retirement party?'

Stamps to Ryan: 'Sure. Can you ask her to bring her dog?'

At Norfolk's Scope Arena, Borg whipped Tanner in straight sets before a packed house of 8,200. But, alas, at the retirement party after the match in the presidential ballroom of the Hotel Madison, neither Navratilova nor K.D. was anywhere to be found. Nor were any stars. Where were the stars? 'We got some big-cheese NATO commander coming later on,' said Bleeck. That's no star. 'Hey, if there's a war, he'll be a star.'

At his only retirement party, Borg sat in a corner, far away from the smoke, the noise, the chaos and the revolting 125-pound yellow tennis-ball cake. He signed his name approximately 48,000 times on items Stamps handed him. 'I hate like hell to make this a cattle call,' yelled Stamps at the crowd through the haze. 'But look, you got Bill Stamps, hard hat, or' – he took off his Panama – 'convertible.' A quick attendance check disclosed not one Mr. or Mrs. Rogers.

Following one of his numerous pastings by Borg at Wimbledon, Connors said, 'I'll follow the sonofabitch to the ends of the earth.' One of the ends apparently was to be Baton Rouge on Saturday night and among Connors' demands of promoter Billy McGehee Jr. was that the match be only two of three sets and that immediately afterward Connors be furnished a private jet from Baton Rouge to Providence. McGehee is the publisher of a Louisiana sports tabloid, even though, he says, 'I've never enjoyed reading in my life.' But he can read bottom lines, and he had sold more than 9,000 seats at the Centroplex arena.

Unbeknownst to Connors, however, Ryan changed the private flight to Sunday morning because he wanted to 'party' in Baton Rouge. On the trip to Louisiana, Borg and his gang whiled away the hours betting on which question would be asked first in each city's press conference and how quickly recently resigned Philadelphia Eagles Coach Dick Vermeil's name would come up. 'I know this Vermeil,' said Borg on Eastern Flight 519. 'Was he really burnt out? I am not burnt out.' Passengers filed by Borg, recreating the art of the double-take. A blonde in a red sweater returned, pencil poised. 'O.K., which one are you?' she said. Obviously a Dick Vermeil fan.

Upon arriving in Baton Rouge, everyone headed for the Sheraton, where Connors, who had checked in the day before, was furious about the plane change and was threatening to take a hike. He was heard to announce, 'Ryan doesn't run the show. I run the show.' *Voilà*. A compromise. Connors will take the private plane on Saturday night; Borg and Ryan will go commercial to Providence on Sunday morning.

Borg and Connors saw each other for the first time outside the hotel. 'Jimbo, man,' said Borg. 'What's happenin', replied Connors. 'What is this, the NBA on CBS?'

In the dressing room before that night's match, Borg slumped into a soft armchair while Connors small-talked with his brother, John, and some local friends. Borg asked Connors who was playing in the finals at Philadelphia. Connors asked Borg what his plans were and how Tanner was hitting. Then it was game time.

The opening set was a revelation for whoever questions the motivation of two sturdy champions when they toil against each other, be it in exos or dominoes. Connors took a 5-3 lead, but Borg rallied after a wondrous backhand. 'And you're going to *retire* after that –,' roared Connors across the net.

With Borg up 5-4 in the first-set tiebreaker, Connors' return of serve was a foot deep, but the linesman signaled good. Borg fell over backward in disbelief. The umpire promptly overruled the call, making the score 6-4 Borg. Both players then approached the chair and unwittingly staged a rather remarkable microcosm of their careers. A furious Connors grabbed the microphone and screamed, 'Keep your mouth shut. Get down from the chair. You're through.' A placid Borg shook the umpire's hand. The umpire stayed put.

Borg won the tiebreaker on the next point. But soon Connors gained control, and he went on to win 6-7, 6-4, 6-4, but not before his exhausted opponent, subsisting on three hours' sleep and some vital pride, nearly overcame a 1-5 deficit in the final set. The following night Connors defeated a weary Borg 6-4, 6-4 before 9,800 spectators at the Providence Civic Center. After the match Borg said that he had tried his best but that he was glad the five days had finally come to an end.

Before Borg left Baton Rouge for Rhode Island, a journalist asked him, 'When will I see you again?' The reporter first had visited Borg in Sweden when he was 17, and only now, on a cold, rainy night in Louisiana, did it occur to the journalist that this could be the end after all.

'I don't know,' said Borg. 'It might be quite some time.' And just like that he was gone into the darkness, into the shadows of his future – to another limo, another plane, another exo and perhaps another life as well. The question lingers still. Has the great Borg left the building for good?

MONTE CARLO FAREWELL
Richard Evans

The shot which ended Bjorn Borg's career was the shot that made him famous. And when he missed it, to go down 4-6, 7-5, 7-6 to the nineteen-year-old Frenchman Henri Leconte in the second round of the Jacomo Monte Carlo Open, one sensed the symbolic passing of an era.

I believe the history of the game will record it as such despite the fact that within fifteen minutes of Borg's disappearance he was replaced on the majestically designed center court of the Monte Carlo Country Club by another blond Swede with a double-fisted backhand.

Mats Wilander, who duly beat his compatriot Henrik Sundstrom and went on to win his fourth straight title on European clay, is destined for great things in the game but he will never be another Borg and is, thankfully, enough of an individual never to seek nor to relish any comparison.

Borg was unique – an immensely dignified champion who somehow overcame the handicap of a moderate volley to win Wimbledon five consecutive times – a feat which still has his peers shaking their heads in disbelief when they think about it. The fact that Bjorn never came close to joining Don Budge and Rod Laver in their terribly exclusive Grand Slam club said more for the opposition he had to face than his own standing as one of the great champions of all time. No matter what the old timers' say Jimmy Connors and John McEnroe, plus a few of today's supporting cast, would have given Budge and Laver plenty to think about and it was Connors twice and McEnroe twice who stopped Borg one match short of the U.S. Open crown he never won.

It was interesting to note that Borg rated his loss to Connors in the 1976 U.S. Open final which, of course, was played on clay at Forest Hills, as the most disappointing defeat of his career even though he was not in line for the Grand Slam that year, having been beaten by Adriano Panatta in the quarterfinal of the French Championships.

'It was my match and I let it go,' Borg said, referring to the 6-4, 3-6, 7-6, 6-4 defeat he suffered at Forest Hills. 'I had breaks in both of the last two sets and didn't take advantage of them. That was my most disappointing defeat.'

But his five Wimbledons and six French titles in eight years were achievements that required incredible self-discipline and strength of character and these attributes were still evident as he carried himself cooly through the near hysteria that surrounded his matches in Monte Carlo.

Tennis had not seen a media event of this magnitude since Billie Jean

King defeated Bobby Riggs in the Houston Astrodome in 1973. Borg was a stripling then but in the decade which followed his reputation grew to such an extent that his pending retirement brought reporters, photographers and television camera crews flocking to Monaco in barely manageable hoards.

His first round match against Jose-Luis Clerc was delayed several minutes while the stampeding media were cleared from the court but those of us who were anticipating the final curtain were a day too early. Clerc, playing possibly the worst match of his life, was simply too bad to allow Borg to slide gracefully from the scene. The maestro had no option but to accept a 6-3, 6-1 victory through the simple expediant of keeping the ball in play.

'Given his talent, it would have been easier for Jose-Luis to play better,' said Clerc's coach, Patricio Rodriguez. Having watched Clerc drive forehand after forehand three yards or more past the baseline, one knew what Pato meant.

But if Clerc was nervous and pressured by the occasion, Borg showed no signs of any kind of emotion either then or on the following afternoon when the sun shone and another 8,000 people packed every available corner of the spacious center court.

Like Clerc, Leconte made errors, too, but they were generously interspersed with inspired flashes of a forceful talent that is unmistakably reminiscent of the young Rod Laver. A Borg of 1981 would have handled it through the sheer relentless consistency and accuracy of his own game. But this Borg, with his skills unprimed and his mind on other things, could only counter the threat with momentary bursts of his own. The result, of course, was an uneven match that Leconte served for at 5-4 in the third and still seemed incapable of grasping when he led by five points to one in the deciding tie break. By that time much of the tennis was of the highest class and the drama was real. Despite Leconte's nationality, the crowd, containing the usual high percentage of Italians, was unashamably pro-Borg and the cheers echoed off the encroaching skyscrapers as the Swede fought back to four-five. Was he going to escape? Was Leconte unable to claim the strange honor of ending so illustrious a career? Apparently not for, with the sun dipping away over Cap Ferrat, where Borg has one of his many homes, the time was drawing near. Subconsciously or not Bjorn had decided it was time to go. A badly mishit forehand gave Leconte two match points and, on the first, Bjorn drew back his trusty Donnay to set himself for the famous backhand and sent it arcing crosscourt to land several inches wide.

Many were thirsting after a Borg–Wilander quarterfinal but, on reflection, I think it was better that it never occurred. A lop-sided victory for Mats – which would have been in the cards – would have proved nothing. Better that these two great Swedes simply passed each other by one cool evening as dusk settled over their adopted Principality; leaving it for others to argue who was king.